IS THIS **ANY WAY** TO RUN A

DEMOCRATIC GOVERNMENT?

IS THIS **ANY** TO RUN A
WAY
DEMOCRATIC
GOVERNMENT?

STEPHEN J. WAYNE, EDITOR

Georgetown University Press

Washington, D.C.

Georgetown University Press, Washington, D.C.
© 2004 by Georgetown University Press. All rights reserved.
Printed in the United States of America

10 9 8 7 6 5 4 3 2 1   2004

This book is printed on acid-free paper meeting the requirements of the American National Standard for Permanence in Paper for Printed Library Materials.

Library of Congress Cataloging-in-Publication Data

Is this any way to run a democratic government? / Stephen J. Wayne, editor.
      p. cm.
Includes bibliographical references and index.
   ISBN 1-58901-005-1 (pbk : alk. paper)
   1. Democracy—United States. I. Wayne, Stephen J.

    JF1726.I8 2004
    320.973—dc22

                    2003019468

Contents

CONTENTS

Figures

Tables

Preface

Americans believe that democracy is the most desirable form of government. They have confidence in the people and think that their judgments should influence government officials in the making of public policy. When Americans are asked if elected and appointed officials should follow what the majority wants, even if it goes against the officials' knowledge, 54 percent said yes (*Public Perspective* 2001a). Democracy has become such a fundamental American value that the United States has tried to impose it on other countries. In the words of President George W. Bush,

> There was a time when many said that the cultures of Japan and Germany were incapable of sustaining democratic values. Well, they were wrong. Some say the same of Iraq today. They are mistaken. The nation of Iraq—with its proud heritage, abundant resources and skilled and educated people—is fully capable of moving toward democracy and living in freedom.
>
> The world has a clear interest in the spread of democratic values, because stable and free nations do not breed the ideologies of murder. They encourage the peaceful pursuit of a better life (Bush 2003).

Is the president right? Is democracy the most desirable form of government? Even more basically, how democratic is the government of the United States? Does it work well? Should it be a model for others?

This book cannot answer all of these questions, but it does examine the theory and practice of American democracy and the dichotomy that currently exists between theory and practice. The contributors to this book assess the reasons for such a dichotomy and its consequences. The focus is on the here and now. The goals are to evaluate the democratic character of the system and some of the normative questions that such an evaluation raises, some of which the president posed in his plea for a democratic Iraq.

This book is about the institutions, processes, and policies of government: how well they work, whether they meet the criteria for a viable democratic system, and the extent to which they contribute to good public policy.

This book is organized in five parts. The first examines the fundamental values and assumptions upon which American democracy rests. Beginning with a discussion of its three basic tenets—personal liberty, political equality, and the collective good—chapter 1 explains why these tenets are necessary in theory but have produced so much conflict in practice.

The first chapter also frames the discussion for the rest of the book. It does so by enumerating three criteria by which the democratic character of the governing system can be assessed: representation, responsiveness, and decisional rules. Together these criteria tie public input to policy output and thereby link government to the governed.

In many ways, chapter 1 also is the most difficult to read and comprehend because it is the most theoretical. Although it is illustrated by examples, key elements in the discussion may become clearer after a closer look at the way American democracy operates in practice—which is the focus of the remaining chapters in the book. Therefore we recommend that you reread the first chapter after you have completed the book. We believe that you will gain a deeper understanding of the theoretical issues and their practical application in the American system of government if you do so.

Chapter 2 turns to the structure of civic society and its impact on democratic politics. The principal questions the author of this chapter, Beth Stark, addresses are these: What kinds of group activities condition and strengthen the political environment and the governing system? What role do religious institutions play? Do they help organize and activate citizens, or do they lead to more tension and conflict within society among competing and often contentious groups? Stark takes the position that such organizations are essential as integrating mechanisms. Without them, she argues, government would be more prone to domination by the few and less likely to generate broad support for its policies and actions; without them, generating the civic culture so necessary to a vibrant democracy would be more difficult.

As you read chapter 2, ask yourself why the framers of the U.S. Constitution protected religious beliefs but separated church and state. Do you think they believed that religious groups were necessary or that they were dangerous and in need of constraint?

Part II begins the study of the institutions of the national government by turning to Congress. Collectively the chapters in this part of the book explore one of the most contentious issues with which contemporary democracy in America has had to contend over the years: money—specifically, the fact that financial resources are unequally distributed within society. What is the impact of resource inequality on the principle and practice of

political equity? How has that impact affected the composition, disposition, and decisions of government in general and Congress in particular? To what extent are Americans with greater resources able to use those resources to maintain their own financial advantage? Is the United States a government of, by, and for the fortunate few, the special interests, the economic and politically elite?

Chapter 3 opens this discussion by exploring the connection between campaign contributions to members of Congress and personal contacts people have with their congressional representatives. It examines who gives, how much, and, most important, what they get for their money. The authors of this chapter—a group of political scientists who have been studying donations to congressional campaigns for several years—identify the characteristics and attitudes of two groups of donors: those who gave more than $200 to a single candidate and those who gave the most money to the most candidates. After describing these donors, the authors turn to the donors' personal contacts with members of Congress. Do campaign contributions "buy" access? Is access a vehicle for exercising influence on legislative outcomes?

Michael Bailey also addresses these questions in chapter 4. He assembles an impressive body of scholarship and his own case studies to explore the linkage between contributions and policymaking. Although Bailey does not dismiss the pernicious effect of money, he suggests that its perceived impact may be overstated. Perhaps campaign contributions are not as damaging to the principle of political equality as we have been led to believe. Perhaps contributions result in more people becoming better informed about the candidates and the issues. Perhaps more people vote as a result. If so, then private money may *invigorate* rather than undercut a democratic legislative process by educating and mobilizing the electorate. By making such an argument, Bailey forces us to think about whether inequitable resources distort legislative outcomes, have little influence over them, or indirectly produce a more informed voter who can more clearly distinguish and evaluate the qualifications of candidates seeking elective office.

Money is only one of the reputed sources of representational distortion. Systemic bias is another. Consider the underrepresentation of women in elective office, for example. In the United States women constitute more than half of the population and the electorate but much fewer than half of the elected officials. Why? Does it matter? Is it fair?

In chapter 5, Courtenay Daum explores the impact of unequal representation on legislative issues and policies. Can a legislative body enact laws that are fair for everyone if some people are excluded or underrepresented in that legislature? Citing a broad body of scholarly literature, Daum asserts that descriptive representation, the proportion of a group in the body as a whole, is a prerequisite for equitable substantive representation—the impact the law has on a particular group. She makes several interesting proposals for improving the representational imbalance for women and minority groups in Congress.

Part III moves to the presidency and the executive branch. Here too, several chapters examine representational and responsiveness issues. In chapter 6, Joseph A. Ferrara looks at the executive branch and asks if it mirrors America. In presenting a wealth of data on the composition of the federal workforce, survey research on the attitudes of civil servants, and opinion polls on the public's attitudes toward people who work in government, Ferrara addresses three basic questions: Does the federal bureaucracy *look* like America? Does it *think* like America? And do Americans *trust* those who work in the executive branch of government?

Chapter 7 examines a related issue: the relationship between public opinion and presidential actions. Do presidents lead or follow? Should they lead or follow in a democracy? Obviously, if government reflects public sentiment and is responsive to political demands, it will engender public support. That certainly is desirable. But does public opinion always, usually, or infrequently generate the best policy for the country? The framers of the Constitution did not think so, but a majority of the American people today apparently do. When Americans were asked how much confidence they have in the public as a whole with regard to making judgments about what general direction elected and governmental officials should take on various issues facing the nation, 54 percent of respondents said a great deal or a fair amount, whereas 45 percent indicated not too much or none at all. Regarding the economy, health care, and education more than 66 percent of the respondents indicated that the public can make a sound judgment; 50 percent believed that the public could do so on foreign affairs as well (*Public Perspective*, 2001b).

In chapter 7 authors Jeremy Mayer and Lynn Kirby direct their attention to the relationship between the president and the public. They examine the increasingly important role that pollsters have assumed as presidential advisers—the information they convey, the advice they give, and the reaction of presidents to that information and advice. Mayer and Kirby use two case studies—one involving the Reagan administration's Central American policy, and the other the Clinton administration and welfare reform—to illustrate the impact of public opinion on these two important presidential priorities. Although two examples do not provide conclusive evidence of whether presidents lead or follow, they do suggest, at least in these cases, that even when presidents follow the polls, they do not always act on the basis of them. Whether they should do so is another important question.

Chapter 8 builds on the theme of president as leader by exploring the unilateral actions presidents take to circumvent the legislative process and control executive branch decision making. Author Margaret Tseng documents the increasing tendency of presidents to make recess appointments; issue declarations, proclamations, findings, and executive orders; and maintain continuous oversight over the regulations that the departments and agencies of government use to implement public policy. Do unilateral presidential actions undermine the underlying norm of a system of separate institutions sharing powers? Do they undercut the "invitation to struggle" that the framers built into the constitutional design? Do they suggest that presidents have become too powerful, or not powerful enough to persuade Congress and others to support their policy judgments?

The final chapter in part III, chapter 9, looks at another aspect of presidential decision making: the way in which presidential priorities are made and imposed on the executive branch department and agencies in the annual budgetary process. Author Lynn Ross, a former budget analyst, points to three tensions that regularly divide the president and executive branch agencies: the administration's perception of the national interest versus the departments' and agencies' views of the special interests that they serve; the Office of Management and Budget's (OMB) desire for an efficient, decisive, and internal budgetary process versus the needs of interest groups to have a more open, accessible, and public policymaking process; and the president's orientation to impose his political perspective on budget decision making versus the policy experts' inclination to base their judgments solidly on the merits of the issue.

In describing the ground rules of the budget battle, the skirmishes that routinely occur, the mechanisms for resolving them, and the goals that undergird the entire process, Ross asks whether a budget can meet the OMB director's bottom line (limit government expenditures), incorporate the president's major policy initiatives (adjust revenue and spending to national needs), and fulfill the agencies' mission of serving their clientele's interests simultaneously.

Part IV turns to the judiciary and the concept of judicial review—the power of the courts to declare acts of Congress and state legislatures unconstitutional. The problem with the courts negating laws is that nonelected federal judges are overturning the decisions of elected public officials. That's not democratic—or is it?

When a court acts to protect political liberties and civil rights, especially for people who cannot do so themselves because they are in the minority or because they have been perpetually underrepresented in government, are such decisions really inconsistent with democratic values? In chapter 10, author Emily Hoechst argues that they are. She contends that judicial review seriously undermines the democratic assumption that the people, through their elected representatives, are best capable of looking out for themselves, not some legal elite in a marble palace.

Steve Glickman presents a different perspective in chapter 11. He also explores the political ticket the Supreme Court jumps into when it declares legislative acts unconstitutional. Focusing on cases that involve legislative reapportionment and redistricting, Glickman argues that the Supreme Court has muddied the waters, confusing rather than clarifying the issues, and ultimately has decreased the quality of substantive representation for underrepresented minorities. Glickman's arguments raise serious questions about the Supreme Court's qualifications for deciding political controversies, such as the outcome of the Florida vote in the 2000 presidential election.

So how democratic is the U.S. system today? Does the government operate in a democratic manner? Is it representative, responsive, and equitable? Does it also promote efficiency and other tenets of good govern-ment? Should an American president promote, prescribe, and even try to impose democracy as the best form of government for all people in all times in all countries?

The chapters that follow are intended to help you answer these questions. They will give you ideas on how to improve the U.S. system—how to make it more democratic and more efficient at the same time.

References

Bush, George W. 2003. "President Discusses the Future of Iraq." White House news release. Available at www.whitehouse.gov/news/releases/2003/02/20030226-11.html (accessed September 3, 2003).

Public Perspective. 2001a. "Lead or Follow?" July/August, 18.

———. 2001b. "Government by the People," July/August, 16.

Part I

DEMOCRATIC THEORY

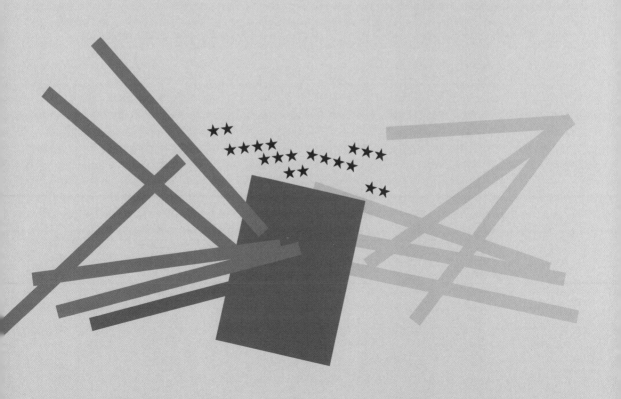

★★★

Chapter 1

Issues of Democratic Governance

Stephen J. Wayne

Most of the theoretical and empirical studies of American democracy focus on participation by the public in electoral and governing processes. Such studies examine the structure, conduct, and consequences of elections; the turnout and behavior of voters; the role of parties in organizing electoral choice, mobilizing political supporters, and influencing the outcome of the vote; and the agenda-setting and accountability function of elections. They also explore the accessibility of government, public attitudes about it, the ways in which individual and groups try to influence it, and the extent to which outside influence, directly or indirectly, affects the formulation, implementation, and adjudication of public policy.

This book does not duplicate those efforts. It does not focus primarily on the inputs to government but on how government reacts to those inputs and converts them into public policy outputs. It is concerned with the composition of governing institutions—particularly their representational character, the structure and processes of those institutions, and especially their decisional rules—and, finally, with the congruence of social needs, public inputs, and policy outputs. In each area the contributors to this book are concerned with the following questions: To what extent is the American system of government democratic, and how well does that system work?

To answer these questions we examine basic democratic values and then apply those values to the operation of the national government. We do so by first discussing the foundations of democratic governance; then we propose three criteria by which the character of that government can be assessed: the way in which government represents and responds to the public, the rules by which it operates and makes policy decisions, and the policy itself and its impact on society. In this way, we evaluate the degree to which the American system of government is of, by, and for the people.

The Foundations of Democratic Government

What is a democratic government? On what assumptions is it based? Simply stated, a democratic government is one that is based on popular consent—"a government of, by, and for the people," to use Lincoln's words from the Gettysburg Address. A government of the people should encourage public dialogue, be accessible to individuals and groups and responsive to them, and make decisions that benefit the society as a whole. Moreover, it must have the capability to convert public expression and group interests into acceptable and desirable policy outputs that are regarded as legitimate by those affected by them.

Strictly speaking, government is a conversion mechanism. It exists for all of the people, not just for those in positions of authority—but especially for those who do not hold such positions. It enables the public to control its own destiny. That is why government is necessary and democratic government is desirable.

Basic Values: Life, Liberty, and Self-Fulfillment

Acknowledging the worth of every human being living within a governing system is an underlying premise of democracy. Such an acknowledgment requires, at the least, that government protect and preserve human life. Personal security must be an ongoing concern; it is a precondition for the pursuit of other needs and desires.

That pursuit, often referred to as self-fulfillment, is most apt to flourish in an environment that maximizes free choice and rewards individual initiative and effort. Borrowing from English philosopher John Locke, Thomas Jefferson summed up these principles in his famous phrase in the Declaration of Independence, "life, liberty, and the pursuit of happiness." Life comes first; freedom is second. Both are essential to the pursuit of happiness, the third component in Jefferson's trinity of fundamental and unalienable rights.

If *individual liberty* represents one pillar of a democratic system, *political equality* is another. When Jefferson wrote that "all men are created equal," he was expressing the belief that all human lives must be considered to be of equal value. His words, which were designed to support the revolutionists' claim that American colonists had been unjustly denied the rights of Englishmen, have subsequently been used by others—nonproperty owners, religious minorities, slaves, women, and, more recently, those whose sexual orientation differs from that of the majority—to claim their lawful and just rights.

Although Jefferson presented a theoretical argument, today the principle of equality has been widely accepted as an operative norm and incorporated into the law of the land through the Fifth and Fourteenth Amendments to the U.S. Constitution. The terms "due process of law," "equal protection of the law," and "equal opportunity under law" are now recognized as legal precepts derived from the concept of political equality and are part of the fabric of our constitutional system.

Political equality does not suggest, however, that everyone has the same skills, abilities, initiative, perseverance, or will. Obviously, people do not. Instead, the concept assumes that everyone's skills, resources, and desires, whatever they may be, are equally important to each person, and that importance must be considered in rendering public policy decisions.[1] No one should be regarded as superior; everyone is equal under the law.

It follows from the equality principle that everyone also should have equal opportunities to express their views through words, actions, and votes. Here, however, we run into a practical problem: the unequal distribution of resources within society. Citizens with greater resources have a better chance of being heard and getting their way. The freedom to spend one's resources to influence who is elected to government and the policy decisions made by that government runs counter to the principle that everyone should exercise equal influence because everyone is of equal worth.

In short, individual liberty and political equality are basic values, but they do not easily coexist with one another. One person's liberty can directly or indirectly impinge on another's and in the process produce an unequal consequence: someone gains, someone else loses; one person or group is advantaged, others are harmed. One of the most difficult problems for a democratic society is when the freedom to use unequal resources perpetuates the advantages of those who are advantaged and does so for an extended period of time.

However the tension between liberty and equality is resolved, it should be done in a way that benefits the society as a whole. The *collective good*, often referred to as the general welfare, is the third pillar of democratic government—one that must be considered in making policy decisions. The collective good is a concept that is discernible in theory but more difficult to agree on in practice. It is not simply the product of what benefits the majority; it is that which has the greatest social value.

For example, homeland security is a collective good. But not all attempts to provide such security are equally desirable. Should suspected terrorists be incarcerated indefinitely without the presentation of evidence? Congress said "no" in the U.S.A. Patriot Act enacted in the aftermath of the terrorist attacks against the World Trade Center and the Pentagon on September 11, 2001. Should Japanese Americans have been placed in detention camps during World War II? At the time, the government felt it was necessary to do so, and the Supreme Court held the action constitutional. Many years later, Congress and the Court had a change of heart.

The Rule of Law

Government must not only contend with the perpetual conflict between the exercise of liberty versus the maintenance of equality, with protecting the rights and interests of individuals versus those of the society as a whole, it must do so in a way that peacefully resolves contentious issues. This objective is achieved through the rule of law: the Constitution, federal and state statutes, and accepted precedent—by which social values are protected, costs are allocated, and resources are distributed.

Law designates the norms and boundaries of acceptable behavior. It is a stabilizing force within society that connects the past with the future through the precedent it establishes. Law reduces arbitrariness and its undesirable psychological and social consequences; it provides behavioral guidelines that protect political activity but also prevent that activity from getting out of hand.

Not all laws are equal. There is a hierarchy that begins with the U.S. Constitution. The Constitution empowers government but also constrains those in government from abusing their authority.

Although the Constitution is the supreme law of the land, it is not absolute or inviolable. It is subject to formal amendment, continuous interpretation, and, theoretically, termination because the people retain the ultimate authority to alter or abolish the political system if they choose to do so. In practice, however, the amendment process that is written into the Constitution makes termination extremely unlikely because those sworn to defend the Constitution would have to initiate the amendment process to end it.[2]

Public Accessibility

For a government to be considered democratic, it must be open, accessible, and responsive. As societies evolve, government must evolve with them. Otherwise a disjunction can occur between public opinion, social needs, and public policy. Such a disjunction has the potential to undermine support for government and the policies it promulgates.

Obviously, a system that discourages the people from making their preferences known or impedes government from responding to those preferences would not be consistent with a democratic process. How open does the system have to be, however, to permit, even encourage, public involvement? Some observers say that it must be completely transparent to facilitate accurate transmission of public opinion and to hold those in power responsible for their actions. Yet the more open the government, the more difficulty it may have in reaching decisions efficiently and effectively. Deliberation and compromise may give way to public posturing and logrolling if public officials pander to those who hold sway over them by virtue of the electoral clout they exercise or other political and personal benefits they provide.

The impediments to decision making that complete visibility produces led Vice President Cheney to refuse to reveal the names of the individuals with whom he consulted in developing the Bush administration's national energy policy. The General Accounting Office had requested such information on behalf of a congressional committee. Cheney argued that the administration should be judged by the merits of its policy and its consequences for society, not on the basis of its decision-making processes or the individuals involved in those processes. Do you agree with the vice president?

Another problem—exacerbated by the tendency of the government to be overly responsive to outside influence—is the general public's indifference, inattention, and even ignorance on many issues. Citizens who feel strongly and tend to be more knowledgeable about an issue frequently constitute only a small proportion of the population. Yet the influence of these people may be disproportional to their numbers because of the unequal distribution of resources within society. Should groups such as the National Rifle Association, the Tobacco Institute, and the Teamsters union be permitted to pursue their interests at the expense of others who are less wealthy, less organized, or less skillful? If your answer is "no," how would you constrain such groups, protect their rights to petition government, and maintain an open and accessible political system simultaneously?

The allegation that the U.S. political system is prone to special interest politics is one of the most persistent public complaints voiced today. That complaint was a driving force behind the campaign finance legislation that Senator John McCain advocated during the 2000 Republican primaries and the 107th Congress enacted in 2002. The objective of this legislation was to ban "soft money" and limit issue advocacy advertising in which candidates were mentioned by name in the period leading up to the election, to reduce the advantages that wealthy individuals and groups enjoy during elections.[3] Yet the very restrictions that Congress imposed in regulating federal elections also limited political expression and, indirectly, public participation at a time when more and more people are turning off to politics. How would

you balance the desire to achieve greater equality with the goal of getting more people involved in politics?

If unequal access is a problem, is a more restrictive governing system the solution? A government that inhibits public access may be more efficient, make better use of policy experts, and take a longer-term perspective, but it also may be less sensitive to public demands, less concerned with the here and now, and less tolerant of persons whose views are not in accord with its own.

In theory, the government closest to the people would be the people themselves. When a community meets together to decide on public policy issues, that process often is described as direct democracy. It is direct because the people are the decision makers; there are no intermediaries, no elected representatives. Town meetings at the local level and policy initiatives, legislative referendums, and recall petitions at the state level are examples of this form of government at work. There are no national examples, however, for a country as large and diverse as the United States.

Direct democracy is neither feasible nor desirable for the country as a whole. It is not feasible because it would require continual plebiscites; it is not desirable because the populace lacks the interest and knowledge to make informed judgments. Nor could such information and expertise be easily communicated to the entire community because most people do not have the time, skills, and incentives to master it. Thus, there is little alternative to representative government at the national level—which, of course, is why we have it.

Government *of* the People: Representation and Responsiveness

There must be a close relationship between representation and responsiveness for the government to be considered democratic. In this section we examine that relationship between the composition of government and the policy decisions it makes. Our focus is on the characteristics public officials possess and the representational roles they assume when they make policy judgments.

Representing Overlapping and Competing Constituencies

The constituency is the key unit for connecting those in government with those outside it. In the United States, the U.S. Constitution creates population and geographic constituencies. The Congress and the president represent population groups within designated geographic areas. With the exception of the Senate and the Electoral College, electoral constituencies must be based on population, predicated on the principle of political equality: one person, one vote.

Electoral constituencies are not the only relevant ones for government, however. All federal officials theoretically also should consider the country as a whole in making policy judgments. Yet only the president and vice president represent a national constituency—even though, under the Electoral College system, they are not directly elected by it.

Keeping the entire country in mind when deciding public policy issues is a challenge because elected officials represent specific geographic constituencies. Within those constituencies, there also are demographic, partisan, and ideological groupings of which elected representatives must be cognizant, from which they gain political support, and to which they need be responsive. Thus, even though most members of Congress complain about excessive government spending, they still enact legislation in which the "pork" is spread around. To put constraints on itself, Congress also has enacted legislation that puts limits on overall spending or restricts its own ability to modify certain types of legislation such as military base closings or international agreements the president has negotiated.

Governing also creates functional and issue constituencies that cut across electoral boundaries and bridge institutional divisions. Examples of functional groups include farmers, labor unions, small and large businesses, and various professional organizations. Issue constituencies comprise citizens who share similar interests. Often these functional and issue constituencies reinforce population and geographic constituencies, thereby orienting government officials toward serving similar needs and considering overlapping interests in their policy decisions. The problem arises when these constituencies do not overlap—when divergent constituencies create cross-pressures that must be reconciled in these decisions.

Members of Congress try to minimize cross-pressures by focusing their legislative activities in the areas that benefit their districts the most. They jockey for committee assignments that will give them the largest electoral payoff. Many federal executives work in highly specialized policy areas in which they too interact on a regular basis with the same clientele groups, led by the same people with expertise and professional interests similar to their own. This dynamic produces an effect in which federal officials become advocates when there is agreement among the groups seeking to affect public policy and referees and arbiters when there is not. Even judges find their own decisional structures reinforced by the norms of the legal system to which most of their profession adhere, by the rule of law grounded in precedent and current interpretation, and by their own judicial attitudes.

A very important and difficult part of the representative function is weighing the various interests to make the best and most responsive policy judgment. The constituency's size is almost always a factor that receives consideration in the weighing process. In a democracy, numbers matter. The operationalization of the equity rule suggests that those in greater numbers should prevail. How much greater do those numbers need to be? Should intensity of beliefs be also taken into account? How should a strongly held minority view be balanced against a much less intense majority opinion? Should officials allow their own values and beliefs to be factored into their decisional equations? Should informed opinion take precedence over uninformed opinion? Should the views of policy experts be weighed more heavily than those of the general public? And what is an appropriate time frame in which to evaluate policy impacts: the here and now, the foreseeable future, or the long term?

Consider the Social Security trust fund, for example. It is currently producing a surplus but is expected to run out of money as baby boomers retire. Which of these considerations, the short- or the long-term, should policymakers today weigh more heavily in deciding what to do with this fund?

These questions are not easy to answer. Much depends on the role perceptions, basic values, and governing orientations of the person making the decision. Recent history often serves as a guide though certainly not as a straightjacket. Nor is it a guarantee for a satisfactory judgment.

The way in which public officials translate public preferences into policy decisions obviously is an important component of democratic government. The relationship between those officials, their decisions, and the constituencies they represent is another. This relationship often is assessed on the basis of the comity between descriptive and substantive representation.

Descriptive versus Substantive Representation

Descriptive representation refers to the relationship between the demographic and attitudinal characteristics of public officials and the people they represent. Substantive representation refers to the relationship between the policy decision and the constituencies that are affected by it, directly or indirectly.

Is descriptive representation a necessary condition for effective substantive representation? Can public officials perceive and respond adequately to constituency demands and needs if they lack their own constituents' characteristics? Can they truly be responsive to issues they personally have not experienced

on some intellectual or emotional level? In a contemporary context, can a predominantly male legislature be responsive to the needs of a society made up of more than 50 percent women? Similarly if African Americans, Hispanics, or another racial or ethnic group are underrepresented in government, can they receive fair treatment by that government? Public perceptions, supported by empirical data, suggest that the answer to both of these representational questions is "no."

Support for government and its decisions relates in part to the confidence people have in public officials to understand their problems and respond to them accordingly. One of the signs of cynicism toward government in American society is the perception that many people have that "most elected officials [don't] care what people like me think."[4] Thus, one argument for broadening representation in government is the belief that it will increase the legitimacy of government and build more support for its policy decisions if a broader cross-section of society were represented in those decisions. Would you agree with this proposition?

There also is evidence that substantive representation suffers when descriptive representation is lacking.[5] Gender, race, ethnicity, age, and social and economic status affect the priorities given to specific issues as well as orientations for dealing with them. Public opinion polls have found consistent policy differences among demographic groups on a wide range of policy matters. Women, for example, tend to be more supportive of government social programs and favor a larger government role in the economy, but they also are more risk adverse and skeptical of military action than are men. These differences carry over into the institutional behavior of public officials: Women tend to be more liberal and men more conservative on these and other issues (Flanigan and Zingale 2002, 122–23).

This connection between descriptive and substantive representation suggests that the composition of government matters. It is an important component of government's democratic character. In theory, the more the government reflects the composition of the society, the more able it will be to make, implement, and adjudicate policy that accords with the desires and needs of that society. Practice, however, does not always follow theory.

Consider the Voting Rights Act of 1986, which was designed in part to improve minority representation in Congress. In implementing this legislation, the Justice departments of the Reagan, George H. W. Bush, and Clinton administrations urged states to redraw their legislative boundaries to create as many "majority-minority" districts as possible. In such a district, a minority group, such as African Americans or Latinos, would constitute the majority of voters and presumably have a better chance to elect one of their own as its representative.

Following the 1990 census and continuing throughout that decade, southern states reconfigured their congressional districts, ostensibly to increase the number of African Americans in Congress. That objective was achieved—but at a high price for the group it was intended to benefit. By concentrating minority voters who usually vote Democratic in certain legislative districts, states "whitened" their other districts, making them more conservative and more Republican. As a result, moderate Democratic legislators were replaced by conservative Republicans who were less sympathetic to the interests and needs of the African American community. State and national governments are still struggling with this representational issue, as is the federal judiciary (see chapter 11).

Delegate versus Trusteeship Roles

In addition to the demographic and attitudinal characteristics that representatives should have to provide for effective substantive representation, there is the additional question: How should they represent their constituents? What role should a public official assume in translating constituency interests, needs, and demands into public policy? These questions strike at the heart of the representation-responsiveness issue. Interestingly, they pertain to officeholders in all three branches of government—to elected, appointed, and career officials in their legislative, executive, or adjudicatory capacities.

Roles vary from *delegate* on one hand to *trustee* on the other. Delegates hew to public opinion and reflect it as much as possible in their policy decisions. They lead by following. Trustees, on the other hand, use their superior "knowledge, experience, and skills" to make decisions that they believe will be in the best interests of those they represent. They lead by exercising their own judgment and then educating people about its merits, not by following the preferences of the moment.

Members of Congress increasingly have assumed the delegate role. When they perceive a consensus in their electoral districts, they follow it. When there is no discernible constituency interest—because the issue is of little interest, has little impact, or is one on which opinion is divided—they will look to others for cues on how to decide. These other sources of input include their political party, their regional interest, the persuasiveness of the president or legislative leaders, staff advice, or their own conscience or best judgment.

To the extent that adhering to the delegate role hardens positions, to the extent that democratic processes open decision making to greater public scrutiny and make compromise more difficult, to the extent that ideology has combined with partisanship to reinforce political stands, the consequence of more democracy may be less deliberation in reaching policy judgments and quicker, more reactive decisions that provide tangible benefits for those who exercise electoral clout. The framers of the Constitution would be unhappy with such a result. They were leery of a government that was overly responsive to public pressure.

Officeholders in the executive and judicial branches, on the other hand, have tended more toward the trustee role, relying on the expertise of those with whom they interact on a regular basis—civil servants, group leaders, and political appointees in the executive branch and lawyers, precedent, and higher judicial authority in the courts—to guide them.

For persons charged with making executive and judicial decisions, there is no right role to assume, but there is a right attitude to take and there are proper criteria to employ. Decision makers should be open to points of view, time frames, even constituencies that differ from their own. Moreover, policy decisions should be made on the basis of their substantive or political merit, not by virtue of the personal, professional, or partisan benefits that might accrue to the person making the decision.

Government *by* the People: Rules for Decision Making

The relationship between representation and responsiveness is only one dimension of democratic governance. The rules by which people in government make policy decisions is another. Structure, process, and modes of operation all contribute to the transformation of public opinion and group pressures into public policy.

Constitutionalism and Democracy

In the United States, a principal impediment to democratic government is the constitutional framework itself: federalism, the separation of national institutions and their sharing of powers, and the internal system of checks and balances. Such a framework prevents any one group from easily or permanently exercising dominance.

The framers were sensitized to the dangers of despotism whether they emanated from one, few, or many. They were in an economic and social minority themselves, so they were especially fearful of majority tyranny because they knew from personal experience that minorities could not adequately protect their rights if numbers alone determined public policy outcomes. Although the framers real-

ized that a determined minority might also prevent a plurality or majority from getting its way in a system in which power was divided, they were willing to take that gamble. In a country composed largely of self-sufficient farmers, perhaps they believed that no policy was preferable to bad policy. They certainly believed that policy that denied people their basic rights should not be permitted by any government.

In addition to the constitutional framework that, in effect, establishes a set of hurdles over which legislators must jump to legislate, each institution adopts its own rules for decision making. These rules balance political equity, operational efficiency, and judgmental factors, all of which affect the policy output. The rules vary within institutions and over time, although most have been stabilized by the tradition of that legislative body and reinforced by partisan preferences.

Decisional Rules

The concept of political equality requires that every representative exercise an equal vote. In a legislative body, the side with the most votes should prevail. But what if *most* is less than a majority of the entire body? Would there still be sufficient consensus for proceeding, for making public policy? The answer depends on the size of the plurality and the number of ways in which opinion is divided.

In theory, majority rule would be the most equitable way of making public policy, with one more than half being the minimum basis for agreement. There are several problems, however, with imposing majority rule as a decisional mechanism. One relates to the diversity of opinion within the country. Perhaps there is no majority—then what? Building a majority through a combination of education, persuasion, and compromise takes time and often requires money—lots of it, if the private sector is involved—and, as we have previously noted, that really gives an advantage to people who possess the most resources and are willing to spend them to influence the formulation of public policy.

Even then, there is no guarantee that such a majority can be built, much less sustained.

To make it easier to reach decisions, the majority rule frequently is relaxed to allow a plurality—the side with the most votes—to prevail. Plurality rule still incorporates the equality principle, but it lessens the consensus requirement. Because a sizable proportion of the population may have no opinion, little interest, or much concern for many issues, such a relaxation of the consensus rule makes sense and counts all votes equally.

Safeguards are still necessary, however, particularly with respect to rights. Should basic rights be subject to a majority or plurality vote or excluded from the reach of government entirely? The answer to this question was critical for the ratification of the U.S. Constitution. Without the promise of a Bill of Rights that precluded the national government from eliminating or curtailing individual freedoms, ratification probably would not have occurred. Later amendments extended this ban on government policy to the states, as well as expanding suffrage rights to all citizens, eighteen years or older.

Decisional rules also should incorporate the components of wise policymaking: information, expertise, and the time necessary for reflection, deliberation, and judgment. The technological nature of contemporary society enhances the role of people who possess the knowledge, skills, and temperament for making sound policy decisions, but it also can shorten the time frame in which those decisions have to be made. The problem is how to mediate between what the public thinks it wants and what policymakers think would be best. Such mediation may require that the government restrain its democratic impulse to respond to public pressures directly, quickly, and efficiently in the interests of seeing and acting on the basis of a larger perspective with a longer time frame. On the other hand, failure to respond to a problem and demands for its resolution may be perceived as a failure to govern effectively. Such a perception usually leads to declining performance ratings as well as loss of public trust and confidence in government. Approval ratings for Congress almost always go down when the House and Senate are unable to agree on legislation or when Congress and the president disagree. Yet policy agreement per se may not serve the public interest or solve the problem at hand.

In short, decisional rules are an important component of democratic government. They contribute to the capability of government to make sound policy judgments as well as to the support those judgments receive from the public. For policy judgments to be followed, there must be a consensus on the validity of the decisional process that led to the policy as well as the right of government to make such decisions. For policy judgments to be approved, there also should be a consensus on the merits of the decision itself, although that consensus may be short-lived if undesirable consequences result.

Legislative Processes and Democratic Government

Over the years Congress has adopted a variety of rules that have undercut the majoritarian principle. These rules, which must be formally accepted by every new Congress on the basis of a plurality voting decision, have been designed for a variety of reasons: to decentralize power; to maximize the advantages of seniority and the expertise that may go with it; to facilitate or terminate legislative debate; and to permit, limit, or prohibit changes to legislation as it moves through the policymaking process. The Senate requires a supermajority (60 of 100 senators) to end debate on most issues; the Constitution imposes a two-thirds rule for the Senate's ratification of treaties and two-thirds of both houses for initiating constitutional amendments.

Do the benefits of these rules compensate for the inequality they produce by undercutting the majority or plurality rule principle? Do they encourage the legislative branch to follow public opinion, or do they give minority groups disproportionate negative power?

This minority rule precept has incurred the most criticism.

The greater the voting requirements for making a policy judgment, the more power minorities exercise over those judgments. A determined minority can prevent change more easily than it can achieve it. Preventing change works to the advantage of whoever benefits from the existing arrangement. For a minority that already enjoys economic, social, or political advantage, having—in effect—a veto reinforces its advantage.

Critics chide Congress for allowing individuals and groups to exercise so much power over public policy outcomes. Through its decentralization of power in the form of a large and complex committee system (consisting of authorization and appropriation committees and subcommittees, select committees, and joint committees), diverse legislative calendars, and conference committees (if both houses do not agree to the same legislation), Congress has created numerous hurdles that must be overcome for a bill to survive the legislative process and move to the president's desk.

This multistage process makes legislating difficult, and that difficulty has been enhanced by the divided partisan control of Congress and the White House—the rule, not the exception, between 1968 and 2002. No wonder the number of new laws has declined during most of this period (Ornstein, Mann, and Malbin 2001–2002, 149) On the other hand, logrolling has increased: Bills have become larger and more complex, giving the executive branch more administrative discretion and Congress more incentive for overseeing its implementation. Are these outcomes desirable?

These institutional changes mirror the increasing diversity of American society and the representation of that diversity in government. Congress has become more atomized. Public approval of Congress as a legislative body usually is lower than most constituencies' approval of their legislative representatives. This disjunction between public perception of Congress and perception of its component parts has serious implications for democratic government. It has enhanced the representational role that members of Congress play, but at the expense of decreased legislative output and increased oversight activities. It also has contributed to the public perception that Congress is beholden to special interests.

Executive Power and Democratic Governance

Like it or not, much of the burden for formulating policy proposals, building majorities across institutional lines, and implementing bills once they become law lies with the president. Regarded as the principal agenda setter, coalition builder, and executive overseer, the president is expected to provide leadership to overcome what the Constitution separates and what partisan divisions within government often reinforce. These expectations, often inflated by promises made by candidates in their campaigns for the presidency and by the personal images they try to project, raise performance goals but do not, in and of themselves, increase the power to attain those goals.

The gap between public expectations and institutional and political resources places presidents in a leadership dilemma that is most severely tested in a "politics as usual" environment such as the situation in which George W. Bush found himself when he became president. Without a clear mandate from the voters—nor even a popular vote victory— Bush did not have much political capital to spend on his legislative objectives. As a consequence he was forced to limit his priorities and succeeded in achieving only one of them— tax relief—in his first six months in office.

During crises, however, presidential leadership is easier to attain; Congress is more deferential, the courts are less likely to impose their judgments, and the public is more united and, initially, much more supportive of the president's performance. Thus, Bush was more successful with Congress in the aftermath of the terrorist attacks of September 11, 2001, than he was before the attacks.

A critical issue, central to democratic government, is the role public opinion should play in presidential policymaking and implementation. To what extent should presidents take that opinion into consideration in prioritizing issues, formulating policies, and promoting them?

The Plebiscitary Presidency: To Lead or to Follow?

The case for following public opinion is most persuasive following a presidential election, particularly when the winning candidate receives a much larger percentage of the popular and electoral vote than his or her opponent (such as in 1964 or 1980). Such an election often is claimed by the winner as a mandate for the type of change that candidate had proposed during the campaign. The claim of a mandate frequently is illusionary, however, even when the margin of victory is substantial. People vote for candidates for different reasons and expect the winner to do different things once elected. Often candidates contribute to that perception by purposely fudging issues, clouding their priorities, and making contradictory promises—and even some on which they cannot possibly deliver.

As the election fades into the past, so do many of the election issues; thus, the campaign agenda is less likely to serve as a governing agenda. How, then, should salient issues be determined and policy solutions devised? Increasingly, presidents have turned to public opinion polls to identify the major concerns of the populace and focus groups for a deeper understanding of people's perceptions of the problems, wants, needs, and rhetoric that will turn them on. Here's how political strategist Dick Morris describes Bill Clinton's use of polls:

> Clinton . . . consults polls as if they were giant wind socks that tell him which way the wind is blowing. And then he asks the pollster to help him determine which current he should try to harness to move him closer to

his destination. He sails with that air current until he has gone too far to the left. . . . He polls again, reverses his tack, and this time aims a little to the right . . . he ends up . . . in the middle (Morris 1997, 84).

Although national surveys and small, interactive groups are useful sources of information, the question remains: Should they be used to design policy initiatives and the rhetoric needed to sell them? Should they be a *modus operandi* for presidential action? Those who argue that they should point to this opinion as setting realistic boundaries for policymakers, the details of which often are provided by interest group representatives as well as government policy experts. Given that public support is critical for policy success, why not act when the fire is hot? And why not use pretested words for their maximum effect?

Critics, however, see presidents who hide behind public opinion polls and focus groups as abdicating their leadership responsibilities and wasting valuable institutional resources in the process. Moreover, presidents who allow others to set their agenda and frame their issues limit their perspective to the contemporary time frame, their vision to what is popular here and now—not what may be better in the long run. They also may fall victim to a form of mob rule that does not adequately protect citizens who do not subscribe to the popular sentiment of the moment.

Regardless of their propensity to follow public opinion or go their own way, presidents are still held accountable if the policy does not produce the desired results. Job approval, reelection, the judgment of history, and, in extreme cases, impeachment are instruments of accountability—inducements for making considered judgments rather than unthinking, "knee-jerk" reactions to events and the moods they generate.

The Crisis Presidency and the Suspension of Personal Rights and Civil Liberties

The dilemma of how to exercise strong presidential leadership in ordinary times is replaced by the danger of how to constrain that leadership during crises—when presidential prerogatives expand, institutional checks are relaxed, partisan politics are muted, and the public looks to the president for direction, resolve, and a response consistent with the threat posed. Given the enhanced expectations and demands placed on the president in such situations—to unify the country, serve as its spokesperson, design the policy reaction, and manage the crisis—it is difficult simultaneously to be as sensitive to diverse domestic pressures, particularly those emanating from a minority that has a different perspective on the problem or has been disproportionately and adversely affected by it. Residents of Japanese and German ancestry during World War II and people of Middle Eastern origin following the terrorist attacks on September 11, 2001, would fit into this category.

Expansion of presidential power is inevitable in situations that jeopardize the country's security. Precedent for the Bush administration's responses to the terrorist threat after September 11 was established in the Lincoln, Wilson, and Franklin Roosevelt administrations. Democracies can tolerate authoritative actions during crises, but only if they are assumed to be temporary. One of the perennial issues—one that followed each of the crises in the United States in which liberties were suspended and enforcement was inequitably applied—is determining when the crisis is over, when normalcy can return. Frequently the executive and the legislature, particularly the opposition party in Congress, have differing perspectives and political incentives on this issue. With broad popular support, congressional and judicial concurrence, increased authority, and the benefits derived from strong and successful crisis management, presidents are reluctant to return quickly to a politics-as-usual environment in which their powers are substantially reduced and their ability to formulate policy is constrained by other partisan, institutional, and public pressures. A good example is the Bush administration after September 11,

2001, which maintained the public's focus on antiterrorism and national security concerns through the midterm elections and into the next presidential election cycle. On the other hand, if domestic pressures persist they will need to find expression and eventually will force those in government to be responsive to them. That is what democratic government is all about.

Executive Branch Decision Making: How Open Should It Be?

The structure and operation of the executive branch also are relevant to democratic governance. Here we are concerned primarily with functional, not electoral, democracy—although there is an electoral tie, albeit an extended one, between appointed officials and the electorate through the processes by which these officials are nominated and confirmed and by whom their performance will be judged during the next election.

Nonetheless, the division of the executive into separate departments and agencies, its functional specialization, and the culture of public service encourage actors outside of government to try to affect policy implementation (as well as its formulation) and orient the bureaucracy to its clientele and their special interests. In other words, these factors keep government tied to those it represents and serves. That tie is the key to a viable democratic institution.

Alliances among executive officials and interest groups extend to Congress through interest group lobbying and congressional oversight of the executive branch, Senate confirmation of political appointees, and annual budgetary politics. Such alliances lead to issue networks in which executive branch officials, interest group leaders, congressional committee members and their staffs, and specialized media interact on a regular basis. The networks are semiautonomous; they operate largely independent of one another. The bonds of these institutional relationships are strengthened by personal ties, common assessments of needs and interests, norms of acceptable behavior, and recognized and stable policy processes.

The policy networks constitute a functional democracy in which input from affected groups is expected and encouraged. One democratic issue for Congress and the executive branch is whether that input is equitable. Do certain groups—by virtue of their size, resources, or even motivation—have a consistent advantage in affecting the making or implementation of public policy? Does the American Association of Retired Persons (AARP) exert a dominant influence on Social Security and Medicare policy? Should it, with approximately 35 million members? Do the rules by which the system operates and policy judgments are made favor those with access, clout, and money such as the pharmaceutical industry, which spent $28.3 million in the 2002 elections (Center for Responsive Politics 2003)?

A second issue pertains to the relationship between special interests and the public interest—assuming there is a discernible public interest. Does the whole, the collective good, equal the sum of its parts: the array of special interests that compete for favorable policy decisions? How do public officeholders weigh offsetting interests in reaching policy judgments? Equally important, how does the public perceive that they do so? Unfortunately, the answer to the last question is "cynically." Public opinion polls suggest that as many people believe that the government is not run for the benefit of all the people as believe that it is (Pew Research Center for the People and the Press 1999).

The Judiciary as an Antimajoritiarian Institution

Like the other branches of government, the judiciary is subject to external influence; unlike Congress and the presidency, however, it is not nearly as sensitive to public opinion or as reactive to the political pressures that flow from that opinion. The avenues by which judicial decisions may be affected also are different. Initiating test cases, filing briefs, and even participating in a debate in a law review or legal journal are considered acceptable ways to try to affect public policy within the judicial system. Direct lobbying in the form of personal contacts on cases under review, grassroots mobilization, protests in front of the Supreme Court, and public relations campaigns are not. An exception may be the political campaigns that seek to influence the nomination and confirmation of federal judges and the confirmation process itself—in which questions asked, answers given, and, in rarer cases, promises made concerning a candidate's judicial philosophy, constitutional interpretation, and hypothetical disposition of cases could impact on that judge's later decisions.

Although federal judges serve during good behavior for life and therefore are not subject to the ongoing political pressures that elected and appointed officials must consider in making their policy judgments, judges still come to their jobs with partisan allegiances, ideological beliefs, judicial orientations, and a host of activities within the legal and political arenas, which presumably contributed to their nomination and confirmation. It is difficult for judges to escape from their past beliefs and behavior in rendering their judgments.

Judicial Review and Democratic Values

The courts are considered the least democratic of the three institutions of the national government because their decisions can reverse the policies or actions of elected officials. Does judicial review of legislative statutes or executive actions always or usually result in consequences that undermine a democratic society? The answer is complex. It relates to cohabitation of the three basic values on which democracy rests: individual liberty, political equality, and a broad-based sense of community, past, present, and future. The Constitution is designed to protect and promote these values for everyone. To do so, its primacy as the law of the land must prevail. The courts make decisions that protect this primacy. These decisions may conflict with the judgments of other government bodies—hence the tension created by judicial review.

In one sense, striking down legislation or declaring executive actions null and void undercuts all three democratic values for the majority: the right of an elected government, which operates on the basis of political equality, to formulate and implement its own policy for the good of the society. On the other hand, the courts also are applying these same values to the people who face the greatest and most persistent threat of being denied these rights: minorities.

Our system of government tends to slow policymaking but does not prevent it from occurring over time. A determined majority usually can get its way, but a determined minority may not. Its only recourse is the judicial arena—the court of last resort.

By interpreting the Constitution, the document that places certain rights beyond the reach of any one group of elected or appointed officials, the judiciary in effect guarantees these rights to the entire community, not just to the plurality or majority. In this sense, judicial review does not undermine democratic government as much as it prevents that government from committing an error, confusing consensus for the interests of the society as a whole. On the other hand, judicial review does elevate the rights of some citizens and, in the process, may undermine those of others, undercut the deliberative process in which legislative and executive officials engage, and weaken the social psychology on which a democratic system is predicated—that the people through their elected representatives are in the best position to decide on policy that is in their own interests.

Government *for* the People: The Adequacy, Equity, and Civic Virtue of Public Policy

The adequacy of representation and the fairness and efficiency of decisional rules should be reflected in the evaluation of public policy

outcomes. Does the policy solve the problem? Does it meet the needs and satisfy the demands of those who have been most interested and involved in the policy process and should be most affected by the solution? On balance, how does the policy outcome affect the society as a whole? Who gains and who loses? How does the policy affect perceptions of and attitudes toward government? Do people place more or less faith in government as a consequence of its policy decisions?

Policymakers gauge the public reaction by the response they receive, the surveys they examine, and the focus groups they and their political parties use. They are interested in whether the issue fades quickly, slowly, or not at all; whether it will spill over to the next election cycle; and the extent to which it will continue to be a subject of public concern after the election.

Good and Bad Policy

In evaluating public policy, an important consideration is the adequacy of the policy itself. Does it rectify the problem and, if so, to what extent and for how long? Does it generate other consequences—intended or unintended, beneficial or harmful—and for whom? The 1979 amendments to the Federal Election Campaign Act are a case in point. Designed to provide political parties with additional funds to enhance their organizational and grassroots activities at the state and local levels, the legislation created a huge "soft money" loophole in the contribution limits for individuals and groups and a way around the expenditure limits placed on presidential candidates who accepted federal funds. Thirteen years passed before Congress enacted legislation to correct the problem it had unintentionally created with these amendments.

Whereas policy might be considered legitimate if it were made by officials chosen in an open and honest election or appointed by those who were, and if it were done in accordance with established decisional rules and procedures, its impact in terms of costs and benefits may run counter to the perception of fairness or be inconsistent with other democratic norms and values. Generating or perpetuating social, economic, or political inequality—such as tax benefits for certain individuals or groups—might be considered an undemocratic outcome, yet it is likely as long as the Constitution protects the expenditure of unequal resources, which are spent to influence government.

Another persistent allegation about U.S. national policy is that it is usually incremental in character, minimally feasible rather than maximally optimal—frequently policy at the level of the lowest common denominator. The implication of this criticism is that political compromise somehow undercuts effective policy solutions. Yet compromise also contributes to political support for that policy. Besides, what is the alternative? Dominance by whoever is in power would not necessarily result in better policy or more tolerance of that policy, especially if it were perceived to be a failure.

The public places a premium on the efficiency with which government deals with the problem, not with the deliberation that may be required to solve it. As an institution, Congress tends to be evaluated more on its productivity—which requires consensus building and takes time—than on its representation of diverse interests, which often stands in the way of reaching a policy agreement or turning it into a huge "pork barrel" with something for everyone. Similarly, presidents are assessed more favorably for their decisiveness, confidence, and consistency than for their reflection, nuance, or hesitation in rushing to judgment. Government officials who act primarily to satisfy the public propensities of the moment may not be exercising good judgment, let alone producing good policy, even though the public desires quick fixes to problems.

The process of policymaking also affects the reception given to the policy: whether it is considered fair, wise, and legitimate. Fairness is enhanced by a perception of adequate descriptive representation and adherence to regular and accepted modes of operation. These institutional components, along with the perceived adequacy of the policy in dealing with the problem it was intended to address, affect the public's trust and confidence in government in general—as well as those responsible for making and implementing it. If unrealistic performance promises are made or unsubstantiated claims announced, if a gap exists between expectations and results, then cynicism toward government is a likely outcome. Over time, cynicism undermines political support and perceptions of legitimacy. If cynicism toward government is combined with unacceptable economic and social conditions, it could actually threaten the system itself—as it did with the Third French Republic and Weimar Germany.

Undoing a Democracy

Because the people or their elected representatives have a right to create and an obligation to maintain whatever form of government they desire, theoretically they could choose to change to a nondemocratic government. In the short run, such a decision might be perceived as legitimate if the government effectively coped with the problems at hand. Over the long haul, however, it would be much more problematic because such a decision could be irreversible. Once a nondemocratic system was created, the people would lose their power to change it because that government would no longer rest on popular consent. Nondemocratic governments could perpetuate themselves indefinitely, if those in power wished and were able to do so. Thus, the alternative to a democratic government that is perceived to be malfunctioning is to fix it, not replace it.

Governing in a democratic manner, particularly within the framework of the U.S. constitutional system, is not easy. It is usually efficient. It produces perceptions of inequality. It frequently encourages a rush to judgment. Yet, in the absence of a viable alternative that would protect, preserve, and promote the basic values upon which American democracy rests, there are few options other than examining the democratic character of the governing system, its strengths and weaknesses, and trying to improve it. The remainder of this book is dedicated to that task.

Notes

1. Robert Dahl (1988) regards political equality as a moral judgment—the normative belief that everyone's life, liberty, and happiness ought to be intrinsically equal to one another's.
2. The framers of the U.S. Constitution faced a similar problem when they desired to replace the Articles of Confederation with the document they had drafted in Philadelphia in 1787. Amending the Articles required a unanimous vote of the states. Fearing that they would not obtain that vote—two states were not even represented when the Constitution was finally completed—the framers incorporated a new amendment process into the Constitution that did not require unanimous consent and then used that process to ratify the Constitution.
3. The Bipartisan Campaign Finance Reform Act (McCain-Feingold bill) prohibits issue advocacy advertisements from mentioning federal candidates by name thirty days or less before a primary election and sixty days or less before a general election. This restriction was challenged on the grounds that it violated freedom of speech as defined by the Supreme Court in its landmark decision in the case of *Buckley v. Valeo*, 424 U.S. 1 (1976). The Supreme Court, however, in *McConnell v. FEC*, no. 02-1676 (2003), upheld this and other major provisions of the law.
4. Over the past decade approximately six of ten people subscribe to this proposition, according to surveys conducted by the Pew Research Center for the People and the Press, published in its report "Retropolitics" (1999), 139.
5. See, for example, Darcy, Welch, and Clark (1987); Dodson (1991); Swers (1998); Thomas (1994); Thomas and Wilcox (1998).

References

Center for Responsive Politics. 2003. "Election Overview, 2002 Cycle, Top Industries." Available at www.opensecrets.org/overview/industries.asp (accessed October 15, 2003).

Dahl, Robert A. 1988. *On Democracy*. New Haven, Conn.: Yale University Press.

Darcy, Robert, Susan Welch, and Janet Clark. 1987. *Women, Elections, and Representation*. New York: Longman.

Dodson, Debra, ed. 1991. *Gender and Policymaking: Studies of Women in Office*. New Brunswick, N.J.: Center for Women and Politics.

Flanigan, William H., and Nancy H. Zingale. 2002. *Political Behavior of the American Electorate*. Washington, D.C.: Congressional Quarterly.

Morris, Dick. 1997. *Behind the Oval Office*. New York: Random House.

Ornstein, Norman J., Thomas E. Mann, and Michael J. Malbin. 2001–2002. *Vital Statistics On Congress*. Washington D.C.: Congressional Quarterly.

Pew Research Center for the People and the Press. 1998. "Deconstructing Distrust." March. Available at http://people-press.org.

———. 1999. "Retropolitics." November. Available at http://people-press.org.

Swers, Michele. 1998. "Are Congresswomen More Likely to Vote for Women's Issues Bills Than Their Male Colleagues?" *Legislative Studies Quarterly* 23: 435–48.

Thomas, Sue. 1994. *How Women Legislate*. New York: Oxford University Press.

Thomas, Sue, and Clyde Wilcox, eds. 1998. *Women and Elective Office: Past, Present, and Future*. New York: Oxford University Press.

Further Reading

Bealey, Frank. 1988. *Democracy in the Contemporary State*. Oxford, U.K.: Clarendon Press.

Berg, Elias. 1965. *Democracy and the Majority Principle*. Stockholm, Sweden: Scandinavian University Books.

Brennan, Geoffrey, and Alan Hamlin. 2000. *Democratic Devices and Desires*. Cambridge, U.K.: Cambridge University Press.

Dahl, Robert A. 1989. *Democracy and Its Critics.* New Haven, Conn.: Yale University Press.

Held, David. 1987. *Models of Democracy.* Stanford, Calif.: Stanford University Press.

Kelso, William Alton. 1978. *American Democratic Theory: Pluralism and Its Critics.* Westport, Conn.: Greenwood Press.

Lublin, David. 1997. *The Paradox of Representation.* Princeton, N.J.: Princeton University Press.

Pennock, J. Roland. 1979. *Democratic Political Theory.* Princeton, N.J.: Princeton University Press.

Pennock, J. Roland, and John W. Chapman, eds. 1983. *Liberal Democracy.* New York: New York University Press.

Pitkin, Hanna. 1967. *The Concept of Representation.* Berkeley: University of California Press.

Sartori, Giovanni. 1987. *The Theory of Democracy Revisited.* Chatham, N.J.: Chatham House.

Verba, Sidney, Kay Lehman Schlozman, and Henry E. Brady. 1995. *Voice and Equality: Civic Voluntarism in American Politics.* Cambridge, Mass.: Harvard University Press.

Warren, Mark, ed. 1999. *Democracy and Trust.* Cambridge, U.K.: Cambridge University Press.

★★★

Chapter 2

The Civic Foundations of American Democracy

Beth Stark

In 2001 the New York City chapter of the League of Women Voters was about to shut its doors. A declining and aging membership, along with dwindling funds, had nearly done in the organization. Now, thanks to a few dedicated members and an article in the *New York Times*, the city's League is enjoying a reprieve. The road back to its former strength is long and uncertain, however. Such a story could be told about many of the organizations that have traditionally constituted American civic culture. Similar evidence, both empirical and anecdotal, is receiving intense scrutiny because of the implications of such a trend for the health and integrity of American democracy.

Clubs such as the League of Women Voters have long served as the lynchpin of participatory politics in this country. Its members are concerned about their community; many are active in their churches and synagogues, belong to other clubs, and use their contacts to get things done. Through their involvement in the League , they have learned about city politics, studied issues, influenced government, and worked to encourage the education and participation of their fellow New York City residents.

This chapter examines the meaning of civic life in a democracy and its potential benefits for democratic institutions of governance. It begins with an explanation of the concept of civil society and how, at its best, it supports and strengthens the participatory nature of our political system. First, Ameri-

cans' civic ties help to integrate them into their communities, while increasing their resources and inclination for political engagement. As an example, I look specifically at how membership in a religious organization plays this important role. Second, civil society enhances the quality of political representation by providing a location for citizens to coordinate action and acquire power. Finally, to understand how these benefits can be realized we must determine which characteristics of association activity are most productive and how civil society itself can be sustained and improved.

The democratic political principles we value cannot flourish without the social practices that support them. The achievement of liberty, equality, and the collective good must be based on a foundation of trust, cooperation, and consent. A democracy cannot survive unless its citizens feel that they can affect their system of government and see their preferences enacted. A robust civil society cultivates the political integration and responsive representation this system of government requires.

The Concept of Civil Society and Its Benefits

When Americans come together for the sake of mutual interests or shared goals, the foundations for healthy democracy are formed. The ties that are fashioned among citizens as a result of association generate benefits for members within the clubhouse and for society beyond. This phenomenon was the subject of Alexis de Tocqueville's writing in *Democracy in America*, and in the decades since it has prompted renewed awareness of the key role of associations as the origin of many of our democratic tendencies and practices.

Americans take an interest in their neighbors' well-being because they understand that their prosperity is bound together. This phenomenon, Tocqueville writes, is "self-interest rightly understood," and the partnership it forms among citizens is the key to democracy's success. Self-interest rightly understood can be realized only in meeting with the "other"—coming face to face with those to whom one's fate is tied—and this coming together requires involvement in local life.

Although democratic institutions may provide for political liberty and equality, they cannot by themselves create the cooperation among citizens that is necessary for successful governing. In fact, liberty and equality can lead citizens to individualism and, in turn, to isolation and disengagement. Without an active citizenry, democracy becomes susceptible to despotism and risks failure. Tocqueville claims that the organizations that structure local life solve democracy's problem of isolation, bringing citizens to act together and depend on one another (Tocqueville 1988, 511). As citizens work for common causes, they meet their neighbors and form ties and obligations. According to self-interest rightly understood in a democracy, not only does each citizen regard the prosperity of the nation as his or her own work, he or she understands that the welfare of each citizen is linked to that of other citizens (Tocqueville 1988, 237). Therefore, each citizen participates in the nation's management not only out of pride or duty but out of a sense of his or her own well-being.

Tocqueville describes how, first, smaller matters demonstrate to the citizen the importance of this relationship; the building of a road, for example, will impact a citizen and his or her property directly, and the citizen can see the benefit of involvement. The citizen becomes involved in political life first by necessity—to influence the building of the road—and then by choice; what starts out as calculation becomes, in the American heart, an instinct to participate (Tocqueville 1988, 512). Thus, Tocqueville discovered in America a nation of joiners, and this characteristic was the secret to a successful democracy.

Today scholars are revisiting Tocqueville's observations to elucidate the importance of this "partnership among citizens" for governing almost 200 years later. At the heart of this discussion is the concept of civil society, which seeks to define the communal and associational life that takes place in a sphere between the state and the market.

Michael Walzer has called civil society "the space of uncoerced human association and also the set of relational networks—formed for the sake of family, faith, interest and ideology—that fill this space" (Walzer 1995, 153).

Dekker and van den Broek define civil society further, seeking to clarify its defining elements. They write that voluntariness is the "guiding principle" of civil society, distinguishing it from the involuntary nature of one's relations with family or the state. They refer to associations as civil society's "dominant collective actors" because the concept of civil society seeks to describe what we do in more or less formal organizations, rather than individually or in intimate social interaction. They also emphasize the interactive nature of associational relations, from which its benefits derive. "Decision making ideally takes shape through debate . . . arguments being the medium of exchange" (Dekker and van den Broek 1998, 13).

Robert Putnam has found that communities with a robust civic life make for a more successful democracy. He argues that horizontal relationships, overlapping networks of associations, and high levels of civic engagement are related to trust, tolerance, and solidarity. These communities possess political systems that are more democratic than neighbors where interaction is limited to clans and mistrust of outsiders is high (Putnam 1993).

The relationships and ties formed in associational life create the social capital necessary for democracy to thrive. Social capital is a resource, like other forms of capital, that individuals or groups can draw on and use to reach desired ends. Putnam (1996) names networks, norms, and trust as three forms of social capital; Coleman (1988, S98) describes them as obligation structures, information channels, and norms/sanctions. Coleman uses the example of the diamond trade among New York City's Hasidic Jews. An exceptionally tight-knit community, with a dense network of ties, enables group members to trust other members and engenders a responsibility to be trustworthy. Diamonds are loaned for inspection without security within the community with the expectation that the borrower's ties to the group will keep him honest. The cost of breaking this trust is high and goes well beyond the trade. Benefits are accrued to the community as a whole in the form of facilitated business practices and reinforced obligations among members.

In short, social capital "increases the capacity for action and facilitates the production of some good" (Paxton 1999, 93). It does so because of the relationships members of the group have with each other as well as collectively as a group (Paxton 1999, 100). Those relationships must involve some type of mutual obligation felt by members of the network, such as gratitude, friendship, or loyalty. Moreover, the ties among members must be generally positive. Tocqueville took note of the goodwill generated: "Feelings and ideas are renewed, the heart enlarged, and understanding developed only by the reciprocal action of men one upon the other" (Tocqueville 1988, 515).

Through membership in a group, we can meet people and expand our range of contacts, create bonds with others through the experience of shared interests or efforts, learn the benefits of coordinated action, develop confidence in those relationships that can be generalized beyond the group, and learn behavior that allows us to remain part of the group. Social capital is the benefit we derive from association that enables us to take some action or produce some good. The resulting goods can be private, solidaristic, or public—such as a business contact developed through a professional organization, the brotherhood experienced by members of a fraternal club, or community parks cleaned by an environmental group's combined effort.

Civil Society and Democracy

The benefits generated in American civic life enhance the democratic nature of our political system by enabling citizen participation and augmenting our representative processes. First, civic activity leads to increased political participation. Americans who meet with their fellow citizens at church or in clubs also are more likely to vote, write a letter to an elected official, take part in a political campaign, and more. The social capital gained in associational life helps them effectively utilize the political institutions we have for democratic representation. They are better positioned vis-à-vis the electoral process and representative bodies to make their voices heard by those who govern. Second, where those institutions fall short, the organizations that constitute civil society help individuals combine limited resources to overcome the often high cost of participation or, in some cases, provide appropriate alternatives or supplements to state governing structures.

Political Participation

Active and authentic engagement in the democratic process requires that citizens possess considerable resources. To make our voices heard and participate effectively, we must have knowledge about the issues that affect us, the skills to communicate our preferences, and the belief that our participation can affect outcomes. Civil society creates a space where those resources often are developed. The projects we undertake as members of our community groups help us gain the knowledge, skills, and personal efficacy necessary to act as democratic participants. Carol Pateman writes:

> The theory of participatory democracy is built around the central assertion that individuals and their institutions cannot be considered in isolation from one another. The existence of representative institutions at the national level is not sufficient for democracy; for maximum participation by all the people at that level socialization, or "social training," for democracy must take place in other spheres in order that the necessary individual attitudes and psychological qualities can be developed. This development takes place through the process of participation itself. The major function of participation in the theory of participatory democracy is therefore an educative one, educative in the very widest sense, including both the psychological aspect and the gaining of practice in democratic skills and procedures (Pateman 1970, 42).

Tocqueville called America's myriad civic organizations "schools of democracy," where the skills and character needed for effective political engagement are learned. He referred to the "human results that accrue from the participatory process" (Tocqueville 1988, 43). Each citizen is benefited individually by the practice he or she performs in civic life that in turn enables that citizen to participate more successfully in the political process. Our democratic system is improved when its citizens are well prepared for their role in governing.

The primary psychological benefit of civic engagement is increased efficacy, or a sense of general personal effectiveness. Some people may be able to achieve this feeling through employment. Not many people, however, may enjoy a sense of autonomy or the opportunity to see the fruit of their labor at work—especially people in low-level or unskilled positions, for example.

When we lead a bible study or coordinate a school fundraiser, we are more likely to feel that "someone like me" can make a difference. That efficacy will then make it more likely that we will see the value of our own political participation.

Coordinating the school fundraiser also allows us to practice the skills required for active citizenship in a democracy. Conducting a meeting, coordinating volunteers, writing a letter on behalf of the fundraising committee—all of these activities foster talents that can be translated to the political process. We can rely on the skills we learn in our associations when we communicate with our legislators, mobilize our neighbors, or run for elective office, for example.

Verba, Schlozman, and Brady (1995) found in their Civic Participation Study that members of nonpolitical organizations (identified by respondents as groups that do not take political stands) are able to exercise civic skills in their groups and that attaining such skills does increase political participation. Forty percent of respondents reported attending meetings where decisions were made, and approximately 20 percent had the opportunity to plan a meeting, write a letter, or make a presentation (Verba, Schlozman and Brady 1995, 312). What's more, these researchers found that the acquisition of civic skills in associations is much less stratified by race, income, and sex than it is in the workplace—suggesting a lot of potential for disadvantaged segments of society to gain important resources (318). Finally, these authors were able to show, using the statistical technique of ordinary least squares regression, that the possession of civic skills significantly improves the likelihood of political activity, even after controlling for a person's level of political engagement (352).[1]

Although most people do not choose membership in civic organizations to pursue political aims, their involvement nevertheless can increase their political interest and knowledge. Only about one-third of group members claim that their organizations "take stands on or discuss public issues or try to influence government actions" (Baumgartner and Walker 1988, 922). But if membership in an organization leads to exposure to issues in the community that might be affected by politics, a member might become interested inasmuch as that issue relates to her organization's goals. New relationships formed with people as a result of group membership also can provide increased opportunities to discuss political topics and be introduced to new information. O'Connell (1999) points out that "though groups start out, and may remain, focused on mutual interests such as hobbies, sports, or the Bible, their 'social talk' often deals with broader subjects leading to awareness and action" (O'Connell 1999, 60). Verba, Schlozman, and Brady (1995) confirm this phenomenon; in their study, 12 percent of members of nonpolitical organizations reported that political discussion had been on the agenda of a meeting of their group, and 30 percent reported that politics was discussed informally in the group (Verba, Schlozman, and Brady 1995, 373). Dekker and van den Broek (1998, 33) find in the 1990 World Values Survey study of thirteen countries in western Europe and North America that "[t]he effects of membership and of volunteering in general reveal a clear impact of membership on trust, political interest, and discussing politics." Moreover, "In almost all cases, membership of nonpolitical organizations is related to political interest and discussing politics" (Dekker and van den Broek 1998, 35). In addition, they conclude that being a member is just as important a factor for gaining social capital as volunteering after one becomes a member. When an organization is politically oriented, however, the impact on the political engagement of its members is considerable (Baumgartner and Walker 1988, 924).

The formation of new contacts through civic involvement also can increase opportunities for recruitment into political participation. The wider our network of relationships, the more likely it is that we will know someone who asks us to join them on a campaign, make a contribution to a candidate, or vote

in a particular election. An average of approximately 10 percent of members of nonpolitical organizations report being asked to vote or take some other political action by someone in their group, according to Verba, Schlozman, and Brady (1995). They emphasize, however, that a nonpolitical organization can include anything from a soccer team to a garden club. The rates of reported recruitment actually range from a high of 39 percent in unions and 27 percent in neighborhood associations to a low of 6 percent and 4 percent in charitable and youth-oriented groups, respectively (Verba, Schlozman, and Brady 1995, 378). In overtly political organizations, as many as two-thirds of members are asked to become politically involved (374).

Whereas Verba, Schlozman, and Brady (1995, 316) assert that these benefits also accrue to a significant extent in the workplace, especially by workers in upper-level positions, Ayala (2000) finds that the voluntary nature of our civic groups is important. Ayala claims that "activity in more voluntary groups has the greatest effect on political participation, especially time-based and volunteer oriented activities" (Ayala 2000, 100).[2]

Civil Society and Religion in America

America's robust religious institutions are widely considered to serve as a critical foundation for the vitality of our civic life and as fertile ground for the seeds of increased political engagement. Although some scholars have suggested that some segments of U.S. civil society are in decline—a point we return to later in this chapter—our commitment to religious organizations remains strong (Putnam 1996, 2000; Wuthnow and Hodgkinson 1990). Furthermore, religious institutions are ideally situated to provide their participants with opportunities, resources, and incentives for action beyond the congregation, suggesting the central role of such groups in forming and maintaining social and political ties.

Other countries may have high levels of religiosity or a great variety of religious faiths represented among their citizens, but "among advanced industrialized countries, none equals the United States in overall levels of religious commitment and the range of religious diversity" (Wuthnow 1990, 4). As a testament to the strength of organized religion in the United States, between 65 percent and 75 percent of adults claim to belong to a church or synagogue. There are approximately 250,000–300,000 congregations in America; the density varies geographically from one congregation for every 1,000 persons to as high as one for every 300 in some areas (Wuthnow 1990, 4). We boast more than 200 major denominations and faiths, in addition to as many as 1,000 smaller sects and cults, with new ones springing up all the time to meet the needs and preferences of potential followers (Wuthnow 1990, 7).

Moreover, membership is not merely symbolic for Americans; we attend, we value religious participation, and we take part in activities. In surveys conducted by the Pew Research Center over the years 2000–2002, almost 60 percent of Americans reported having attended religious services in the previous seven days, and nearly half attended on a weekly basis or more often (Dimock, Craighill, and Rogers 2002, 30). Furthermore, 60 percent of respondents agreed that religion was very important to them (Dimock, Craighill, and Rogers 2002). One-fifth of Americans report doing some sort of volunteer work related to a religious organization, and 40 percent say taking part in a church-related activity is very important—compared with only 15 percent in Great Britain, for example (Wuthnow 1990, 7).[3] Such healthy statistics prompt Wuthnow to write that "on the whole, the religious sector constitutes one of the strongest and most dynamic segments of the entire voluntary effort in American society" (7).

All of this activity is of interest to scholars of civil society not only for the civic life that occurs in and around the practice of faith but for the potential for that civic engagement to go beyond the congregation and into the public sphere of political participation. Two dominant theories regarding the possible relationship between religion and political participation have been suggested and investigated. The first is that membership in a religious organization leads to increased levels of nonreligious civic activity, which in turn improves the likelihood of political participation. The second is that membership directly increases political participation by increasing one's exposure to political issues or opportunities for political action.

The 1988 *Giving and Volunteering Study* found that members of religious congregations were 50 percent more likely to volunteer than nonmembers (Hodgkinson, Weitzman, and Kirsh 1990, 103). Of the 12 percent of adults who volunteer more than five hours per week (27 percent of volunteers), "78 percent were church members" (11).[4]

Religion also provides an organizational context that offers structural benefits to members. Institutional characteristics help by lowering the costs of participation and providing resources. Many denominations feature an administrative hierarchy that links members at the national, state, and local levels. This arrangement provides an extensive infrastructure that ties otherwise disparate grassroots efforts undertaken by various congregations. A federated structure can disseminate information regarding needs in other parts of the country or world, and it broadens the perspective of its membership. Some large denominations foster political ties directly by lobbying in Washington and taking stands on political issues. Some also have established links with nonprofit organizations to facilitate the contribution of time and money.

A local congregation also provides an amenable environment for civic activity. It offers to its members and neighbors a facility for meeting, professionally trained clergy to lead, and an established community presence to lend clout and attract contributions. Furthermore, a congregation aggregates people and helps to form a social network from which volunteers can be recruited and personal ties that motivate people to help, such as when a church member is ill or bereaving. Wuthnow calls these connections "first-order mecha-nisms of caring." He writes, "In an otherwise atomized and commercialized society, churches and synagogues remain one of the few places in which members of different families, age groups, occupations and neighborhoods can interact at a deeply personal level over extended periods of time" (Wuthnow 1990, 12).

Furthermore, a religious institution can encourage civic activity by including such activity in its mission. In other words, the extent and range of community activism already undertaken by a congregation can provide a ready-made opportunity for participation. There is ample evidence to suggest that opportunities are common, in fact. Wuthnow contends that religious groups do not usually confine themselves to purely religious goals but that the voluntary activities of congregations "respond to recent community needs as well as traditional commitments" (Wuthnow 1990, 16). This type of activity could include endeavors such as shelters, food banks, clinics, substance abuse counseling, day care, or international refugee and peace work. "In effect, religious participation not only encourages people to give and volunteer, and to do so more generously than the majority of unchurched Americans, but it does so in ways that are deeply woven into the fabric of civil society at the community, national, and international levels, both within and beyond the context of individual congregations" (Wuthnow 1990, 16).[5]

For these reasons, when we volunteer most often we do so through a religious organization. In fact, religious groups receive nearly one-half of all volunteer time donated in the country (Hodgkinson, Weitzman, and Kirsch 1990, 93). Almost half of that time is committed to nonreligious philanthropic efforts. American congregations reported a force of 10.4 million volunteers who worked an average of ten hours per month; a full 48 percent of those hours were devoted to nonreligious programs. "These findings suggest that many Americans and their families get the first introduction to voluntary service and

responsibility to engage in community activities through participation in a religious congregation" (Hodgkinson, Weitzman, and Kirsch 1990, 97).[6]

In *Voice and Equality,* Verba, Schlozman, and Brady (1995) study the relationship between religion and political participation more directly. They ask specifically whether church participation can help us gain skills or opportunities for recruitment that could be translated into political action. It appears that important skills can be practiced by members of congregations. When respondents were asked what activities they had undertaken at their church or synagogue within the past six months, 32 percent said they had attended a meeting where decisions were made; 17 percent had planned a meeting; 12 percent reported writing a letter; and 18 percent made a speech or presentation (Verba, Schlozman, and Brady 1995, 312).

Verba, Schlozman, and Brady also find that members encounter political issues at church or synagogue. One-third of religious members reported that they had been asked to vote or take some other political action by someone with an official position within their institution. In addition, 12 percent of respondents reported attending a meeting about a political issue at their church or synagogue, and 25 percent reported that clergy frequently discuss political issues (Verba, Schlozman, and Brady 1995, 373).

Political Representation

Not only does civil society have the potential to enhance the citizen's democratic capabilities; it also holds the possibility of carrying out democratic functions of its own. Although civic organizations operate in a separate sphere from the state, for the most part, they often contribute to political equality and representation in a variety of ways.

The networks among and within associations facilitate the flow of information through society. New ideas can spread and extreme ideas can be more easily challenged. As associative relationships help us realize our common goals, or "enlightened self-interest," we will be more likely to consider the public good. The resulting sense of greater responsibility will lead in turn to political participation that is more tolerant, moderate, and publicly motivated (Paxton 1999; Mansbridge 1992).

These same networks also create a context of generalized trust and obligations that has enabled democracy to thrive in the United States. "[O]verlapping collective activities provide a framework in which it is difficult to free ride without provoking punishments. In such a tight knit society, each citizen must actually meet obligations . . . in order to avoid punishments meted out to defectors. In such societies, trust and trust worthiness are closely linked" (Scholz 1998, 138). Not only is a citizen's trust in government and each other improved; so is the likelihood that he or she will comply with rules and behave in a law-abiding manner.[7] This increased trust allows us to have reasonable expectations about political outcomes and to have faith in and submit to the rules of our governing system; it also increases the range of potential cooperation among citizens working toward shared goals.

Civic groups also serve as the location of many meaningful functions for everyday life. In such groups smaller matters can be negotiated without the intrusion of state institutions and in a manner that is more satisfying and empowering than formal political participation. Michael Walzer points out:

> Politics in the contemporary democratic state does not offer many people a chance for Rousseauian self-determination. Citizenship, taken by itself, is today mostly a passive role: citizens are spectators who vote. Between elections, they are served, well or badly, by the civil service. . . . But in the associational networks of civil society, in unions, parties, movements, interest groups, and so on, these same people make many smaller decisions and shape to some degree the more distant determinations of state and economy (Walzer 1995, 164).

In addition, associations function as problem solvers; they can take on responsibilities that would otherwise fall to the state and improve efficiency. "They help to formulate and execute public policies and take on quasi-public functions that supplement or supplant the state's more directly regulatory actions" (Cohen and Rogers 1992, 425). The professional association, for example, provides licensing and standards for members and implements sanctions for noncompliance.

Tocqueville noted the importance of the association for helping to voice the political will of the American people. He wrote, "As soon as several Americans have conceived a sentiment or an idea that they want to produce before the world, they seek each other out, and when found, they unite. Thenceforth they are no longer isolated individuals, but a power conspicuous from the distance whose actions serve as an example; when it speaks, men listen" (Tocqueville 1988, 516). Especially for citizens in the political minority, the ability to unite greatly improves their ability to impress their preferences on the political system. By pooling their resources, they are able to ameliorate material inequalities as well. Groups also are better able to communicate the effectiveness and impact of public policy to elected officials. In an increasingly complicated world, often it is the groups that form around an issue that have the information and technical expertise needed for good policymaking.

Civic organizations also can provide important settings for organizational experimentation. For constituencies that are outside the mainstream or are not politically powerful, an association can serve as a platform for forming novel identities and innovative strategies that might give challengers to the status quo the momentum and critical mass to instigate change in political institutions.

Civil society helps citizens utilize their democratic institutions for fulfillment and supplement them when necessary. As a result, these institutions are made more effective at governing, more authentically representative, more legitimate in the eyes of citizens, and therefore more stable over time. Democracy is healthier when it is based on a social structure of cooperation and shared endeavor and supported by an active and engaged citizenry.

Understanding Associations and Their Effects

Not all groups formed by citizens are going to provide equal benefit—or any benefit, in some cases. Because the concept of civil society is focused on relational networks that generate mutually positive obligations and collective responsibility, it is important to delineate which groups are likely to contribute. Many organizations may have the potential to promote high intragroup trust accompanied by low intergroup trust. Positive effects may be realized for members within the group, without extending to society as a whole (Paxton 1999, 97). This dynamic may take the form of a special interest group—or faction—seeking to extract exclusive goods for its members. Individuals could learn skills that would improve their political participation or form ties with others that lead to future coordinated endeavors; the external objectives of an organization in this context, however, often are counter to the public good.[8] Clearly undesirable are groups whose main activities skirt or even violate the laws; gangs, militias, and mafias fit into this category. Our understanding of how associational life supports democracy therefore is conditioned on an appreciation for which group characteristics and activities are most productive.

To this end, Mark Warren (2001), in *Democracy and Association,* has created a typology of group traits to determine the nature and extent of democratic effects that can be engendered by associational activity of varying kinds. Warren recommends evaluating the degree to which participation in a group is voluntary. The ease with which members can exit the group when conflict arises will determine how much politics is practiced within. Must members stay and work to have their voice heard, or is debate avoided when dissatisfied individuals simply opt out of the group? The medium an association uses to achieve its ends also can have implications for its democratic potential. Warren classifies "the means through which collective decisions are made and collective actions organized" as coercive power backed by the state, such as with interest groups or political pressure groups; economic exchanges in the case of unions or consumer groups; and associational relations constituting churches, social movements, and hobby clubs. Finally, as the benefits sought by a group vary along a spectrum from scarce, individual, material goods to inclusive social goods, so too will the anticipated democratic by-products. "All other things being equal," Warren writes, "associations that pursue public goods are the most likely to contribute to a broad range of democratic effects" (Warren 2001, 129).

Groups differ qualitatively "with respect to such features as the pattern of their internal decision-making, their inclusiveness with respect to potential membership, their relations to other associations, and the nature and extent of their powers. The art of associative democracy consists in . . . cultivating those characteristics appropriate to functions consistent with the norms of egalitarian democracy" (Cohen and Rogers 1992, 428).

Concern for the Civic Future

Knowing which characteristics produce desirable effects would help us identify the kinds of groups that should be nurtured for a healthy democracy and provide insight into how they might be encouraged. Recent research has identified a startling trend of civic decline. In *Bowling Alone,* for example, Robert Putnam recounts a thorough exploration of the American civic landscape and determines that it is not what it used to be. After looking at the time we spend in (for example) fraternal organizations, service clubs, social groups, political organizations, sports teams, neighborhood associations, and even leisure activities with friends, Putnam declares that

"Americans have been dropping out in droves" (Putnam 2000, 64). He reports that, compared to thirty years ago, Americans are spending one-third less time in organizations, and half as many Americans are participating in organizations at all. The decline in group membership has been steady over the past quarter-century or more and is largely attributable to generational replacement.

Although there are many more organizations on the scene these days, because of the "professionalization" of associations that is common today, many have few active members. Putnam calls this phenomenon the "proliferation of letterheads" (62). Increasingly, many memberships consist of little more than writing a check. No social capital is generated if there are no local chapters with meetings among members, and a quarterly fundraising appeal does not bring citizens together for "self-interest rightly understood." The deterioration of civic life is so dramatic that Putnam writes, "If the current rate of decline were to continue, clubs would become extinct in America within less than twenty years" (62).

Other authors argue, however, that there has been an increase in civic participation in some sectors of associational life (Ladd 1996) or that the standard wording in repeated waves of national surveys fails to capture the nuance of multiple memberships in similar groups or the emergence of new kinds of groups (Baumgartner and Walker 1988). Pettinico (1996) has written that environmental groups, which have had considerable success generating support through direct mail, in fact foster member interaction through regular meetings, and he describes "a vibrant grassroots culture involving countless individuals who are actively engaged in their communities" (Pettinico 1996, 27). Using the General Social Survey from 1975 to 1994, Paxton (1999) does not find that association membership, or the time people spend with friends and neighbors, has changed.

Even if the civic culture is not declining in the aggregate, it certainly is shifting and changing shape. This type of transformation still could have serious implications for the social capital participants are able to gain and whether they are able to translate it into political empowerment. The success of the democratic project depends on the quality of citizen participation and representation in its system of government. As Tocqueville warned, civil society provides the necessary context that gives this engagement meaning. He wrote, "If the inhabitants of democratic countries . . . did not learn some habits of acting together in the affairs of daily life, civilization itself would be in peril" (Tocqueville 1988, 514). The democratic character of America, which this book aims to examine and critique, grows out of this environment, is nurtured by it, and is relatively successful and stable as a result.

Notes

1. Verba, Schlozman, and Brady (1995, 352) use political interest, information, efficacy, and partisan strength as measures of political engagement.
2. Ayala finds that "the effect of civic skill-acts exercised on the job are [*sic*] roughly half as strong as those performed in religious groups and other nonpolitical organizations. Furthermore, controlling for occupation level has no effect" (Ayala 2000, 10). Ayala also finds that civic skill-acts from nonpolitical organizations are similar in magnitude to socioeconomic variables for explaining political participation.
3. Wuthnow (1990) cites both a 1988 Gallup study and the 1988 *Giving and Volunteering Study* by Independent Sector.
4. I believe "church" is being used here to connote institutions of all religious faiths.
5. See also McCarthy (1999).
6. See also Peterson (1992).
7. See Scholz (1998) for a discussion of tax compliance in this context.
8. For a discussion of "rent-seeking" interest groups, see Mansbridge (1992).

References

Ayala, Louis J. 2000. "Trained for Democracy: The Differing Effects of Voluntary and Involuntary Organizations on Political Participation." *Political Research Quarterly* 53: 99–115.

Baumgartner, Frank R., and Jack L. Walker. 1988. "Survey Research and Membership in Voluntary Associations." *American Journal of Political Science* 32: 908–27.

Cohen, Joshua, and Joel Rogers. 1992. "Secondary Associations and Democratic Governance." *Politics and Society* 20, no. 4: 393–472.

Coleman, James S. 1988. "Social Capital in the Creation of Human Capital." *American Journal of Sociology,* 94 (suppl.): S95–S120.

Dekker, Paul, and Andries van den Broek. 1998. "Civil Society in Comparative Perspective: Involvement in Voluntary Associations in North America and Western Europe." *Voluntas: International Journal of Voluntary and Nonprofit Organizations* 9: 11–38.

Dimock, Michael A., Peyton M. Craighill, and Melissa Rogers. 2002. "Temporary Turnabout: Religion and the Crisis." *Public Perspective* (September/October): 29–33.

Hodgkinson, Virginia A., Murray S. Weitzman, and Arthur D. Kirsch. 1990. "From Commitment to Action: How Religious Involvement Affects Giving and Volunteering." In *Faith and Philanthropy in America,* ed. Robert Wuthnow and Virginia A. Hodgkinson. Washington, D.C.: Independent Sector.

Ladd, Everett C. 1996. "The Data Just Don't Show Erosion of America's Social Capital." *Public Perspective* 7, no. 1: 5–22.

Mansbridge, Jane. 1992. "A Deliberative Theory of Interest Representation." In *The Politics of Interest: Interest Groups Transformed,* ed. Mark P. Petracca. Boulder, Colo.: Westview Press.

McCarthy, Kathleen D. 1999. "Religion, Philanthropy and Political Culture." In *Civil Society, Democracy and Civic Renewal,* ed. Robert K. Fullinwider. Lanham, Md.: Rowman and Littlefield.

O'Connell, Brian. 1999. *Civil Society: The Underpinnings of American Democracy.* Hanover, N.H.: University Press of New England.

Pateman, Carol. 1970. *Participation and Democratic Theory.* New York: Cambridge University Press.

Paxton, Pamela. 1999. "Is Social Capital Declining in the United States? A Multiple Indicator Assessment." *American Journal of Sociology* 105, no. 1: 88–127.

Peterson, Steven A. 1992. "Church Participation and Political Participation: The Spillover Effect." *American Politics Quarterly* 20, no. 1: 123–39.

Pettinico, George. 1996. "Civic Participation Alive and Well in Today's Environmental Groups." *The Public Perspective* (June/July): 27–30.

Putnam, Robert D. 1993. *Making Democracy Work: Civic Traditions in Modern Italy.* Princeton, N.J.: Princeton University Press.

———. 1996. "The Strange Disappearance of Civic America." *American Prospect* 24: 34–48.

———. 2000. *Bowling Alone: The Collapse and Revival of American Community.* New York: Simon and Schuster.

Scholz, John T. 1998. "Trust, Taxes and Compliance." In *Trust and Governance,* ed. Valerie Braithewaite and Margaret Levi. New York: Russell Sage Foundation, 135–66.

Tocqueville, Alexis de. 1988. *Democracy in America,* ed. J. P. Mayer. New York: Harper Perennial.

Verba, Sydney, Kay Lehman Schlozman, and Henry E. Brady. 1995. *Voice and Equality: Civic Voluntarism in American Politics.* Cambridge, Mass.: Harvard University Press.

Walzer, Michael. 1995. "The Civil Society Argument." In *Theorizing Citizenship,* ed. Ronald Beiner. Albany: State University of New York Press, 153–74.

Warren, Mark E. 2001. *Democracy and Association.* Princeton, N.J.: Princeton University Press.

Wuthnow, Robert. 1990. "Religion and Voluntary Spirit in the United States: Mapping the Terrain." In *Faith and Philanthropy in America,* ed. Robert Wuthnow and Virginia A. Hodgkinson. Washington, D.C.: Independent Sector.

Wuthnow, Robert, and Virginia A. Hodgkinson, eds. 1990. *Faith and Philanthropy in America.* Washington, D.C.: Independent Sector.

Further Reading

Dionne, E. J. 1998. *Community Works: The Revival of Civil Society in America*. Washington, D.C.: Brookings Institute.

Eberly, Don E. 1998. *America's Promise: Civil Society and the Renewal of American Culture*. Lanham, Md.: Rowman and Littlefield.

Gamm, Gerald, and Robert D. Putnam. 1990. "The Growth of Voluntary Associations in America, 1840–1940." *Journal of Interdisciplinary History* 29, no. 4: 511–57.

Newton, Kenneth. 1997. "Social Capital and Democracy." *American Behavioral Scientist* 40, no. 5: 575–86.

Steinberg, Richard. 1989 "The Theory of Crowding Out: Donations, Local Government Spending, and the 'New Federalism': Studies in Varieties and Goals." In *Philanthropic Giving*, ed. Richard Magat. New York: Oxford University Press, 142–56.

Part II

A DEMOCRATIC CONGRESS?

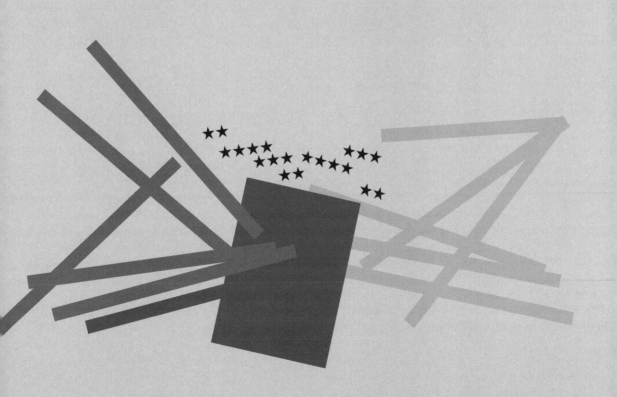

Chapter 3

Campaign Contributions and Democracy

*Peter Francia, John C. Green, Wesley Joe, Paul S. Herrnson,
Lynda W. Powell, Benjamin Webster, and Clyde Wilcox*

There's no doubt that special interests and their representatives have taken over the legislative process, and more and more money is pouring into political campaigns from these interests. . . . We will have blood all over the floor of the Senate until we exceed to the demands . . . of the American people to be represented in Washington again.

—John McCain, interviewed by Jim Lehrer, August 1, 2000

On March 27, 2002, President George W. Bush signed the Bipartisan Campaign Finance Reform Act. The bill sought to limit the influence of well-financed interest groups by banning large contributions to political parties and by regulating advertising by groups before election campaigns. The logic of the bill was simple: Large contributions by corporations, unions, and interest groups are made in an attempt to influence policy, and the larger the contribution the more likely it is to corrupt politicians. If the "special interests and their representatives" that John McCain worried about couldn't give as much money, they might get less access and fewer government favors. Almost immediately the law was challenged by a diverse coalition of politicians and groups. A divided Supreme Court, however, upheld its major provisions in 2003 in the case of *McConnell v. FEC*.

Almost thirty years earlier the Supreme Court had reviewed an earlier campaign finance law that imposed contribution limits on individuals and limited groups to spending money that they could raise in small contributions from their members. In seeking a delicate balance between protecting freedom of speech for individuals and candidates and enabling the government to enact laws to control corruption, the Court ruled that large contributions can undermine the integrity of the system of representative democracy and further contribute to the erosion of confidence in the system of representative government.

Smaller contributions were permitted because they are less likely to lead to corruption—both because policymakers are less likely to reward small donors with policy favors and because small donors are less likely to seek such favors. Yet although a contribution of $1,000 may appear small compared to multimillion-dollar soft-money contributions from business and unions, only a small and wealthy elite can give this amount. When only a small and unrepresentative group of citizens engages in a particular form of communication and when government listens disproportionately to this group, the result can be representational distortion of the democratic process.

One comprehensive study of political participation concluded that among the myriad ways for citizens to participate in politics, contributing money creates the greatest representational distortion because it is the exclusive province of wealthy citizens whose economic attitudes and policy priorities do not match those of other Americans (Verba,

Schlozman, and Brady 1995). Consequently, even contributions permitted under campaign finance limits may well distort the democratic process, whether or not they lead to corruption (Wilcox 2001).

Contributing to congressional campaigns is a rare form of political participation. Fifteen to twenty million Americans gave money to some kind of political campaign in 1984, and two to four million Americans made contributions to congressional candidates (Sorauf 1988). One study of political activists found that more than 80 percent did not give more than $250 to all kinds of candidates and political groups combined, and the average contribution was less than $75. The Center for Responsive Politics has estimated that just over 370,000 individuals made contributions of more than $200 in the congressional elections of 1996. This would mean that fewer than 0.2 percent of American adults contributed enough money to a congressional candidate to trigger disclosure.

It is not surprising that giving money to candidates is a rare form of participation. Many Americans are not interested in politics, and only half of those who are eligible to vote in presidential elections actually cast ballots. In addition, many Americans view the process of financing campaigns with distaste (Hibbing 2001) and therefore may be reluctant to give money to politicians. Perhaps most important, giving money costs money. Citizens with large incomes are much more likely to give money to political candidates than those with small incomes.

The common stereotype of a political donor is a wealthy businessman or woman giving money to a congressional candidate, expecting in return favorable treatment for their business. For example, on June 19, 2002, a Republican fundraising event raised more than $30 million, much of which came from drug companies (VandeHei and Eilperin 2002). Only a few days earlier, House Republicans had proposed a bill for prescription drugs for elderly Americans that would greatly benefit drug companies. Democrats often hold similar large fundraisers that attract contributions from groups that have sought to influence legislation. This kind of coordinated group giving is the image that inspires Senator McCain's quote at the beginning of this chapter, and it incites reformers to attempt to limit the role of large contributions in American politics.

Yet we know little about the people who make contributions to congressional candidates or about why they give. In this chapter we report the results of two surveys of congressional donors in 1996: a random sample of all donors of more than $200 to any single candidate, and an oversample of donors who gave the most money or gave to the most candidates (Francia et al. 2000). We refer to the random sample as "all donors" and the most active donors as "major donors." Major donors are represented in the random sample, so when we refer to "all" donors we are describing the entire donor pool. Major donors constitute about 6 percent of all donors, but they account for almost one-third of total contributions by the donors we sampled.[1]

A Small and Steady Pool with a Mild Current

Even among affluent Americans, giving to congressional candidates is uncommon. Instead, a relatively small number of Americans are routine givers to political candidates. There is an enduring donor pool of contributors who have given in past elections and are willing to give again, and this pool provides the vast majority of funds to congressional candidates. Almost all donors to congressional candidates have given before, and many of them contribute regularly to many types of candidates and political committees. Candidates turn first to this pool of regular donors to raise money because although each election brings a trickle of new donors to the pool, past donors are far more likely to give than are citizens who have never given before (Brown, Powell, and Wilcox 1995).

Table 3.1 shows the frequency of giving by all donors and by major donors in 1996.

Table 3.1 Frequency of Past Giving (%)

	All Donors		Major Donors
	In Most Elections	In Some	In Most Elections
Presidential candidates	36	36	72
Senate candidates	38	44	80
House candidates	47	40	75
State and local candidates	45	38	17
Parties	30	36	48
PACs	23	29	40

Source: Congressional Donor Survey conducted by authors.

The portion of donors who give in most elections to different types of candidates is remarkably high: 38 percent of donors in 1996 give in most elections to Senate candidates, and nearly half give in most elections to House candidates. Among major donors, 75 percent give in most elections to House candidates, and 80 percent give in most elections to Senate candidates.

Most of these regular contributors to House and Senate campaigns give to other types of candidates and committees as well. Among those who give in *most* elections to either House or Senate candidates or both, 92 percent give in most elections to some other type of candidate or committee. Among those who give in *some* elections to either House or Senate candidates or both, 96 percent have given at least once to some other type of campaign finance actors. More than 20 percent of all donors in 1996 report that they give in most elections to all four types of candidates in our survey: presidential, senatorial, congressional, and state and/or local. Nearly two in three give in most elections to at least one type of candidate; this core of the donor pool constitutes a steady source of funding for campaigns.

Members of the donor pool give in subsequent elections because they are motivated to give, and they are asked repeatedly to give. All potential contributors must weigh the opportunity costs of contributing against an array of political, social, or material benefits that such a contribution might produce.

Those who have decided in the past that the benefits of contributing outweighed the costs are more likely to make a similar decision in the future. Thus, those who have a propensity to contribute in one election will probably have a propensity to do so next time (Brown, Powell, and Wilcox 1995). Moreover, members of the donor pool are repeatedly asked to give by candidates, in solicitations that often are carefully crafted to appeal to the motivations and values of the donor.

Table 3.2 shows the frequency of solicitation and giving among members of the donor pool. Only 9 percent of donors were asked to give by only a single candidate; more than 30 percent were asked by more than six candidates. Candidates begin their fundraising by contacting donors who have given to them in the past. Many candidates also identify new potential donors from lists of those who have given to party committees, political action committees (PACs), and other candidates. The extent of candidate solicitation is most evident among the most active donors; an astonishing 67 percent were asked to give by eleven or more candidates—the highest category provided in the survey.

Yet all donors are selective about giving in response to the many solicitations they receive. Table 3.2 also shows that 37 percent of donors gave to only a single congressional candidate, although 91 percent were asked to give by two or more. Moreover, although nearly one-third were asked to give by more

Table 3.2 Solicitation and Giving in 1996

	All Donors (%)	Major Donors (%)
Number of candidates by whom donor was solicited:		
1	9	0
2–5	59	14
6–10	19	18
11+	13	67
Number of candidates to whom donor gave:		
1	37	7
2–5	56	26
6–10	4	29
11+	4	38
Asked by 6 or more	32	86
Gave to 6 or more	8	67

Source: Congressional Donor Survey conducted by authors.

than six candidates, only 8 percent gave that often. Selectivity is evident among the most active donors as well: Although two-thirds received requests from more than eleven candidates, only 38 percent actually gave to that many candidates.[2]

Some donors may be giving for the first time to congressional candidates. Although our data do not permit a precise estimate, we can put an upper boundary on the number who gave for the first time in 1996. No more than 5 percent—and probably many fewer—were new recruits to the donor pool. The donor pool changes slowly as new donors trickle into the pool and others trickle out—either because they lose interest in politics, their circumstances change, or by death.

Why Do Donors Give? Ideologues, Investors, and Intimates

What leads Americans to give money to candidates? Our data show that the common image of political contributions flowing from businessmen who seek narrow benefits for their business is partially true, but donors are far more diverse than this image would sug-

gest. We asked donors several questions to determine their motives for giving. Table 3.3 shows the percentages of donors and major donors who indicated that each factor was "very important" in one set of questions or "always important" in another.

We can classify donors on the basis of their responses to these questions. Our analysis reveals three major sets of motives that are consistent with many earlier studies. One identifiable group of donors gives in an effort to help elect candidates who will pursue broad public policies. These ideologues often hold extreme policy views or care deeply about a few issues, such as abortion, gun rights, or taxes. One ideologue emphasized environmental protection:

> To me the bottom line is environmental policy: If we don't stop despoiling the air and the water, there will be no political system to worry about in the future. So, I have a kind of test for candidates—namely, where do they stand on the environment? Now, this is a fairly complicated thing because there are lots of environmental issues. My evaluation is sort of a sum of the issues I care about.

Table 3.3　Donor Motives
Percentage who say reason is "very important" in making contributions

	All	Major
Purposive motives		
To make a difference in the outcome of an election	61	78
To influence the policies of government	61	80
Material motives		
For business or employment reasons	8	16
It is expected of someone in my position	4	7
Solidarity motives		
Enjoyment of friendships and social contacts	3	4
It gives me a feeling of recognition	1	1
Percentage who say factor is "always important" in making contribution		
Purposive motives		
Candidate's ideology	69	67
Candidate's stand on particular issues	35	38
Candidate's party	31	31
Material motives		
Candidate is friendly to my industry	25	26
So my business will be treated fairly	23	22
Solidarity motives		
Know candidate personally	47	54
Asked by someone I knew personally	25	32
Invitation to an event	4	3
(Weighted)[a]	*(1047)*	*(281)*

[a]Number of respondents weighted to reflect unequal probabilities of selection.

Source: Congressional Donor Survey conducted by authors.

Investors give in an effort to help their business. In some cases they give to members of Congress who can help or hurt their company, and in other cases they give because the person who asked them to give can help or hurt their company. An investor explained:

> My business is heavily regulated, and it is important that we be treated fairly—both my firm and my industry. Most people have no idea how hard it is to get bureaucrats and leg-islators to pay attention, and being part of the process helps.

That investors would give to members of Congress to influence the bureaucracy might seem surprising initially because the president appoints department heads. Yet members of Congress do meet at least occasionally with bureaucrats on behalf of constituents and contributors.

Finally, intimates give because of friendship with the candidate or the solicitor or because they enjoy socializing with other like-minded donors at fundraising events. An engineer and self-described "people person" remarked:

> I really enjoy politics. I like to write checks, lick stamps, shake hands, and argue about issues. . . . I am most influenced by friends, and I influence them as well. . . . I really do it all: I write [members of Congress], I talk, I testify, and I meet these guys socially. I spend a lot of time intervening for people I raise money from. I'm always making calls, setting up meetings, introducing people to government officials.

Ideologues make up the largest group of donors, followed by investors and then intimates. About one-quarter of donors lack distinctive or strong motivations; they often are intermittent participants in the donor pool who are motivated by particular candidates or local issues.

Who Gives?

The Bipartisan Campaign Reform Act eliminated unlimited contributions from individuals and groups, but it also raised the legal limit for contributions from individuals from $1,000 to $2,000. During the debates over this provision, supporters sometimes asserted that donors who give $1,000 to a political candidate are "average citizens."

Our data show that political donors are anything but average. In table 3.4 we show the demographic characteristics of all donors and the oversample of major donors. When possible, we compare these characteristics to those of respondents to the 1996 National Election Study (NES), representing all Americans.

Donors have much more formal education than the average citizen. Fully 44 percent of the public has a high school degree or less, compared with only 5 percent of all donors and 1 percent of major donors. Nearly half of all donors and more than half of the most active donors have some form of advanced degree—most frequently business, medicine, law, or a Ph.D.—compared with less than 10 percent of the general public.

The contrast on income is even greater. Fully 65 percent of NES respondents had incomes of less than $50,000, but only 5 percent of donors and none of the most active donors had incomes this low. The NES does not bother to ask respondents about extremely high incomes because they are too rare to appear frequently in samples of citizens, but only 8 percent have incomes of more than $100,000. In contrast, more than three in four donors and 96 percent of the most active donors have incomes of more than $100,000. Indeed, 14 percent of all donors had incomes of more than half a million dollars, as did more than half of the most active donors.

Donors also are significantly older, more likely to be male, and more likely to be white than the general public. Four in ten donors are 61 years or older, as are more than half of the most active donors; these figures compare sharply with those for NES respondents, of whom only 22 percent are 61 years or older. Only 1 percent of donors are 30 years or younger, compared with 19 percent of NES respondents. More than three-quarters of donors are male; this figure reaches 82 percent among habitual donors and the most active donors. Fewer than half of NES respondents are men. More than 95 percent of each category of donor is white, compared with 85 percent in the NES. Less than 0.5 percent of donors are African Americans, compared with 12 percent of NES respondents and a larger portion of the general population. There is a slight geographic bias among the donor pool, with the Northeast overrepresented. This distortion is even greater among the most active donors; more than a third are from that region.

Despite years of electoral mobilization by the Christian Right, only 12 percent of donors and only 5 percent of the most active donors are evangelical Christians, compared

Table 3.4 Social Characteristics of Donors and General Public, 1996 (%)

	All	Major Donors	NES
Education			
High school or less	5	1	44
Some college	10	6	27
College degree	23	29	19
Some graduate	11	13	NA
Graduate/professional degree	48	51	10
Income			
$50,000 or less	5	0	65
$51,000–$99,000	17	4	27
$100,000–$249,000	40	17	8
$250,000–$500,000	2	28	NA
More than $500,000	14	52	NA
Age (years)			
18–30	1	1	19
31–45	17	6	39
46–60	42	39	20
61+	40	54	22
Sex			
Male	77	82	48
Female	23	18	52
Race			
White	95	96	85
Region			
Northeast	25	36	20
Midwest	20	17	24
West	21	18	22
South	35	29	35
Religious faith			
Evangelical Protestant	12	5	27
Mainline Protestant	41	32	23
Catholic	23	12	27
Jewish	11	39	2
Secular	8	6	12
Other	6	5	9
Frequency of religious attendance			
More than weekly	10	4	12
Weekly	27	16	14
Monthly	16	13	27
A few times a year	25	39	18
Seldom or never	23	28	29

Source: Congressional Donor Survey conducted by authors.

with more than one-quarter of all NES respondents. Mainline Protestants are overrepresented: They constitute 41 percent of all donors and 32 percent of the most active donors, compared with 23 percent of NES respondents. Jews are even more overrepresented; they make up only 2 percent of NES respondents but 11 percent of all donors and a remarkable 39 percent of the most active donors. Donors are actually more likely than nondonors to attend religious services than are NES respondents, although among the most active donors there is a very sizable contingent who attend a few times a year or less (primarily concentrated among Jewish respondents).

There are a few differences in the social characteristics of ideologues, investors, and intimates, but these differences generally are small. Women are more likely than men to be ideologues, as are evangelical Christians. Investors have slightly less formal education than other donors, and slightly higher income. The similarities among donors far overshadow their differences, however.

Clearly contributors are an unrepresentative elite, with a very distinctive demographic profile. Although candidates and parties have raised money in amounts that increase dramatically from year to year, they appear to be receiving money from the same narrow elite that has always given. When we compared the characteristics of donors in 1996 with those of an earlier survey of House donors in 1978, there was surprisingly little change. Donors have a variety of resources to bring to bear in politics—their education, their time, their social connections—and they have an additional route to access through their contributions.

Party, Issues, and Ideology

If donors do not look like America, do they think like America? If donors' political views are similar to those of the general public, their demographic profile may be less important. If the political preferences of donors differ from those of the general public, however, they are likely to present government with a distinctive voice.

Among all donors, Republicans outnumber Democrats by 51 percent to 31 percent, and conservatives outnumber liberals by 50 percent to 35 percent. Among the smaller group of major donors, these figures are reversed: Democrats outnumber Republicans by 50 percent to 30 percent, and liberals outnumber conservatives by 46 percent to 32 percent. Democrats depend more on a smaller cadre of very active donors who give larger contributions to many candidates, whereas Republicans depend more on the larger pool of donors who give to fewer candidates.

We cannot directly compare the responses of donors to the general public because we have no identically worded questions in the NES or other surveys. In table 3.5 we summarize responses to the specific policy questions among all donors, showing first the percentage that took conservative positions and then the percentage that took liberal positions. There also was a neutral category in each question. The wording of the question is reproduced in abbreviated form in the table, to help readers interpret the results.

The right-hand column shows the percentage of all donors who take conservative and liberal positions on the issues. Among all donors, conservative voices outnumber liberal voices on all economic issues except the gold standard (which appeals only to Christian conservatives seeking absolute standards in economics as well as morality). Liberal voices are more numerous on social issues, however, including gay rights, abortion, and women's roles. The donor pool is generally liberal on affirmative action and supportive of free trade but opposes cuts in defense spending.

The left side of the table shows these data separately for donors who identify with or lean toward the Republican and Democratic parties. In recent years scholars have pointed to a growing divergence between the parties

Table 3.5 Political Attitudes: Conservatives/Liberals, All Donors
(% who took conservative positions on five-point scales)

	Republicans		Democrats		All	
	Con	Lib	Con	Lib	Con	Lib
Economic issues						
Reduce taxes even if it means cut services	75	13	8	82	51	37
U.S. needs comprehensive national health insurance	73	16	11	76	49	37
Federal government should spend more to reduce poverty and hunger	64	16	9	77	44	38
More environmental protection even if it means fewer jobs	65	19	7	78	45	39
U.S. should return to gold standard	20	42	3	67	15	50
Social/moral issues						
Homosexuals should be allowed to teach in schools	46	33	10	76	33	48
Abortion should be outlawed except to save mother's life	40	46	8	86	27	63
Women should have equal role in business, industry, and government	10	78	1	95	7	83
Racial issues						
Country has gone too far in helping minorities	59	24	7	71	30	50
Foreign/defense issues						
Free trade is important even if loss of jobs (free trade position is liberal)	24	57	29	45	26	52
U.S. should sharply reduce defense spending	72	14	25	49	55	26

Source: Congressional Donor Survey conducted by authors.

in Congress, as well as in the general public (Fleisher and Bond 2000; Jacobson 2000). The parties' donor bases hold very different attitudes on economic issues, and Democratic donors are far more liberal than Republican donors on social issues and affirmative action.

Table 3.6 shows these same data for major donors. Because there are many more Democrats than Republicans among this smaller set of active donors, overall attitudes are liberal on economic issues and very liberal on social issues. What is most interesting is the difference between Republican major donors in this table and average Republican donors in table 3.5. Major Republican donors are more conservative than the sample of all Republican donors on economics, but they are far more liberal on social issues. Indeed, a

Table 3.6 Political Attitudes: Conservatives/Liberals, Major Donors
(% who took conservative positions on five-point scales)

	Republicans		Democrats		All	
	Con	Lib	Con	Lib	Con	Lib
Economic issues						
Reduce taxes even if it means cut services	80	11	6	92	37	57
U.S. needs comprehensive national health insurance	84	9	10	77	39	50
Federal government should spend more to reduce poverty and hunger	79	9	10	82	37	53
More environmental protection even if it means fewer jobs	75	17	10	70	36	47
U.S. should return to gold standard	16	54	1	74	7	66
Social/moral issues						
Homosexuals should be allowed to teach in schools	37	38	3	88	18	65
Abortion should be outlawed except to save mother's life	27	57	5	95	15	79
Women should have equal role in business, industry, and government	10	78	3	95	7	87
Racial issues						
Country has gone too far in helping minorities	60	13	16	75	25	61
Foreign/defense issues						
Free trade is important even if loss of jobs (free trade position is liberal)	16	67	19	63	19	64
U.S. should sharply reduce defense spending	14	72	3	95	7	87

Source: Congressional Donor Survey conducted by authors.

plurality of Republican major donors is liberal on each of the social issues, and the gap is quite large on abortion. Democratic major donors are significantly more supportive of free trade than those in the random sample.

Overall, these data tell us that the voices Congress hears at fundraising events are largely conservative on economics and more liberal on social issues, although the most active donors are more liberal on most issues than the donor pool as a whole. Perhaps more important, the donor base of each party differs in attitudes. The average Democratic donor is wealthy and a member of a business group, but that donor also is likely to support additional spending for welfare and civil rights protections for gays and lesbians. The attitudes of donors are as diverse as their motives.

Table 3.7   Group Membership of Donors and General Public (%)

	All Donors	Major	Civic Voluntarism
Fraternal	18	15	18 (service, fraternal)
Civic	49	54	3 (civic nonpartisan)
Community	41	41	
Church	64	47	
Professional	63	52	23 (business/professional)
Business	63	65	
Labor union	2	3	12 (union)
Political			14 (political/issue)
Environmental	26	34	
Women's	14	17	4 (women's rights)
Prochoice	17	35	
Civil Rights	15	26	
Gun owner group	23	19	
Profamily	12	13	
Prolife	11	8	
Christian conservative	6	4	
Party	42	50	5 (party, candidate)
Conservative	2	18	1 (liberal, conservative)
Liberal	10	21	

Source: Congressional Donor Study conducted by authors.

The social characteristics of donors make it inevitable that they are involved in social and political networks. We asked donors whether they were members of a variety of types of political and social groups; their responses are summarized in table 3.7. Although we do not have these types of questions for the general public from the NES, we also present data from the Civic Voluntarism study by Verba, Schlozman, and Brady (1995) for comparison, where available. The categories for this latter study do not always match perfectly, but we include them for their heuristic value.

Donors are active citizens who are involved in a wide variety of groups. Large majorities of donors are members of professional and business groups and churches, and significant minorities are members of civic groups, community groups, and party orga-nizations. The economic interests of donors are evident in this table: Nearly two of every three donors are members of business groups, but only 2 percent are members of unions. Although unions have other resources to bring to elections, their members do not directly contribute to candidates.

A significant number are members of ideological groups as well—prochoice and prolife, civil rights, women's groups, environmental groups, and gun groups. Here liberal groups are slightly better represented than conservative groups, and this is especially true among major donors. Among all donors, for example, members of prochoice groups outnumber members of prolife groups by 17 percent to 11 percent, and among major donors this gap increases to 35 percent to 8 percent. There are comparatively few members of prolife, profamily, and Christian conservative groups among congressional donors, although previous research has shown them to be more numerous in the presidential donor pool (Brown, Powell, and Wilcox 1995).

Comparisons to the Civic Voluntarism Study must be made cautiously because the categories of groups do not quite match. That study reported, however, that 23 percent of citizens are members of business or professional groups, whereas nearly two-third of contributors are members of each type. In contrast, union membership is six times more common among the general public than among the donor pool. Other comparisons suggest that donors are especially more likely than the general public to be active in political/issue groups, in candidate or party groups, and in ideological groups.

On average, donors were members of between 4.5 and 5.5 categories of groups, and of course they may have been members of several organizations in each category. In contrast, in the 2000 NES, the average respondent was a member of approximately two organizations. Clearly the donor pool is more active in community, economic, and political networks than the general public.

The extensive organizational involvement of donors provides them with political skills, information, political allies and support networks, and other resources that are useful in political processes. Mark Warren (2000) has argued that some but not all types of groups help build individual political skills and values in participants, and the wide range of groups of which these donors are members doubtless multiply those potential effects.

Donors of both parties are active in business and professional groups, as well as in community and civic organizations. Fully 71 percent of GOP donors are members of business groups, but so are 46 percent of Democratic donors. More than 60 percent of donors in both parties are members of professional organizations, more than half are members of civic organizations, and more than 40 percent are members of community organizations. Thus, although the donor pool is divided by ideology, donors do

share common interests arising from their social location and are likely to interact frequently in business, professional, and community settings.

These data also suggest that members of certain groups are heavily represented among donors to one or the other party and therefore are likely to have a large voice in party politics. Among Democrats, half of all donors were members of environmental groups, more than one-third were members of prochoice groups, and one-third were active in civil rights groups. One-quarter of Democratic donors were members of women's groups.

Among Republicans donors, 28 percent of donors were members of gun groups, 17 percent were members of prolife groups, 15 percent were members of profamily groups, and 8 percent were members of Christian conservative groups. These lower figures suggest that the social ideological base of Republican politics has not yet become active in financing congressional campaigns. This finding suggests an asymmetry in the financial bases of the parties: Democrats draw more heavily from members of ideological groups, whereas Republicans depend more heavily on business groups. Although unions overwhelmingly support Democratic candidates in elections, Democratic donors are far more likely to belong to business groups than to unions.

Pluralists such as David Truman (1958) believed that membership in overlapping groups would help contain group conflict in the United States. If members of the Sierra Club frequently interacted with members of the National Rifle Association (NRA), they would be more likely to understand each other's views and therefore would be more likely to fight their political battles within a set of rules. Diana Mutz has reported evidence that cross-cutting social networks promote political tolerance, arguing that they help build "formalized ways in which people agree to disagree" (Mutz 2002, 123).

Donors are members of crosscutting networks. For example, 25 percent of members of business groups are also members of environmental groups, 20 percent of environmental group members are also members of gun groups, and 17 percent of members of profamily groups also are members of civil rights organizations. Moreover, some donors are members of groups that are not normally associated with their party. For example, 15 percent of Republicans are members of environmental groups, 5 percent are members of civil rights groups, and 9 percent are members of women's groups. Similarly, 3 percent of Democratic donors are members of prolife groups, and 10 percent are members of gun groups.

Contributing and Voice

Although there is much debate over whether contributions influence the content of public policy, it is almost incontrovertible that contributing leads to greater access to policymakers (see, e.g., VandeHei 2002). Indeed, many of the contributions in this study were made at fundraising events, which provide the donor with a chance to meet the candidate face-to-face. The contributors in our study are active in contacting elected officials.

Donors are political activists who not only give; they also contact Congress. Eighty-one percent of all donors have tried to influence an act of Congress, and a majority have spoken directly with their member of Congress or their senator. Contributors advocate for policy not only by contributing and by voting but also by contacting elected officials directly. Eleven percent of donors have testified before Congress. Contributors also work through groups in exerting influence: 28 percent had worked through parties, 41 percent worked through other formal groups, and 19 percent worked through informal groups.

The extent of donor voice is evident in table 3.8, which shows the number of contacts that donors had with representatives and senators over the preceding two years. More than 40 percent of all donors contacted two or more members of the House, and a similar number contacted two or more senators.

Among major donors, more than one-quarter contacted eleven or more members of the House, and a similar number contacted eleven or more members of the Senate. More than three in five had contacted their own House member (although many do not belong to the party of that member), and about the same number contacted at least one of their senators. Perhaps most striking is the fact that more than half of all donors, and two-thirds of major donors, claim to know personally their member of the House and at least one senator.

Clearly donors have disproportionate access to policymakers, but some donors are extremely active in contacting Congress and some are far less so. In a multivariate statistical model (not shown), we have estimated a model predicting the total number of representatives and senators contacted by each donor. Members of political groups were more likely to contact members of Congress; members of business groups, environmental groups, prolife and gun groups each contacted more members than did donors who were not members of those groups. Material motives did not predict more contacts, nor did conservative positions on economic issues. Instead, ideologues—especially donors who are liberal on social issues such as abortion and gay rights—contacted officeholders more often. Strong partisans also contacted more members than did weak partisans or independents.

Of course, the sheer number of contacts that a particular donor makes is less important than the results of the contacts. Prolife groups and social liberals might flood Congress with phone calls, letters, and personal visits, but the less frequent but more substantial visits of investors may influence policy more. Regardless of the policy impact of contacts, surveys show that the public believes that donors have special access to policymakers and that policymakers reward donors with special favors. Indeed, a majority of donors in our survey agreed with statements that donors regularly pressure officeholders for favors and that most donors seek access to government.[3]

Table 3.8   Contacting Members of Congress (%)

	All	Major Donors
Contacted during last two years		
Number of House members		
None	29	16
1	25	8
2–5	36	29
6–10	5	18
11+	5	30
Number of Senators		
None	37	17
1	17	7
2–5	39	39
6–10	3	11
11+	4	26
Contacted House member from own district	61	60
Contacted senators from own state		
None	40	31
One	23	21
Both	36	48
Know personally		
Own House member	58	69
One of own senators	27	25
Both of own senators	23	50

Source: Congressional Donors Survey conducted by authors.

Thus, the special access given to donors contributes to the "appearance of corruption" that the Supreme Court recognized as a corrosive force on democracy.

Conclusions

Donors are an elite group: rich, well educated, white, male, and middle aged. They tend to be conservative and Republican, although there is a very active subset that is disproportionately liberal and Democratic. Donors overall hold conservative positions on economic issues and moderate to liberal positions on social issues, but there are sharp disparities among Democratic and Republican donors. Donors vary with regard to their motives: Ideologues seek to shape broad public policies, investors pursue narrow policies to benefit their businesses, and intimates value personal connections with solicitors and candidates. Finally, donors have disproportionate access to members of Congress.

What do these data tell us about the role of campaign money in democracy? One important conclusion is that donors are far more varied than they often are portrayed. The group that is most commonly singled out for concern we have called investors, who seek to give to pursue narrow business interests. Yet investors are not a plurality of the donors to either political party, and many donors are motivated by very different considerations.

Ideologues are more numerous than investors and are concerned not with narrow material benefits but with broader policies. Intimates give because of friendship and social contact—the personal side to fundraising.

A second conclusion is that although donors are a rich and advantaged elite, there are many voices in the donor pool in favor of national health insurance, increased spending on programs to end poverty, and maintaining higher taxes to pay for government services. Donors do not universally seek their own narrow economic self-interest; many are motivated by broad ideological positions about the role of government in helping disadvantaged people.

Yet the divergent economic views among the donor pool do not mean that their voices do not create representational distortion. It is one thing for a wealthy Democratic businesswoman to advocate more spending for antipoverty programs, but it is quite another for a member of Congress to actually talk to someone who receives aid from these programs and who actually encounters the problems of poverty on a daily basis. Moreover, as Verba, Schlozman, and Brady (1995) point out, when affluent Americans—even those as liberal as the major donors in this study—contact policymakers, they are far less apt than their poorer fellow citizens to raise issues of concern to disadvantaged elements of society. Indeed, when we asked our donors to list issues of special concern to them, nearly half mentioned taxes—an issue that the 1996 presidential campaign proved did not resonate with average Americans.

Members of Congress spend a large and increasing portion of their time raising money, which means talking with and interacting with donors. The donor pool does not look like America, and its life experiences and major concerns do not reflect the range of experiences and concern of the American people. The unequal voice of contributors poses a problem for democratic governance. The diversity of donor motives and views helps to somewhat mitigate that problem, but the policy priorities of donors do not reflect those of average citizens, so members of Congress hear a distorted echo of the public's voice.

Notes

1. For details of the survey, contact the authors.
2. Even donors who did give to more than eleven candidates may have said no to at least a few, but this may be disguised by the categories of the survey question. For example, a donor may have been solicited by thirty candidates and have actually given to twelve, but this outcome would appear in our data as having been asked by and given to eleven or more.
3. A majority also agreed that donors are motivated by ideology, suggesting again the diverse motives of donors. Indeed, almost half agreed that most donors are motivated by ideology *and* that donors regularly pressure elected officials for favors.

References

Brown, Clifford W., Jr., Lynda W. Powell, and Clyde Wilcox. 1995. *Serious Money: Fundraising and Contributing in Presidential Nomination Campaigns*. New York: Cambridge University Press.

Fleisher, Richard, and Jon R. Bond. 2000. "Congress and the President in a Partisan Era." In *Polarized Politics: Congress and the President in a Partisan Era*, ed. Jon R. Bond and Richard Fleisher. Washington, D.C.: Congressional Quarterly Press.

Francia, Peter, John C. Green, Paul S. Herrnson, Lynda W. Powell, and Clyde Wilcox. 2000. "Dissent from the Donors? Congressional Contributors and Campaign Finance Reform." *The Public Perspective* (May/June), 29–32.

Hibbing, John. 2001. "The People's Craving for Unselfish Government." In *Understanding Public Opinion*, 2d ed., ed. Barbara Norrander and Clyde Wilcox. Washington, D.C.: Congressional Quarterly Press.

Jacobson, Gary. 2000. "Party Polarization in National Politics: The Electoral Connection." In *Polarized Politics: Congress and the President in a Partisan Era,* ed. Jon R. Bond and Richard Fleischer. Washington, D.C.: Congressional Quarterly Press.

Mutz, Diana. 2002. "Cross-Cutting Social Networks: Testing Democratic Theory in Practice." *American Political Science Review* 96 (March): 111–26.

Sorauf, Frank J. 1988. *Money in American Elections.* San Francisco: Scott, Foresman and Co.

Truman, David. 1958. *The Governmental Process.* New York: Knopf.

VandeHei, Jim. 2002. "GOP Monitoring Lobbyists' Policies; White House, Hill Access May Be Affected." *Washington Post,* June 10, A1.

VandeHei, Jim, and Juliet Eilperin. 2002. "Drug Firms Among Big Donors at GOP Event." *Washington Post,* June 19, A1.

Verba, Sidney, Kay Lehman Schlozman, and Henry E. Brady. 1995. *Voice and Equality: Civic Voluntarism in American Politics.* Cambridge, Mass.: Harvard University Press.

Warren, Mark. 2000. *Democracy and Associations.* Princeton, N.J.: Princeton University Press.

Wilcox, Clyde. 2001. "Contributing as Participation." In *A User's Guide to Campaign Finance Reform,* ed. Jerry Lubenow. Lanham, Md.: Rowman and Littlefield, 109–27.

★★★

Chapter 4

Money and the Possibility of Democratic Governance

Michael Bailey

On almost any day of the week you can find members of Congress locked away in cubicles in their national party headquarters. Why are they there? To escape the stress of the job? To study policy? Hardly. They spend the hours calling wealthy individuals who might contribute to their campaigns. They do this because running a competitive campaign for the House requires more than $1 million—an amount that requires candidates to raise an average of $1,300 per day throughout their two-year term. For the Senate the demands are higher; competitive races can cost $10 million or more.

Is this any way to run a democratic government? Many observers say no. They argue that there is too much money in the system, that fundraising distracts politicians, that only the wealthy—or those supported by the wealthy—can be elected, and that policies are decided on the basis of money instead of what is good for the people. As Gore Vidal (2001, ix) puts it, the system "is rotten and corrupted to its core, because organized money has long since replaced organized people as the author of our politics. And most of it comes from rich people and corporations, who now own our political process—lock, stock, and pork barrel."

Not everyone agrees. Some observers say that money improves governance by promoting vigorous electoral competition. They say that, if anything, too little is spent on politics. They also argue that there is little evidence that money has undermined democratic governance, and even if it did, regulations on political spending conflict with the liberty that is a foundation of American democratic government.

The goal of this chapter is to explore how money affects the operation and outputs of Congress. The focus is not on the manner in which money affects elections but the manner in which money—including money spent on elections—affects the policies Congress enacts. I argue that, unsavory as much of the fundraising process may be, the connection between money and outcomes is complicated and not necessarily all negative. I begin with background facts about money in U.S. politics. I then discuss ways money can affect governance. Finally, I look at congressional activity on the Patients' Bill of Rights to explore how money and governance interact in practice.

Money in American Politics— The Basics

An extraordinary amount of money is spent on American politics. In the 2000 election, the average major-party candidate spent more than $1 million for House races and $5.4 million for Senate races (Federal Election Commission 2001). As figure 4.1 demonstrates, these numbers are the culmination of years of increases.

Such eye-popping numbers need to be put in context, however. What, exactly, is the standard against which we judge campaign spending? In 2001 major league baseball players earned almost $2 billion in salaries alone (Canoe Internet Network 2001). How much

Figure 4.1 Spending on House Campaigns

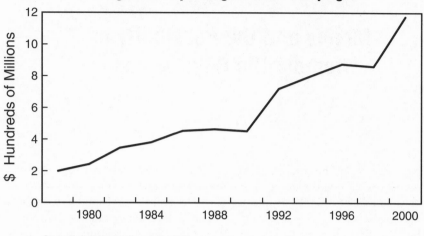

Source: Federal Election Commission 2001.

was spent on federal election campaigns in the two preceding years? Less: about $1.5 billion per year (Center for Responsive Politics 2002a). Such examples are not hard to generate. Brubaker (1998, 36) tells us that spending on perfume was twice that of campaign spending in 1995–96. Smith (1996, 1060) indicates that spending on ads for *Seinfeld* reruns topped spending on presidential campaigns and that Proctor and Gamble and Philip Morris spent more on ads than all federal and state political candidates and parties in a two-year election cycle.

In addition, the "explosion" of campaign spending is less impressive when it is adjusted for inflation, population growth, and economic growth. Figure 4.2 plots the ratio of spending in 2000 to that in 1980. In raw terms the ratio is huge: there was six times as much spending in 2000. If we account for population growth, the ratio shrinks to under five. If we account for population growth and inflation, the ratio drops under two. Finally, accounting for gross domestic product (GDP) growth as well pushes the ratio down to almost one.

In light of the foregoing analysis, serious examinations of money in politics tend to focus more on the sources than the amounts of money. Congressional campaign money comes from four sources: individuals, politi-

cal action committees (PACs), "unregulated" givers (a category I expand upon below) and politicians themselves. The largest share comes from individuals who contribute directly to candidates. These individuals are an exceptional group. Figure 4.3 shows the results from a survey of congressional donors in the 1995–96 election cycle (see chapter 3). Ninety-nine percent were white, 76 percent were male, 40 percent were older than 61, 78 percent earned more than $100,000, and 38 percent earned more than $250,000 (Francia et al. 2000). As a point of reference, the median income in the United States in 1996 was about $35,000.

PAC contributions also are important. Business PACs contributed almost $200 million in the 2000 cycle (Center for Responsive Politics 2002b). Many business PACs, such as Microsoft and Citigroup, give substantially to candidates from both parties. Labor union PACs contributed about $60 million in 2000, almost all of it to Democrats. Ideological PACs associated with interest groups such as the National Rifle Association (NRA) or the Sierra Club contributed $35 million in the 2000 cycle. They tend to give almost exclusively to one party.

Recently the "action" in fundraising has moved away from PACs to less-regulated

Figure 4.2 Ratio of Spending in Congressional Races, 2000 versus 1980

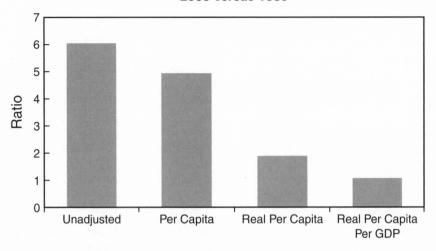

Source: Federal Election Commission 2001 and author's calculations.

forms of spending. One form of such money is "soft money." This money goes to parties for so-called party-building activities that range from "get-out-the-vote" efforts to campaigns ads that do everything but say the words "vote for Smith." The parties raised almost $500 million in soft money, often in donations in excess of $100,000 per donor (Center for Responsive Politics 2002c). Concern about soft money led to the passage of McCain-Feingold campaign finance legislation, which limits soft-money contributions and places restrictions on the ads that can be aired before an election. The Supreme Court upheld in *McConnell v. FEC*, no. 02–1676 (2003) the constitutionality of these limits.

Interestingly—and ironically, given that the Democrats led the charge to ban soft money—Democrats do quite well by big-money contributors. The top ten individual

Figure 4.3 Characteristics of Contributors

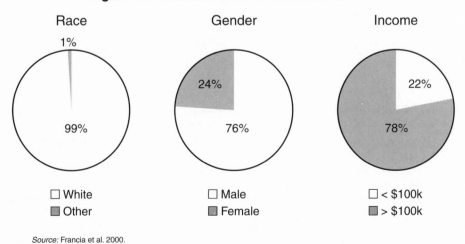

Source: Francia et al. 2000.

contributors gave between $840,000 and $1.6 million (Center for Responsive Politics 2002d). All but one gave overwhelmingly to the Democrats. In fact, soft money is the means by which Democrats have equalized fundraising. Usually, Republicans are able to raise more money than the Democrats. For example, in 1999–2000, Republicans raised $715 million, while Democrats raised $520 million (Center for Responsive Politics 2002c). The difference, though, is in "hard money" (federally regulated money subject to strict per donor limits): The Republicans substantially outpaced the Democrats. Both parties raised similar amounts of soft money.

Issue advocacy spending may continue to be important despite the restrictions imposed on issue advertising by the McCain-Feingold law. Issue ads are funded directly by interest groups and are not, in theory, campaign ads. In fact, however, the ads are used for electoral purposes, telling viewers things like "call your congressman and tell him to stop spending senior citizens' social security checks on clubbing baby seals." As long as there is no coordination with candidates and no explicit appeal for votes, this spending is totally unregulated. The Annenberg Public Policy Center of the University of Pennsylvania estimates that more than $500 million was spent on issue ads in 1999–2000 (Annenberg Public Policy Center 2001).

Politicians themselves also can be major sources of money. The Supreme Court ruled in *Buckley v. Valeo*, 424 U.S. 1 (1976), that the government cannot limit what an individual spends on his or her own campaign. This ruling had led many candidates to contribute large sums to their own campaigns—including the famous example of Jon Corzine (D-N.J.), who spent $60 million of his own money to win his Senate race in 2000.[1] Such prominent examples mask a hard truth about spending one's own money, however: Self-financing guarantees only a lighter wallet, not victory. Table 4.1 shows the campaign outcomes for the top twenty-seven self-funders in 2000 who contributed more than $500,000 to their own campaigns. Twenty lost in the

primary or general elections (Center for Responsive Politics 2002e).

Lest we get too focused on campaign spending, however, we should note that substantial amounts of money are spent on lobbying. The top spenders on lobbying typically are business interests such as the Chamber of Commerce, Philip Morris, and Exxon. In 1997–98, reported expenditures on lobbying were $2.6 billion. This figure rivals the amount spent on federal campaigns. Although this amount is immense, some context is useful. In that same time period, corporations gave more than $17 billion to charity (Milyo, Primo, and Groseclose 2000, 83).

The sources of money are heavily skewed toward business and professional sources. Figure 4.4 provides one indication of this trend by showing the breakdown of campaign money according to source. Clearly, most money comes from business or business-related interests.[2]

How Can Money Affect Governance by Congress?

Knowing the sources and destination of money does not, by itself, tell us whether money undermines the ability of Congress to govern effectively. It does not matter if we spend more on politics than diapers. If money corrupts, we want to spend less. If it improves the process, we want to spend more.

Therefore, to understand how money affects governance we want to know how it affects the people doing the governing. In this section I consider several mechanisms whereby campaign money can affect governance: Fundraising can distract politicians from policymaking; contributions and spending can distort the types of people who get elected; money can distort what representatives do on specific issues; and it can affect the responsiveness of politicians to voters. I consider each in turn.

Table 4.1 Self-Funding Candidates in 2000

Chamber	Name	Party-State	Self-Funding	Total Spent	Outcome
Senate	Jon Corzine	D-N.J.	$60,200,967	$63,209,506	Won general election
Senate	Mark Dayton	D-Minn.	11,772,067	11,957,114	Won general election
Senate	Maria Cantwell	D-Wash.	10,331,911	11,571,697	Won general election
House	James Humphreys	D-W.Va.	6,105,000	6,964,933	Lost general election
Senate	Herb Kohl	D-Wisc.	4,830,800	4,991,364	Won general election
Senate	Michael Ciresi	D-Minn.	4,762,100	5,883,233	Lost primary
House	Phil Sudan	R-Tex.	3,175,000	3,247,033	Lost general election
House	Roger Kahn	D-Ga.	2,960,742	3,859,860	Lost general election
House	Peter Wareing	R-Texas	2,325,860	3,896,840	Lost primary runoff
House	Shawn Donnelley	R-Ill.	2,255,458	2,444,398	Lost primary
House	Darrell Issa	R-Calif.	1,809,864	2,304,833	Won general election
House	Andrew Hochberg	R-Ill.	1,563,400	1,661,177	Lost primary
Senate	Bob Rovner	D-Pa.	1,510,000	1,750,772	Lost primary
House	Terry Lierman	D-Md.	1,465,000	2,131,527	Lost general election
House	Paul Jost	R-Va.	1,266,500	1,334,133	Lost primary
House	William Peacock	D-Calif.	1,259,748	1,373,020	Lost primary
House	Derek Smith	R-Utah	1,207,674	1,681,135	Lost general election
House	Ronald Kapche	R-Tex.	1,119,433	1,116,791	Lost primary
Senate	Ed Bernstein	D-Nev.	988,000	2,449,093	Lost general election
House	Mike Ferguson	R-N.J.	760,000	2,294,820	Won general election
House	Martha Clark	D-N.H.	705,500	1,055,513	Lost general election
House	John Cox	R-Ill.	654,500	702,655	Lost primary
House	Leigh McNairy	D-N.C.	641,000	1,176,161	Lost general election
House	Terry Gladman	R-Ill.	581,868	611,676	Lost primary
House	Tim Johnson	R-Ill.	580,000	1,760,128	Won general election
House	John Brewer	R-Tex.	559,846	645,792	Lost primary
Senate	Rebecca Yanisch	D-Minn.	502,348	1,938,042	Lost primary

Source: Center for Responsive Politics 2002e.

Figure 4.4 Sources of Contributions

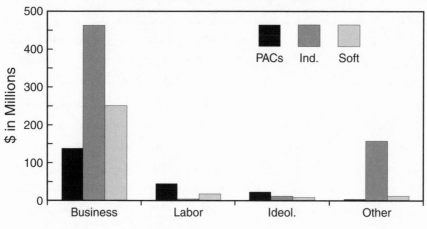

Source: Center for Responsive Politics 2002b.

Does Money Distract Members of Congress from Governing?

There is no doubt that fundraising eats up immense amounts of politicians' time. They spend many hours calling contributors and attending fundraisers. It is difficult to see how this situation could be a good thing. At a minimum, this grind makes politicians' lives less pleasant and thereby may decrease the quality of people who are willing to run and serve. In addition, the process may cause politicians to "go native": Time spent currying favor with big-money insiders may change their view of the world.

It is not clear whether the way to address this problem is by making it harder to raise money or easier. As experienced fundraisers say, "Nibbles take time; gulps take less." For example, Eugene McCarthy's antiwar candidacy in 1968 was bankrolled by contributions of more than $200,000 from a small group of wealthy patrons (contributions worth almost $1 million in today's dollars). Getting money in such big "gulps" freed McCarthy from exhausting fundraising (Smith 2001, 67).

It also is not clear that making politicians' lives easier merits fundamental changes in the system. For all we know, the time spent by politicians "dialing for dollars" takes politicians away from working on their handicap

as much as it takes them away from working for the handicapped. It seems, therefore, that a higher priority should be to look at how money affects who wins and what they do in office.

Does Money Bias Who Governs?

Another way money could affect governance is by deciding who does the governing. That is, money might decide who wins office. This causal relationship would undermine governance by biasing who makes decisions.

The sound-bite version of this debate is quite lively. Of course money buys elections, some observers say; the candidate who spends more wins 95 percent of the time, and winners outspend losers almost three to one in House races and two to one in Senate races. Hold on, others say, we have already seen that self-financed candidates cannot simply buy their way into office. This pattern extends to non–self-financed candidates, as well: In 2000, four of the top ten spenders in House races lost, as did three of the top ten spenders in Senate races.[3]

Really knowing how money affects election outcomes is difficult. The problem is that vulnerable incumbents raise more money because they are vulnerable and get relatively

Table 4.2 Top-Spending Senate Candidates in 2000

Name	Party	State	Amount Spent	Outcome
Jon Corzine	Democrat	New Jersey	$63,209,506	Won
Rick A. Lazio	Republican	New York	40,576,273	Lost
Hillary Rodham Clinton	Democrat	New York	29,871,577	Won
Spencer Abraham	Republican	Michigan	13,028,636	Lost
Mark Dayton	Democrat	Minnesota	11,957,114	Won
Maria Cantwell	Democrat	Washington	11,571,697	Won
Rick Santorum	Republican	Pennsylvania	10,616,262	Won
Dianne Feinstein	Democrat	California	10,346,170	Won
George Allen	Republican	Virginia	9,980,930	Won
John Ashcroft	Republican	Missouri	9,098,581	Lost

Source: Center for Responsive Politics 2002f.

fewer votes—again, because they are vulnerable. This pattern makes it appear that money does little good because many candidates who spend a lot do relatively poorly.

This difficulty has generated controversy among academics. On one side is Gary Jacobson (1978), who argues that incumbent spending has little or no effect on campaign outcomes (everyone agrees challenger spending increases challenger vote share). Green and Krasno (1988) and Gerber (1998) use different statistical methods and find that incumbent spending did increase incumbent vote share. More recently, Erikson and Palfry (2000) argue that statistical headaches are minimized for competitive races. They show that in these races, both incumbent and challenger spending matters.[4]

To say, however, that money increases vote share is not to say that money buys elections. Erikson and Palfry's estimates imply that spending $100,000 more than one's opponent in a competitive race was worth about 0.2 percentage points. This figure is not trivial—especially in a close race—but neither is it overwhelming, to say the least.

More important, to say money influences elections does not tell us how it influences policy. Consider table 4.2, which shows the top spenders in the Senate campaign in 2000. This list includes Jon Corzine, Hillary Clinton, Mark Dayton, Maria Cantwell, and Diane Feinstein. Corporate marauders let loose on the American polity? Hardly. All are liberal, several decidedly so. Yet all these candidates spent more than $10 million on their races. So just because money helps candidates win elections does not mean that money distorts policy toward wealthy interests. To really understand the effect of money on governance, then, we need to ask a different question.

Does Money Bias How Members of Congress Govern?

The crux of the issue is whether money biases legislators. One way it could do so is through campaign contributions. That is, does the fact that interest group X gives money to Congressman Y lead the congressman to be more supportive of X than otherwise? A common way to answer this question is to find an issue of interest to some contributor and to look at how much money the "yea" and "nay" legislators received. Usually there is a strong pattern, with legislators voting with the contributor receiving substantially greater contributions than those voting against the contributor. For example, in 1997 the Senate narrowly voted down a proposal to cut $10 million from the Forest Service's road construction budget ("Case in Point," *Washington Post,* 12 October 1997). Timber companies supported the spending; environmentalists and taxpayer groups regarded it as destructive and wasteful. An analysis by the Center for Responsive Politics showed that nine of the top ten recipients of money from timber interests voted with the timber industry.

The impact of that evidence is reduced, however, when someone inevitably asks, "How would these legislators vote if they didn't get contributions?" More often than not, the people receiving the money are those who ideologically or geographically are committed to supporting the industry in question. In the timber case, the top recipients were Republicans from Oregon, Washington, Alaska, and Idaho. Given their political bases, they would be crazy not to vote with the timber industry, whether they received contributions from the industry or not.

This analysis begs the question of how to disentangle the two effects—the incentives of representatives to vote for contributor interests and incentives for contributors to contribute to ideologically compatible representatives. A large literature in political science addresses this more complex question, often employing advanced statistical techniques. Although researchers have developed many different approaches and findings, the consensus appears to be that contributions do not affect votes on major issues but may affect votes on minor issues (Sorauf 1992; Wright 1990; Grenzke 1988).

This area is ripe for additional research, however. Most studies look at whether legislators who receive contributions are more supportive of the contributor. In theory, however, everyone could be affected by contributions—even those who do not receive them. For example, the NRA could not only cause Republicans to be pro-gun, it also could push Democrats to be less anti-gun in an ef-

fort to minimize the threat that the NRA will enter subsequent campaigns on the side of the Republicans. Thus, looking for influence among only recipients of money is looking at only part of the story. One way around this problem—an approach very much in the spirit of this book—is to look at outcomes. If money can affect all legislators, recipients and nonrecipients alike, we would expect policy outcomes to be more favorable to contributors than to noncontributors. Analysis of state-level contributions and policy is an interesting possibility given that contribution levels and policies vary across states (see Bailey 2002b).

Another way money could influence how Congress governs is via lobbying. Although one component of lobbying is guiding and taking credit for campaign contributions, there are many other facets. One is provision of information. People with money can more easily follow and analyze the tangle of legislation under consideration in Congress. If there is a proposal to their advantage, they can make sure people hear about it. If there is a proposal to their disadvantage, they can go after its weaknesses and make sure people hear about those.

Assessing the impact of lobbying expenditures on policy also is difficult. A widely held view among political scientists is that lobbyists focus on providing information to legislators who are already supportive of their positions. When lobbyists contact legislators who are not already on their side, they do so when there is a strong, sympathetic constituency in the legislator's district (Hojnacki and Kimball 1998). The implication is that lobbying expenditures do not steamroll opposition, but they do reinforce and perhaps increase the salience of existing support.

Does Money Affect the Responsiveness of Members of Congress?

We have considered the main mechanisms whereby money can undermine fair and effective governance. It also is possible, however, that money makes politicians more responsive.

The reason is that campaign money goes toward activities that strengthen—or perhaps even define—democracy. These activities include efforts to inform and mobilize voters during election campaigns.

How could having a lot of money available for campaigns help representation? First note that representation in the United States is primarily anticipatory. Voters are uninformed about almost all policies. They simply do not have the time, interest, or incentives to follow H.R. 2990 or any other obscure (but potentially very important) legislation. Thus, politicians do not receive "instructions" from voters. So why do politicians care about what voters want? They do so in anticipation of what constituents *would* prefer if they were informed, because a failure to do so would allow political rivals to pick up votes by telling voters about the issue (Arnold 1990; Bailey 2002a).

The potential for rivals to mobilize voters drives politicians to respond to the typical (uninformed) citizen. If there is no threat of mobilization, candidates do best by paying attention only to voters who follow politics closely. These voters are the type of people who watch C-SPAN religiously or have an interest group (such as the NRA or a labor union) that is eager to inform them. If there is a threat of mobilization, on the other hand, candidates have to make sure that "regular" people would not be upset to hear about the candidates' positions. Money plays a central role in this story because it increases the capacity of challengers to reach voters (which, in turn, increases the incentive of incumbents to do what voters would want them to). The less money in the system, the less an incumbent has to worry about uninformed voters being mobilized and the less the incumbent has to take their interests into consideration.

An important factor for this model to work is that money spent in campaigns actually informs voters. If money can be spent on successful efforts to dupe voters, politicians could raise money from the most despicable special interests and then cruise to victory on

the strength of ads that trick voters into thinking that the politicians are actually doing what voters want. Of course, if voters can be tricked by ads, we face deeper questions about democracy in the first place. If we do not trust voters to judge information—whether from ads, politicians, the news media, or their neighbors—why should we trust them to choose our leaders?

Fortunately we do not have to delve into these deep questions about democracy because there is considerable evidence that ads do not trick voters but inform them. Research has found that "political advertising contributes to a well-informed electorate" (Brians and Wattenberg 1996, 185) and that campaign ads were more important than television news and local newspaper coverage (West 1994, 1063; Patterson and McClure 1976). Coleman and Manna (2000, 757) sum up their findings by stating that campaign spending "improves the public's ability to place candidates on ideology and issue scales, and encourages certainty about those placements. Rather than permit House members to mask their voting records, incumbent spending helps improve the accuracy of citizen perceptions of the incumbent's ideology."

Note that this argument does not necessarily imply that voters will be informed or that electoral competition will be vigorous in all cases. The argument is that when an incumbent knows that his or her potential challengers could raise a lot of money, the incumbent will be more responsive to voters to avoid providing potential challengers with issues to run on. If the incumbent does this effectively enough—and presents a record with no obvious hooks to run against—top-flight challengers may not run. Yet the potential for raising money might have helped keep the incumbent responsive.

One other requirement for this mechanism to work is that there be multiple sources of campaign contributions. If there is only once source of money, the only candidates who will have resources are those friendly to the contributor. Opponents of the contributor, however sensible or popular their issue positions, will have no resources with which to mobilize voters and will do poorly (see Bailey 2002a). If contributions are available from multiple sources, however, the self-interest of contributors can be used to work against each other. How does this dynamic work? The key is the fungibility of money. Money raised from oil companies does not have to be spent touting energy policy. In fact, a candidate will spend the money touting his or her most popular positions and criticizing his or her opponent's least popular positions. So as long as there is some (possibly obscure) issue on which a candidate can raise money, then he or she can pressure the opponent to be more responsive on the issues voters care about.

In summary, the effect of money on governance may be conditional. If money can be spent on ads that "trick" people into supporting a candidate irrespective of the issue positions of the candidate, money is bad for governance. Money also undermines governance if it comes from only one source. Money can aid responsiveness on major issues, however, if campaigns are informative and money comes from diverse sources.

Money and Policymaking: Patients' Bill of Rights

I now turn to an exploratory case study of the Patients' Bill of Rights, an issue that frequently headlined political debate from 1998 to 2001. This case is useful for our purposes because it features popular legislation that was resisted by wealthy interest groups. The legislation also has yet to be passed, raising a legitimate concern that money is behind the inaction. I discuss the issue in light of the mechanisms discussed above.

Democrats were the primary proponents of the Patients' Bill of Rights. They said that the legislation was necessary to protect people from ruthless insurance companies. They wanted to expand the right to sue health maintenance organizations (HMOs), to improve access to specialists, and to expand the

scope of coverage. Opponents said the legislation would drive up costs and push more than a million people off of health insurance. Their legislative strategy was to shift the debate to Medicare; polling found that key blocs of voters placed a higher priority on overhaul of Medicare (Foerstel 1999a, 1610). Most opponents were Republicans, although there were important differences within the party, as we shall see.

The most active interest groups on the issue were health insurers and business interests opposed to the legislation. They formed an organization called the Health Benefits Coalition. Groups associated with this coalition contributed more than $10 million to Republicans and more than $2.5 million to Democrats in 1999–2000 (Center for Responsive Politics 2002g). They also bankrolled independent issue ad campaigns and lobbying efforts worth several millions more (Carey 2001a).

Interest group activity was not one-sided, however. Doctors and their professional organization, the American Medical Association (AMA), pushed for the bill. Historically, doctors have been closer to the Republican Party, preferring limited government intervention in health care (Koszczuk 1999). Working with HMOs changed their perspective, however, as the insurance firms squeezed compensation and put limits on medical choices. In a survey of doctors and nurses in 2000, 90 percent said that insurers had denied needed coverage to patients, and 75 percent said managed care has reduced the quality of care (Foerstel 1999b). The result was that the AMA moved toward the Democratic Party, with half of its PAC contributions going to Democrats in 1999–2000 (compared to only 28 percent going to Democrats in 1997–98).[5] The AMA also played a leading role in lobbying on behalf of the legislation.

Trial lawyers also tended to favor the legislation, although they did not play a central lobbying role. All told, lawyers and law firms contributed more than $3.6 million in the 2000 cycle, with more than 90 percent going to Democrats (Center for Responsive Politics 2002h). They were interested in other issues, such as reform of tort law.

The bill has had a bruising—and, to date, unsuccessful—legislative history. In 1999 the House and Senate passed different versions of the legislation. The two chambers could not agree on how to resolve the differences in their versions, and the bill died. In June 2001 the Senate passed legislation that allowed patients to sue HMOs for as much as $5 million in damages. The House passed a version with a lower cap on damages in August 2001. Their version was a result of last-minute arm-twisting and dealmaking between President Bush and key lawmakers. Since then the bill has languished, waiting for President Bush and Senate Democrats to reach an agreement.[6]

Our goal in looking at the issue is to explore how money and congressional governance play out in practice. Instead of seeking to answer these questions with technical statistical analyses (for one example of that approach, see Bailey 2002b), I use the case study to spur thinking about the relationship between money and governance.

Did Money Distract Members of Congress from Governing?

The first question to assess is whether the money chase undermined governance by distracting members from legislating. In the House, consideration of the Patients' Bill of Rights was marked by a surprising lack of formal deliberation. In 1998, 1999, and 2001, legislation on the issue did not have markup hearings in any House committees. There were relatively brief deliberations on the floor of the House. However, informal deliberation among members, staff, and lobbyists was intense, even "brutal."[7] In the Senate, informal deliberation was similarly intense, but formal deliberation also was extensive. In 2001 the Senate debated the issue for nine days. Trent Lott probably was not alone when he stated, in the middle of the debate, "I'm tired of debating this. I want this over" (Carey 2001b).

The biggest determinant of whether there was extensive formal deliberation was the position of congressional leadership. The Republican leadership resisted the legislation and wanted to minimize the attention given to the issue. They especially wanted to minimize the number of times their members would have to vote against the politically popular legislation.[8] Hence they minimized the exposure of the bill. Senate Democrats, on the other hand, relished debating the issue because the more attention it got, the more useful politically it was for the party. So whatever role money played was in terms of affecting the leadership, not the members.

Did Money Bias Who Governed?

The second question is whether money from health care firms may have determined elections and thereby skewed the composition of the legislature that considered the legislation. As the foregoing discussion suggests, money probably does increase the odds of winning, but not by an overwhelming margin. Hence, if health insurers were to have had an effect, we would expect them to have had it among the closest races. Yet among these close races, both sides were flush with money. "No race was lost because of a lack of money," said election analyst Amy Walters from *The Cook Political Report*. Consider Michigan's Eighth District, where Republican Mike Rogers beat Democrat Diane Byrum by fewer than 200 votes. Rogers raised $2.2 million; Byrum raised $2.3 million.[9] Rogers raised $63,000 from insurance companies—a large amount, but hardly overwhelming given his overall take. Byrum raised a total of $162,000 from doctors and lawyers—again, hardly a dominant figure. The consensus among political observers is that both candidates had so much money that the marginal effect of more money was tiny.

Moreover, the composition of Congress has not been what has held back the Patients' Bill of Rights legislation. The legislation languishes not for a lack of votes but for lack of will on the part of the congressional leadership and the president. In both chambers, a majority favored serious reform. In the Senate in 2001, fifty-six senators voted in favor of the stringent McCain-Edwards-Kennedy bill. In the House in 1999, a majority of the House, including sixty-eight Republicans, supported legislation that included a right to sue HMOs. Of these sixty-eight Republicans, twenty-one were so committed to passing strong legislation that they also voted against weaker Republican legislation that was regarded as an effort to co-opt the issue (Carey and Adams 2001).

Did Money Bias How Members of Congress Governed?

The third mechanism is that money might bias what legislators did on specific policies. That is, the prospect of a juicy contribution—or the prospect of preempting a juicy contribution to an opponent—could lead members to support policies preferred by big contributors on an issue. In this case, however, it is hard to argue that money pulled members to one side or the other. Although there certainly was a lot of money flowing from health care companies, there also was money from doctors and lawyers. In fact, two Republican leaders of the Patients' Bill of Rights effort did quite well. Charlie Norwood, a Republican dentist from Georgia, raised more than $1.2 million for his race in 2000, including over $300,000 from health professionals. Greg Ganske, a Republican plastic surgeon from Iowa, raised more than $1 million, including almost $200,000 from health professionals.

A related possibility is that lobbying expenditures could skew the debate. There is no doubt that the issue was heavily lobbied. The health industry spent more than twice as much on lobbying as on campaign contributions in 1999–2000—although these contributions do not include issue ad expenditures, which are unregulated and therefore uncounted (Center for Responsive Politics 2002j).

Part of the lobbying effort also involved taking the case directly to voters. Health insurers spent heavily on ad campaigns at strategic points in the debate. These ads argued that the legislation would increase costs and cause 1.5 million Americans to lose health care coverage (Foerstel 1999a). The response from the other side was to publicize HMO problems, including a horrific case in which a six-month-old boy had his hands and feet amputated because of complications that arose when he was denied emergency room treatment by his HMO (Foerstel 1999a).

The net effect? It is hard to tell. Both sides clearly had enough resources to get information to legislators and, to a lesser degree, the public, so neither side appeared to have a decisive advantage. Probably the clearest effect was that the additional money pushed each side away from its weakest points, as the lobbying efforts identified problems in the other side's arguments, forcing them to try to move away from such weaknesses. For example, proponents' ability to hammer away at HMO abuses forced Republicans to favor some kind of reform. At the same time, opponents' ability to hammer on exorbitant lawyer fees pushed Democrats toward limits on what a lawyer could earn from a single case. Without lobbying expenditures, it is not clear that the two sides would have had to compromise as much (although, of course, they have yet to compromise enough to get anything passed).

Did Money Affect the Responsiveness of Members of Congress?

The fourth possible effect of money is positive—that money in the system actually increased legislators' responsiveness to voters on the issue. Did spending make politicians more concerned with what voters wanted? Doing the HMOs' bidding came with the cost of making oneself vulnerable to attack on the issue. For example, FamiliesUSA, a patient advocacy group, targeted moderate Republicans with ads in their districts about the issue (Foerstel 1999a). Business interests emphasize the possibility the legislation could enrich lawyers without benefiting patients.

Fear of such ads is precisely what could push such members to be more responsive. The key to the argument, however, is that such ads do not necessarily have to be funded by doctors. Candidates could raise money from labor unions and telecommunication companies and use those funds in the exact same manner. In fact, most issue ads on the Patients' Bill of Rights were run by the Democratic Party with funds raised from soft money (Annenberg Public Policy Center 2001). Either way, the presence of such money could make it uncomfortable for members from districts where the legislation was popular to oppose it.

In several cases, Republicans who were most subject to big-money campaigns were among the most supportive of the Patients' Bill of Rights. Greg Ganske ran for the Senate (but lost), and Charlie Norwood openly explored doing the same (but chose to remain in the House).[10] Lindsey Graham (R-S.C.) is a conservative who moved from the House to the Senate in 2002. He too favored the legislation that allows patients to sue HMOs (Adams 2001).

Finally, we should note in this context that the political vulnerability of Republicans on the issue, despite all of the money behind the opposition to reform, led Republicans closer and closer to strong legislation. Part of that movement surely is that the Democrats have the resources—from doctors, lawyers, and a myriad of other sources—to publicize the issue in political campaigns. Fearing this possibility, by July 2001 Speaker Dennis Hastert's strategy was to get something passed, even if it meant pushing something very close to what the Democrats wanted. This process led Michael Castle (R-Del.) to comment, "The differences between the [Republican and Democratic leadership] bills are becoming almost nil" (Adams and Carey 2001).

In summary, the Patients' Bill of Rights provides an interesting window on money and governance in Congress. Of course, the case is only a single example, and it has several distinctive characteristics. Among other things, the case features a high-profile issue with contributors on both sides. Yet we see some interesting patterns. One is that the stalemate is related more to leadership (or lack thereof) than to money. Money prevented neither serious consideration of the issue nor the election of a majority that wanted to pass it. This analysis implies that the money and politics literature should give more attention to what money does to leadership policy positions. For the rest of the members of Congress, however, the link between money and governance is hard to discern. In fact, some of the members who were most subject to big money competitive races were the ones who were most likely to oppose the health insurers and support the Patients' Bill of Rights.

Conclusion

The flow of money in American politics raises questions about the ability of Congress to govern fairly. The total amounts are staggering, and the time politicians spend raising money is disturbing. Understanding the effects of money and what we should do about it is difficult, however. Evidence of harm is limited, and even if we could demonstrate that outside money had a pernicious impact, regulating it brings core values of equality and liberty into direct conflict.

In this chapter I have attempted to identify mechanisms by which money can influence governance. I have explored these mechanisms through the scholarly literature and a case study of the Patients' Bill of Rights. By and large, there is less evidence of harm than one might think, given the huge amounts of money coming from self-interested sources that enter the system.

That is not to say, however, that money in politics is of no concern. First, we have not explored all mechanisms of potential influence. For example, money could influence opinion formation by voters. In addition, by looking at a high-profile issue, we have not been able to address the concern that money is more dangerous to fair governance on obscure and complicated issues such as tax provisions and financial regulations than on major wedge issues that divide a large portion of the society.

So what, if anything, should be done about money in politics? The discussion here does not offer the final word on the matter, but it does provide some principles for assessing competing approaches.

One popular approach, embodied in the McCain-Feingold legislation, is to try to reduce the amount of large contributions and expenditures in politics. This approach is risky. First are the obvious constitutional issues raised by potentially limiting what people can say, contribute, and spend in the political realm. Moreover, experience at the state level shows that such efforts fail to achieve their intended goals and often yield undesirable, unintended consequences (Malbin and Gais 1998). At a more practical level, it is reasonable to wonder if reducing money in the system achieves what it is supposed to. Presumably the goal is to give voice to citizens without money. Yet if the threat of campaign spending pushes legislators to take the concerns of uninformed voters more seriously (in the anticipatory fashion discussed above), then making it harder for candidates to raise money may actually reduce the incentives for legislators to be responsive. To put the point in partisan terms, if the goal of reducing money is to help the "middle class" against "the rich," does it really make sense to hurt the Democratic Party, as a ban on soft money almost certainly will (at least in the short term)?

The opposite approach is to increase the amount of money in the system via public financing. Doing so could help provide a baseline level of funding for credible candidates and limit the negative side effects of relying solely on self-interested money. Public funding of presidential elections provides a cautionary tale, however. In 2000 the federal government provided $83 million to Al Gore, $63 million to George W. Bush, and $16 million to Pat Buchanan. It is impossible

to deny that the effort failed to achieve its intended result of reducing the money chase, in light of Bush's and Gore's unrelenting fundraising efforts. Moreover, in failing to achieve this goal, the policy wasted millions on the Buchanan campaign. (If you need to be convinced of this claim, consider the following: Buchanan spent an astounding $89 per vote, compared to $3.66 per vote for Bush, $2.35 per vote for Gore, and $2.69 per vote for Nader.) To top things off, the unintended consequences of the public funding were catastrophic: Public funding put Buchanan and Nader on the ballot (Buchanan because he had funding; Nader because he wanted it) and contributed to the Florida vote-counting debacle.

A better result can occur if public funding is more sensitive to the way representation really works. Representation is anticipatory, and the easier it is for candidates to effectively publicize their differences, the greater the incentives candidates have to be responsive to typical uninformed voters. One idea in this spirit is to devote public resources to creating a political infrastructure that encourages vigorous and credible debate. This infrastructure would include funding of debates and provision of information, perhaps including voting guides in which both sides square off. The logic behind these efforts is not a naïve hope that voters will blossom into A+ civics students. Instead, the goal should be to facilitate credible information transmission. Strengthening the potential for voters to get good information strengthens the incentives for politicians to be responsive. Another idea is to use tax credits for contributions to allow citizens to control how the money is allocated and to minimize the possibility that rules are skewed to protect incumbents or major parties. These approaches would reduce the chance that good ideas go unfunded. They also would not force people to pay for candidacies they do not support. Moving in this direction could improve the incentives of Congress to respond to the public and create policies that serve the people.

Notes

1. Some politicians also pass on money they have raised to other politicians. The politicians who contributed the most to others in 2000 were Nancy Pelosi (D-Calif.), who gave more than $900,000; Tom DeLay (R-Texas); Dennis Hastert (R-Ill.); Dick Armey (R-Texas); and Steny H. Hoyer (D-Md.).
2. Note, however, that individual contributions are linked with the employer of the individual, regardless of whether the individual's contribution had anything to do with the employer's interests.
3. Two more of the top spenders in the House just barely won (Bill Luther and Clay Shaw). Money may well have been behind their margins of victory, although it clearly did not makes things easy for them (see Center for Responsive Politics 2002f).
4. Analyses of state-level legislative races come to the same conclusion (Gierzynski 2000, 60).
5. For all health professionals, it is harder to see a pattern. They contributed $45 million to candidates in the 2000 cycle. About 42 percent of this amount went to Democrats, which was pretty close to historical patterns; in 1990, 1992, and 1994, for example, the percentages going to Democrats were 48, 50, and 45, respectively (see Center for Responsive Politics 2002i).
6. As a practical matter, the differences are small because most states already have caps on damages, and most cases award much less than the caps (see Norwood 2002).
7. Interview with House legislative aide, May 6, 2002.
8. Ibid. On efforts by Republican leaders to structure the legislative process against the Patients' Bill of Rights, see Foerstel (1999a).
9. All data on congressional finances in this section are from Center for Responsive Politics (2002i).
10. On Ganske and Norwood, see Dovere (2001).

References

Adams, Rebecca. 2001. "House Sends Patients' Rights On to Last Critical Test." *Congressional Quarterly Weekly Report* (August 8): 1900.

Adams, Rebecca, and Mary Agnes Carey. 2001. "Speaker Pulls Out All the Stops for a Win on Managed Care." *Congressional Quarterly Weekly Report* (July 7): 1765.

Annenberg Public Policy Center. 2001. *Issue Advertising in the 1999–2000 Election Cycle.* Released February 1, 2001 [online]. Available at www.appcpenn.org/political/issueads/ (accessed May 3, 2002).

Arnold, K. Douglas. 1990. *The Logic of Congressional Action.* New Haven, Conn.: Yale University Press.

Bailey, Michael. 2002a. "Can Representation Be Fair When Campaign Contributions Come Mostly from Business? An Exploration in Multiple Dimensions." Unpublished manuscript.

———. 2002b. "Do Campaign Contributions Lead to Policies That Favor the Wealthy? An Examination of Taxing and Spending in the American States." Unpublished manuscript.

Brians, Craig, and Martin Wattenberg. 1996. "Campaign Issue Knowledge and Salience: Comparing Reception from TV Commercials, TV News, and Newspapers." *American Journal of Political Science* 40, no. 1: 172–93.

Brubaker, Stanley. 1998. "The Limits of Campaign Spending Limits." *Public Interest* 133 (fall): 33–54.

Canoe Internet Network. 2001. *Baseball Salaries.* April 5 [online]. Available at www.canoe.ca/BaseballMoneyMatters/salaries_players.html (accessed May 21, 2002).

Carey, Mary Agnes. 2001a. "Employers, Insurers Pull Out Stops to Defeat McCain-Edwards-Kennedy." *Congressional Quarterly Weekly* (June 6): 1420.

———. 2001b. "Patients' Protection Bills Lock Horns on Employer Liability." *Congressional Quarterly Weekly* (June 23): 1500.

Carey, Mary Agnes, and Rebecca Adams. 2001. "Senate Oks Patients' Rights Bill; Backers Brace for House Battle." *Congressional Quarterly Weekly Report* (June 6): 1579.

Center for Responsive Politics. 2002a. "Summary" [online]. Available at www.opensecrets.org/pubs/lobby00/summary.asp (accessed May 21, 2002).

———. 2002b. "Election Overview, 2000 Cycle, Business-Labor-Ideology Split in

PAC, Soft & Individual Donations to Candidates and Parties" [online]. Available at www.opensecrets.org/overview/blio.asp?Cycle=2000&display=Pacs (accessed May 6, 2002).

———. 2002c. "Soft Money's Impact at a Glance" [online]. Available at www.opensecrets.org/parties/softglance.asp (accessed May 3, 2002).

———. 2002d. "Election Overview, 2000 Cycle, Top Individual Contributors" [online]. Available at www.opensecrets.org/overview/topindivs.asp?Cycle=2000 (accessed May 3, 2002).

———. 2002e. "Election Overview, 2000 Cycle, Top Self Funders" [online]. Available at www.opensecrets.org/overview/topself.asp?Cycle=2000&Sortby=SelfFunding (accessed May 6, 2002).

———. 2002f. "Election Overview, 2000 Cycle, Who Spent the Most" [online]. Available at www.opensecrets.org/overview/topspend.asp?Cycle=2000 (accessed May 6, 2002).

———. 2002g. "Health Care: Patients' Bill of Rights" [online]. Available at www.opensecrets.org/payback.issue.asp?issueid=PB1 (accessed May 6, 2002).

———. 2002h. "Health Professionals: Long-Term Contribution Trends" [online]. Available at www.opensecrets.org/industries/indus.asp?Ind=H01 (accessed May 6, 2002).

———. 2002i. "2000 Congressional Campaign Finance Profiles" [online]. Available at www.opensecrets.org/politicians/index.asp (accessed May 7, 2002).

———. 2002j. "Totals by Sector" [online]. Available at www.opensecrets.org/pubs/lobby00/sectors.asp (accessed May 21, 2002).

Coleman, John, and Paul Manna. 2000. "Campaign Spending and Democracy: Public Boon or Public Bane?" *Journal of Politics* 62, no. 3: 757–89.

Dovere, Edward-Isaac. 2001. "Patients' Rights Puts Ganske in Bind." *The Hill*, August 8.

Erikson, Robert, and Thomas Palfry. 2000. "Equilibria in Campaign Spending Games: Theory and Data." *American Political Science Review* 94, no. 3: 595–609.

Federal Election Commission. 2001. "Congressional Financial Activity Soars for 2000." Press release, January 9, 2001. Available at http://fecweb1.fec.gov/press/post-general2000.htm (accessed May 3, 2002).

Foerstel, Karen. 1999a. "Clinton Pushes to Salvage Partial Victory on Health Care." *Congressional Quarterly Weekly* (August 7): 1609–11.

———. 1999b. "Managed Care Fight Finds GOP Torn Between Doctors, Insurers." *Congressional Quarterly Weekly* (July 7): 1862.

Francia, Peter, John C. Green, Paul S. Herrnson, Wesley Joe, Lynda W. Powell, and Clyde Wilcox. 2000. "Donor Dissent: Congressional Contributors Rethink Giving." *The Public Perspective* 11, no. 4 (July/August): 29–32.

Gerber, Alan. 1998. "Estimating the Effect of Campaign Spending on Election Outcomes Using Instrumental Variables." *American Political Science Review* 92: 401–11.

Gierzynsky, Anthony. 2000. *Money Rules: Financing Elections in America.* Boulder, Colo.: Westview Press.

Green, Donald, and Jonathan Krasno. 1988. "Salvation for the Spendthrift Incumbent: Re-estimating the Effects of Campaign Spending in House Elections." *American Journal of Political Science* 32: 884–907.

Grenzke, Janet. 1988. "PACs and the Congressional Supermarket: The Currency Is Complex." *American Journal of Political Science* 33: 1–24.

Hojnacki, Marie, and David Kimball. 1998. "Organized Interests and the Decision Whom to Lobby in Congress." *American Political Science Review* 92, no. 4: 775–90.

Jacobson, Gary. 1978. "The Effects of Campaign Spending in Congressional Elections." *American Political Science Review* 72: 469–91.

Koszczuk, Jackie. 1999. "Doctors and GOP, Longtime Allies, Part Company on Managed Care." *Congressional Quarterly Weekly Report* (October 10): 2285.

Malbin, Michael, and Thomas Gais. 1998. *The Day After Reform: Sobering Campaign Finance Lessons from the American States*. Albany, N.Y.: Rockefeller Institute Press.

Milyo, Jeffrey, David Primo, and Timothy Groseclose. 2000. "Corporate PAC Campaign Contributions in Perspective." *Business and Politics* 2, no. 1: 75–88.

Norwood, Charlie. 2002. "Break the Patients' Rights Stalemate." *Roll Call*, February 14.

Patterson, Thomas, and Robert McClure. 1976. *The Unseeing Eye*. New York: Putnam.

Smith, Bradley. 1996. "Faulty Assumptions and Undemocratic Consequences of Campaign Finance Reform." *Yale Law Journal* 105: 1049–91.

———. 2001. *Unfree Speech: The Folly of Campaign Finance Reform*. Princeton, N.J.: Princeton University Press.

Sorauf, Frank. 1992. *Inside Campaign Finance*. New Haven, Conn.: Yale University Press.

Vidal, Gore. 2001. "Forward." In David Donnelly, Janice Fine, and Ellen Miller, *Are Elections for Sale?* Boston: Beacon Press.

West, Darrell. 1994. "Political Advertising and News Coverage in the 1992 California U.S. Senate Campaigns." *Journal of Politics* 56, no. 4: 1053–75.

Wright, John. 1990. "Contributions, Lobbying and Committee Voting in the U.S. House of Representatives." *American Political Science Review* 84: 417–38.

★★★

Chapter 5

Women in Congress: Descriptive Representation and Democratic Governance

Courtenay Daum

The majority of the U.S. population and 52 percent of eligible voters—residents age eighteen and older—are women (U.S. Census Bureau 2003). Yet women occupy only 13.6 percent of the 535 seats in Congress. In 2003 there were seventy-three women in Congress—fifty-nine in the House of Representatives and fourteen in the Senate—and this figure was an all-time high. In fact, since the nation's founding only 219 women have served in Congress (Center for American Women and Politics 2003). Like other previously disenfranchised groups, women had to overcome a series of obstacles to gain election to office that white male candidates did not have to face. Although the opportunities for women have expanded rapidly in the past few decades, women continue to struggle to achieve equality in elected offices in the United States. The reality is that at the current rate at which women are increasing their presence in Congress, it will be decades before women achieve parity. The current electoral system is not conducive to the election of large numbers of new female candidates, and this bias impedes effective democratic governance.

This chapter examines the obstacles confronting female candidates running for national office in the United States and discusses alternative electoral systems that may reduce these obstacles and produce a more democratic system of government. First I discuss different theories of representation, including the merits of the descriptive representation of women in Congress. Then I examine the relationship between equitable representation of women and an increase in democratic governance . Finally, I briefly discuss alternatives to the existing congressional electoral system, including quota systems and cumulative voting schemes. I also introduce a third alternative: doubling up, which is designed to increase the representation of women in Congress to reflect the presence of women in the population and thereby further democratization.

Theories of Representation

Since the nation's founding, political philosophers have debated theories of democracy and representation and their application in the United States—including what it means to live in a vibrant democracy and the role that representation plays in such a system. Traditional debates about representation focus on how representatives are expected to act once in office, who should be elected as representatives, and which actions and characteristics translate into legitimate representation. For example, should representatives act as delegates or trustees? As Stephen Wayne notes in chapter 1, the delegate model presupposes that individuals are elected to office to directly convey the interests of their constituents, whereas the trustee model presupposes that voters trust their representatives to act on their behalf and allows representatives a great deal of latitude in their decision making (Hero and Tolbert 1995; Jacobson 1997; Weissberg 1978).

In addition to the delegate/trustee and direct versus indirect representation debates, there is an ongoing dialogue about the merits of substantive versus descriptive representation. This discussion focuses on the demographic and attitudinal characteristics of representatives in addition to how they act once they are in office. Substantive representation is achieved when elected officials represent the needs of their constituent groups, either directly or indirectly, whereas descriptive representation is achieved when the representative body mirrors the demographic makeup of society (Pitkin 1969a; Swain 1995).

In the United States, all federal and most state electoral systems are premised on achieving substantive representation. Candidates are elected to office and expected to engage in either indirect or direct substantive representation of their constituents' interests. This process, however, fails to adequately take into account the interests of various marginalized groups—such as women and racial and ethnic minorities—that have not always benefited from substantive representation because they were systematically excluded from participating in elections and politics throughout much of American history. Members of these groups had to overcome a legacy of disenfranchisement and a variety of obstacles designed to keep them from running as candidates and winning election to political office in the United States. As a result, the structure of the current electoral system and the high value assigned to substantive representation may not be conducive to the election of women or members of racial and ethnic minorities. In contrast, an electoral system that is designed to ensure the descriptive representation of women and racial and ethnic minorities will increase the number of individuals from these groups elected to office, and should enhance the substantive representation of these constituents and their interests, and contribute to a more democratic system of government.

Why Descriptive Representation of Women?

Theories of descriptive representation have achieved particular saliency in the United States in recent decades as increasing emphasis has been placed on the heterogeneity of populations and the problems associated with representation of a diversity of interests in a system of government founded on liberal democratic principles. In accordance with the liberal democratic tradition, difference in a democracy traditionally is regarded as a matter of different ideas. Differences among groups in terms of social and economic equality are considered irrelevant to the functioning of a democratic government because the emphasis in the United States is on political equality. All citizens are equal as individuals, consistent with the one person, one vote principle. The vote is the mechanism by which individuals express their ideas and preferences, and representation is considered adequate when elected officials appear to be both responsive and accountable to the members of the electorate. Thus, although one's preference may not always be commensurate with the outcome of a given election, one accepts the result because it is assumed that each individual had the same means by which to influence the election (Phillips 1991; Swabey 1969).

There are numerous problems, however, with this definition of political equality. It overlooks the fact that until 1919 the individual in the American liberal democratic tradition was male. The belief that the individual is sex-neutral obscures the dominant role that men have played in the United States' political system since its founding and the extent to which a male perspective has conditioned the realm of government involvement and policymaking. There are real differences between the opportunities that are available to men and women. For example, pretending that the individual is sex-neutral ignores the fact that women often are not able to vote on the same terms as men. The liberal state can give women equal opportunity to participate in elections in the form of the vote, but this mere ability to vote does not create the equality of conditions necessary for women to vote or participate in politics. Real political equality requires economic, social, and sexual equality so that women may have access to the same opportunities as men to participate in the political realm as voters, volunteers, employees, or candidates (Eisenstein 1987; Phillips 1991).

Historically, women have been precluded from or had difficulty voting because of their unique family obligations. More recently, women's dual roles as workers and mothers have constrained their political participation more than men's roles as workers and fathers have constrained men's political participation. Similarly, evidence indicates that women historically have been denied access to the educational and occupational opportunities that are the traditional launching pad for political careers, thereby reducing their presence in the eligibility pool for political candidates (Darcy, Welch, and Clark 1994). In addition, women who do run often are at a disadvantage because they predominantly are forced to challenge male incumbents who are difficult to defeat. The reality of incumbency advantage and the less-than-promising races for challengers have systematically worked to keep women out of Congress for decades (Burrell 1997).

A definition of political equality premised on the notion of one person, one vote not only ignores differences between males and females in the public sphere, it obscures social inequities between men and women in the private sphere as well. Defining equality in terms of one's limited access to participation in the public sphere isolates the private sphere from the public realm, and this isolation has a disproportionately negative impact on women.

Men and women have occupied different roles in the private sphere, and although these differences have narrowed in recent years, substantive challenges to equality persist. Women still perform a disproportionate amount of household work in comparison to men, and women's political participation often is restricted by their positions as primary caregivers for their children. Giving women the right to vote in 1920 did not liberate them from many of the constraints on women in the private sphere. Suffragists' demand for the vote challenged the male monopoly on the public arena, yet suffragists silently accepted the feminine character of the private sphere. The goal of the suffrage movement was simply to get women the vote, not to get women elected to political office. In fact, one of the suffrage movement's most popular arguments was the housekeeping argument:

> The housekeeping argument was that the traditional role for the woman gave her responsibility for the moral, spiritual, and physical well-being of her family. In the modern industrial society, however, women could not exercise this responsibility solely from within the home itself. Municipal sanitation, food inspection, the regulation of working conditions, the control of drunkenness and all manner of vice—all were relevant to her duties, and all were manageable only through political action. Women needed the ballot for reform so that women could better carry out their traditional responsibilities to their families (Darcy, Welch, and Clark 1994, 12).

In this sense, even when women achieved so-called political equality in the form of the vote, they continued to be constrained politically by their familial roles while men continued to dominate the political sphere (Darcy, Welch, and Clark 1994; Dubois 1987).

Finally, it is a gross assumption to suggest that political equality—defined in terms of the vote—automatically translates into adequate representation if, in fact, the identity and sociological group membership of representatives are relevant. As Anne Phillips explains in *Engendering Democracy*, the composition of elected bodies matters because "when the characteristics of those elected deviate to any significant degree from those of the electorate as a whole, there is a clear case for saying something is wrong. These 'characteristics' have obviously proved themselves relevant, and some groups have become more powerful than the rest" (Phillips 1991, 149). Thus, theories of substantive representation that place an emphasis on what an individual stands for rather than who the representative is as the measure of true representative democracy are problematic because they fail to take into account the unique historical, cultural, and social positions that groups traditionally excluded from the U.S. political system—such as women—have occupied in the United States.

Some theorists argue that a political system that is designed to elect individuals who substantively represent their constituents' interests is more than adequate, and striving for descriptive representation is impractical and inefficient. For example, Pitkin (1969b) has spoken out against descriptive representation because she believes that a representative's actions are more important than his or her characteristics. Pitkin warns that descriptive representation may place too much emphasis on depictions of representation rather than on the activities of representatives. She believes that men are equally capable of representing women and that women are not necessarily good representatives of women's interests. Pitkin argues that it is unrealistic to expect that members of certain groups will accurately represent the "interests" of their identity group solely on the basis of similar physical or socioeconomic characteristics. All women do not all share the same interests, and no woman in Congress can claim to represent all women. Suggesting otherwise would perpetuate female stereotypes and run the risk of compartmentalizing all female representatives.

Nevertheless, it is important to recognize that a representative's characteristics may matter. Women may have different individual and group interests and experiences, but it is possible to respect the diversity of women's interests while at the same time recognizing that sexual inequality is universal and all women share an interest in eradicating this problem (Phillips 1991, 72). Given the lack of demographic diversity among elected officials in the United States in comparison to the population at large, increasing the number of women and other underrepresented groups in Congress may have real substantive benefits.

This research focuses on the descriptive representation of women because if democracy is defined as majority rule it is essential that women gain a greater voice in the U.S. political system. As John Stuart Mill explains, "In a really equal democracy, every or any section would be represented, not disproportionately but proportionately. A majority of the electors would always have a majority of the representatives" (Mill 1969, 190).

Female members of the electorate face a series of obstacles that are distinct from those confronted by members of racial and ethnic minorities. At-large districts often are most conducive to the election of female candidates but are least conducive to minority candidates. At the same time, single-member districts (particularly those in which the minority is the dominant group) are most likely to ensure the election of minority candidates but are least conducive to the election of women. As a result, solutions that are likely to aid the election of women may be different from those that are helpful to racial and ethnic minorities (Darcy, Welch, and Clark 1994; Gerber, Morton, and Rietz 1998; Welch 1990; Welch and Studlar 1990).[1]

Deepening Democracy: Benefits of Having More Women in Congress

In *Democracy in Capitalist Times*, John Dryzek identifies three criteria that are necessary for further democratization: franchise, scope, and authenticity. He defines each as follows:

1. Franchise—the number of participants in a political setting
2. Scope—the domains of life under democratic control
3. Authenticity—the degree to which democratic control is substantive rather than symbolic, informed rather than ignorant, and competently engaged (Dryzek 1996, 5).

Dryzek argues that increasing the number of women in Congress will increase the franchise, expand the scope of government and democracy, and improve the authenticity of representation. He warns, however, that it is dangerous to pursue one of the three criteria for deepening democracy at the expense of the other two. For example, when women were granted the right to vote in 1920, the franchise was expanded but scope and authenticity were not because elected officials did not consider or substantively represent the interests of women. I evaluate each of Dryzek's three criteria to illustrate how and why the descriptive representation of women in Congress will lead to a deeper and more vibrant democracy.

Franchise

Increasing descriptive representation of women in Congress will expand the franchise by bringing more women into the mechanisms of government. In a system based on proportional descriptive representation, the proportion of women in Congress should increase to at least 50 percent.

One might argue that direct and participatory democracy are equally viable alternatives for deepening democracy and expanding the franchise for women, but there are numerous problems with both options. Reforming representative democracy is a more appealing choice. The merit of a direct democracy is that it enables a large number of individuals to participate directly in politics, but implementation of direct democracy in the United States is difficult because it makes great demands on people's time and is an unwieldy expansion of the franchise at the

national level. It is impractical and perhaps undesirable. If democratic authenticity requires engaged and informed political control, it is unlikely that direct democracy with its expansive franchise will qualify.

Similarly, the requirements of participatory democracy are equally problematic. Participatory democracy places greater demands on more women as a group than on men because women must balance their dual roles as workers and mothers, which reduces the amount of time they can spend attending meetings and deliberating over political matters. Moreover, because the workplace historically has been one of the primary places for organizing, women may be disadvantaged in that a smaller percentage of women work outside the home than men. Thus, the female franchise may not be equal to that of men in a participatory democracy, nor will the scope of the political system be expanded enough to include many of the issues that are important to women (Phillips 1991).[2]

On the other hand, representative democracy "reduc[es] the demands of participation to such a low level, it makes them more genuinely available to all" (Phillips 1991, 162). In this sense, a representative democratic system appears to be more equitable and more likely to engage the greatest number of individuals in politics.

Scope

Expanding the franchise and bringing more women into the mechanisms of government will expand the scope of democracy, and this expansion will benefit all society—women, men, and children. A political system that limits access or shuts out ideas undermines legitimacy and maldistributes benefits. Having more women in Congress will raise the saliency of issues traditionally associated with women and the private sphere, such as marriage, sexuality, and the politics of the welfare state (Pateman 1989, 133).

Women may be better situated than men to develop policy dealing with these and related issues. The evidence indicates that female legislators are more likely than male legislators to assign priority to issues closely associated with the private sphere—notably legislation related to children and family (Burrell 1997; Thomas 1994). Female members of Congress often cite their own experiences in the private sphere—as mothers and wives—as well as their unique experiences in the public sphere—as victims of sexual harassment and sexual discrimination—as influences in the legislative process (Dodson 1998). In addition, women who are elected to Congress often come from very different occupational backgrounds than their male colleagues. According to Burrell:

> Contemporary congresswomen have differed from their male colleagues in their occupational histories.... Lawyering and business backgrounds have predominated among the male members, while education fields distinguished the backgrounds of the female members. Further, 10 percent of female members listed their profession as either homemaker or civic leader (not a paid position) ... [women's] distinctive occupational backgrounds and apparently greater community involvement bring experiential diversity to the legislative arena (Burrell 1997, 78).

Although female legislators often come from distinctive backgrounds and have different life experiences than men, it is important to remember that women in the United States are a diverse group, and no single female legislator is capable of representing all women all the time. Thus, descriptive representation of women in Congress will not translate into representation of all women's interests, but it will expand the diversity of ideas in Congress. Although there are a variety of women's interests, not all of these interests are gender neutral per se. Many are gender specific, such as disparate pay and treatment in the marketplace, exclusion from positions of political and economic power,

women's roles as childbearers and caretakers, and even women's experiences as victims of sexual harassment (Phillips 1995, 67). Increasing the number of women in Congress is beneficial to all female members of the populace in that all women share a common interest in gaining better access to and influence in the public sphere (Phillips 1991).

Authenticity

Increasing the number of women in Congress will increase representational authenticity because more equitable descriptive representation usually translates into greater substantive representation of a variety of constituent interests and may produce substantive results and qualitative differences. Legislation that may not have been drafted or considered without the presence of women in the legislature often will not pass without their commitments as well (Dodson 1998).[3] Furthermore, evidence indicates that in addition to expanding the scope of issues under consideration, women also bring a new voice and perspective to all different types of legislation, and research shows that women and men often cast very different votes on a variety of issues (Clark 1998; Kathlene 1998).[4] In this sense, descriptive representation of women in Congress should move beyond a simple quantitative increase to a truly qualitative change in the legislative process and traditional policy outputs as well (Schroedel and Mazumdar 1998; Swabey 1969).

Getting There

Even if there is universal agreement that proportional descriptive representation of women in Congress will enhance democratic governance, accomplishing this task will be no small feat. The United States' electoral system, premised on single-member, winner-take-all elections, rewards candidates with the greatest amount of name recognition, money, and organization—usually incumbents. Incumbency advantage is the biggest obstacle standing between women and election to

Congress. As long as low turnover rates for members of Congress persist, female candidates for Congress will continue to be disadvantaged (Burrell 1997; Darcy, Welch, and Clark 1994; Jacobson 1997; Rule and Norris 1992). In addition, the current party structure is detrimental to the election of women. Political parties in the United States are relatively weak; their leaders no longer control the nomination process. Female candidates benefit from strong political parties that promote greater sex inclusion (Burrell 1997; Rule and Norris 1992; Welch and Studlar 1990).

Theorists have proposed numerous changes to the U.S. electoral system to enhance democratic governance. Many of these recommendations seek to overcome the underrepresentation of women and minority groups in Congress. For example, Anne Phillips (1995) recommends replacing single-member districts with a system of proportional representation and using quotas to ensure the equitable distribution of seats, whereas Lani Guinier (1994) introduces cumulative voting as an alternative to casting a single vote for each open seat.

Quotas and Cumulative Voting

Anne Phillips proposes a politics of presence to enhance democratic governance. She argues that we need to increase drastically the presence of marginalized groups in government, including women. Phillips believes that a quota system may be the most effective way to do so because it is easy to implement and forces outcomes. She bases her quotas on equal sex representation because the two sexes are fairly evenly represented in other race, ethnic, religious, and class groups. To implement quotas, Phillips places the onus on political parties when they nominate candidates for office. A quota system works best in proportional representation or multimember districts (Phillips 1995). Through proportional representation, political parties can ensure the descriptive representation of certain groups as well as facilitate candidate turnover, neither of which is possible in a single-member

plurality district system (Darcy, Welch, and Clark 1994; Rule 1992; Rule and Norris 1992; Welch and Studlar 1990).

In contrast, Lani Guinier proposes cumulative voting as an alternative to winner-take-all majority rule because it will enhance the electoral prospects and representation of minority and marginalized groups in government. Guinier argues that winner-take-all majority rule leaves winners—the majority—with everything and losers with nothing. She suggests, "Sometimes, even when rules are perfectly fair in form, they serve in practice to exclude particular groups from meaningful participation" (Guinier 1994, 1). According to the system Guinier proposes, each voter is given as many votes are there are open seats. Voters distribute their votes individually or cumulatively as they see fit. If an election consists of six seats with twelve candidates vying for the seats, each individual will be able to cast six votes. The voter may give one vote each to six different candidates or concentrate all six votes on one candidate. By voting cumulatively, an individual increases the likelihood that a candidate who supports her interests is elected to at least one of the six seats. Marginalized groups will not be successful in determining all election outcomes, but Guinier believes that African Americans and women will get some victories and, consequently, better representation than they have now (Guinier 1994).[5]

Phillips' and Guinier's proposals seek to enhance women's participation in the democratic process by increasing the number of female representatives in government. There are problems with each proposal, however, that may undermine the goal of increasing democratization. For example, to enforce Phillips' quotas in a single-member system like that in the United States, political parties will have to declare that congressional candidates running in certain districts must be women. This requirement is problematic because it may constitute discrimination against men (and thus might be unconstitutional), and it also could drastically reduce voters' choices. Critics will argue that this type of quota system denies men the opportunity to run for office in certain districts on the basis of their sex and denies voters the opportunity to vote for certain candidates, thereby hindering democratic governance.

Guinier's solution for increasing the diversity of representation has been criticized because cumulative voting fails to guarantee that groups that are systematically excluded will achieve results that are proportionate to their numbers. Cumulative voting cannot guarantee proportional representation (Zimmerman 1992). This limitation is problematic because a threshold often is required before representatives from marginalized groups are comfortable exercising their voices. Success by women in legislative bodies may require the presence of a critical mass of women, and cumulative voting cannot guarantee that mass, much less the election of women.[6]

Finally, quotas and cumulative voting require a move away from single-member to multimember districts. There are numerous obstacles to abandoning single-member districts, including resistance from the public and the two major political parties—not to mention the major logistical problems associated with this type of change.[7]

A New Alternative: Doubling Up

It is possible, however, to conceive of a new electoral system that guarantees proportional, descriptive representation of women; effectively increases the franchise, scope, and authenticity of democratic governance, and does not require a move from single-member to at-large districts or a move from winner-take-all to a system of proportional representation. Single-member districts serve an important purpose in the American political system, and there are several reasons for maintaining them as such. First, the district system works to enhance effective governance by ensuring that geographical areas receive representation. Individuals residing in suburban, rural, and urban areas all receive equal representation under the district system. It is possible

to imagine, however, how poor individuals or those living in urban areas might be overlooked in a multimember district system. The use of geographical divisions has been beneficial to minority groups seeking to elect representatives that share their characteristics through majority-minority districting as well. Multimember districts might further disadvantage these groups by diluting the strength of majority-minority districts and making it more difficult to elect minority racial and ethnic candidates, thereby undermining their representation in government.

Furthermore, geographical boundaries establish a ratio between the candidate and the number of constituents in his or her district. If single-member districts were replaced with multimember districts, however, members of Congress would be forced to cater to a larger number of constituents, which could threaten to undermine effective governance by making it even more difficult for constituents—especially those in the minority—to contact and receive attention from their representatives.

In addition, there are real logistical problems associated with implementing multimember congressional districts in the United States that might have negative repercussions for democratic governance. Multimember districts would need to be implemented on a statewide basis, so citizens in most states would have to vote for many candidates each election; it would be difficult for citizens to educate themselves about the variety of candidates running for every open seat. Most Americans have a difficult time educating themselves to vote for a single congressional candidate, let alone multiple candidates. In addition, candidates would have a more difficult time attempting to disseminate their messages across large states, and the costs associated with these media campaigns would be higher than they are today. An additional logistical problem is that some states have only a single at-large district for the entire state, so multimember districts cannot be introduced in these states.

Finally, at-large or multimember districts are no more conducive to the election of women than single-member districts on their face. Multimember districts cannot guarantee that a proportional number of women will be elected to office unless proportional representation and a quota system are implemented, options that have difficulties of their own, as noted above.

I propose an alternative solution that will maintain the means by which Americans elect members of Congress but will drastically alter the outcomes and produce a more democratic system of government. This alternative is consistent with the values of the American public; is commensurate with the structure of the current electoral system; and guarantees that the franchise, scope, and authenticity of the U.S. government will be expanded. I suggest that it is time to consider doubling the number of representatives in the House and Senate so that each district has two seats for each previous seat—a male seat and a female seat. The move from single-member to two-member districts will ensure that an equal number of men and women are elected to Congress, thereby enhancing democratic governance, and it will maintain both geographical districts and the winner-take-all system.[8]

The benefits of this solution are many. Each state and each district will maintain the same amount of representation relative to other states, and existing geographical districts will be protected—including majority-minority districts. In addition, because the number of seats will have doubled, critics cannot claim that women used affirmative action to gain election to seats that "belong" to men. Finally, the structure of Congress, the rules governing elections, and the Electoral College system can remain essentially the same. Some changes in committee assignments and size may be necessary, and rules governing debate and discussion may need to be modified, but these matters have all been subject to change before and the adjustments would not seriously disrupt Congress' functions. Initially the increase in membership may slow the deliberative process of government, but the legislative branch would continue to operate; moreover, the presence of 535 women from a variety of backgrounds and areas, bringing a diversity of experiences and ideas, would actually enhance Congress' role as the representative branch of government. In addition, racial and ethnic minorities might benefit from doubling up because they would be in a better position to increase their representation in Congress as well. Predominantly African American single-member districts that usually elect an African American representative would have the opportunity to elect two African American representatives—one male and one female.

Critics will argue that doubling up gives women an unjustified advantage in the electoral and legislative arena. Women are a majority of the population, however, and logically should constitute at least 50 percent of legislators in a democracy. According to the current rate at which women are increasing their presence in Congress, it will be decades before women achieve parity in government. Under this proposed system, hundreds of open seats will be created, ensuring the immediate election of new members of Congress.

Once in Congress, all new members—male or female—would be entitled to the same opportunities and benefits associated with the office. Nevertheless, a certain stigma might be attached to the "new" female members of Congress because critics probably would suggest that the presence of so many new members of Congress would undermine both the policymaking process and the integrity of the whole institution. The stigma might persist for a few electoral cycles, but it would disappear over time—just as the stigma associated with the first women elected to Congress disappeared as women proved themselves highly capable lawmakers. The new members of Congress would prove their merit to their fellow members of Congress and their constituents by providing new perspectives and producing substantive legislation that benefits a variety of constituent groups. Doubling up finally would enable women to achieve guaranteed parity in Congress, and proportional descriptive representation of women has the potential to produce a deeper democracy that benefits the entire society.

Conclusion

Women are underrepresented in Congress because when women received the vote in 1920, the equality of conditions necessary for women to vote and participate in politics did not automatically follow. The persistence of economic, social, and sexual inequities has constrained women from participating in the political realm on the same terms as men. Women have been denied access to the educational and occupational opportunities that are the traditional launching pad for political careers, thereby reducing their presence in the eligibility pool for political candidates and contributing to their underrepresentation in government. The disparity between the female population and the proportion of females in Congress is likely to continue under the existing electoral system because women often have to wait for an open seat to win election to Congress. Incumbency advantage—and the fact that most incumbents are males—has systematically kept women out of Congress for decades, and probably will continue to do so. The electoral system has been biased against women for two centuries, and the time has come to explore electoral alternatives that will increase the representation of women in Congress to enhance democratic governance. To that end, doubling up will create hundreds of open seats and guarantee the election of 535 new members of Congress. Increasing the size of Congress may slow the deliberative process, but the continued exclusion of women from Congress undermines the democratic process.

Notes

1. This research does not propose that the representation of women in Congress be increased at the expense of African Americans, Hispanic Americans, or other underrepresented groups. Instead, this proposal takes into account that it may be necessary to implement different electoral reforms to benefit different marginalized groups. That being said, the electoral reforms to increase the representation of women in Congress proposed at the end of this chapter also may have a positive effect on increasing the representation of African Americans, Hispanics, and other racially segregated groups as well by increasing the number of seats and subsequent opportunities for minority candidates to run for Congress.

2. According to Anne Phillips in *Engendering Democracy*, when women's groups have attempted to employ participatory democracy the results have been problematic. In their haste to reach a consensus, they often have stifled or ignored differences. This type of participatory democracy probably would be especially problematic for women of color, economically disadvantaged women, and lesbians. These women may choose not to express their opinions or may have their concerns dismissed. If that is the case, participatory democracy will expand the franchise only superficially and will not contribute to an expansion of the scope or authenticity of the democratic system (Phillips 1991, 126–27).

3. Female members of the House of Representatives—Democrat and Republican—have acknowledged that they often feel a responsibility to act on behalf of the special concerns of women in addition to the concerns of their geographical constituents. Drawing on her research on female members of the House, Dodson explains, "The acknowledgement by most female members of Congress that women's and men's lives give them different perspectives, combined with the sense of responsibility they felt to represent these different perspectives, provided a foundation for women to have a distinctive, collective, gender-related impact on public policy" (Dodson 1998, 133). Dodson goes on to explain how women in Congress not only play a role in defining the agenda and incorporating a women's agenda into legislation, they also play a major role in ensuring policy victories that likely would have been defeats without the presence of women in Congress (Dodson 1998).

4. A study of state legislators in Colorado illustrates how males and females approach crime legislation from two different perspectives and propose very different solutions. The female legislators tended to perceive criminals as the products of their environments and, hence, favored legislation that would discourage individuals from becoming criminals in the first place. In contrast, the male legislators believed that criminals chose a life of crime and

focused on developing legislation that would improve the administration of criminal justice and hold criminals accountable for their behavior (Kathlene 1998, 194). Kathlene suggests that women's different voice indicates a desire to approach issues from a perspective that may be indicative of women's role as caretakers. Regardless, the Colorado study indicates that women were more interested in solutions that addressed the causes of crime, whereas men were more interested in *post hoc* solutions (Kathlene 1998). Thus, the presence of women in a legislative body can have a substantive impact on defining and managing a variety of policy areas.

5. Single-member districts have proven more conducive to the election of male candidates for office than female candidates. Although single-member districts have proven more advantageous to the election of African American candidates for office than at-large districts, African American women—like white women—are disadvantaged by single-member districts, which promote the representation of African American men but not African American women (Darcy, Welch, and Clark 1994; Rule 1992; Rule and Norris 1992). Research indicates, however, that in multimember districts employing cumulative voting, minority candidates win more seats than they do in straight, one seat, one candidate, one vote elections, and this pattern may benefit both male and female African American candidates. Gerber, Morton, and Rietz (1998) found that in straight voting multimember districts with two open seats and two majority and one minority candidates, the two white candidates placed first and second, whereas the minority candidate came in third. In contrast, when a cumulative voting multimember district holds the same election, the minority candidate has a high probability of winning election. In recent years, local governments that have been charged with diluting the votes of racial minorities have implemented cumulative voting schemes to avoid costly lawsuits. The evidence indicates that this alternative has been successful in improving the diversity of representation. In Alamogordo, New Mexico, for example, cumulative voting has been used to elect Hispanics to office; in Chilton County, Alabama, African American voters have used cumulative voting to increase the number of African American representatives elected to office (Engstrom 1992; Engstrom, Taebel, and Cole 1989; Still 1992).

6. Sue Thomas' research on women in state legislatures indicates that as the percentage of women in a legislative body increases, the percentage of women who are more active than males on legislation related to women, children, and family increases as well (Thomas 1994). Similarly, Dolan and Ford have discussed the critical mass thesis, which indicates that as the number of women in a legislative body increases and moves toward a certain threshold, women begin to act more distinctly and devote more attention to developing and passing policy related to women's concerns and issues (Dolan and Ford 1998, 77). Although increasing the number of women (or racial minorities) in Congress certainly is an improvement over the "tyranny of the majority"—Guinier's terminology for white male domination—simply improving on the existing number of women in Congress may not be enough. The actual number of women in Congress is significant. Descriptive representation of women in Congress will not only ensure that women "get a turn"; it also will guarantee them a permanent seat at the table in numbers sufficient to have a substantive impact. Any female legislator may bring a unique perspective to the legislature, but her "'different voice' is not easily integrated into existing gendered institutions" (Kathlene 1998, 202).

7. This change would eliminate the geographical districts that have played a major role in the American political system since the middle of the nineteenth century. The U.S. Constitution does not require members of Congress to be elected from single-member districts. It was not until 1842 that Congress passed legislation requiring single-member districts for congressional elections. Prior to 1842, multimember districts for congressional elections were common (Gerber, Morton, and Rietz 1998; Rule and Norris 1992). That being said, single-member geographical districts designed to give a minority group a majority in the district have been instrumental in helping African Americans and other members of marginalized socioeconomic groups gain election to Congress, and it is unlikely that members of those groups would support a move to at-large districts in which their voting power may be diluted (Darcy, Welch, and Clark 1994; Gerber, Morton, and Rietz 1998; Welch 1990).

8. Another alternative to doubling the number of senators from each state is to keep two senators per state and allocate one male and one female seat. This approach would maintain the Senate's current size and enable the Senate to continue functioning according to existing rules. This alternative would allow the Senate to remain a relatively small, deliberative body, in contrast to the House of Representatives. There are some complications associated with

this option, however, including the fact that most states now have two male senators and this proposal would require one of the current male senators to surrender his seat to a newly elected female. Similarly, three states have an all female Senate delegation, and one of the women from each state would have to give up her seat in favor of a male candidate. Asking elected Senators to surrender their seats is highly problematic and may raise arguments about affirmative action.

References

Burrell, Barbara. 1997. *A Woman's Place Is in the House*. Ann Arbor: University of Michigan Press.

Center for American Women and Politics. 2003. Fact Sheet. *Women in Elected Office 2003*. Available at www.cawp.rutgers.edu.

Clark, Janet. 1998. "Women in National Office." In *Women and Elective Office*, ed. S. Thomas and C. Wilcox, 118–29. New York: Oxford University Press.

Darcy, R., Susan Welch, and Janet Clark. 1994. *Women, Elections, and Representation*. Lincoln: University of Nebraska Press.

Dodson, Debra. 1998. "Representing Women's Interests in the U.S. House of Representatives." In *Women and Elective Office*, ed. S. Thomas and C. Wilcox, 130–49. New York: Oxford University Press.

Dolan, Kathleen, and Lynne E. Ford. 1998. "Are All Women State Legislators Alike?" In *Women and Elective Office*, ed. S. Thomas and C. Wilcox, 73–86. New York: Oxford University Press.

Dryzek, John S. 1996. *Democracy in Capitalist Times*. New York: Oxford University Press.

Dubois, Ellen. 1987. "The Radicalism of the Woman Suffrage Movement: Notes toward the Reconstruction of Nineteenth Century Feminism." In *Feminism and Equality*, ed. Anne Phillips, 127–38. Oxford, UK: Basil Blackwell Ltd.

Eisenstein, Zillah. 1987. "Elizabeth Cady Stanton: Radical-Feminist Analysis and Liberal Feminist Strategy." In *Feminism and Equality*, ed. Anne Phillips, 77–102. Oxford, UK: Basil Blackwell Ltd.

Engstrom, Richard. 1992. "Alternative Judicial Election Systems: Solving the Minority Vote Dilution Problem," In *United States Electoral Systems: Their Impact on Women and Minorities*, ed. Wilma Rule and Joseph Zimmerman, 129–39. New York: Greenwood Press.

Engstrom, Richard, Delbert Taebel, and Richard Cole. 1989. "Cumulative Voting as Remedy for Minority Vote Dilution: The Case of Alamogordo, New Mexico." *Journal of Law and Politics* (spring): 469–97.

Gerber, Elizabeth, Rebecca Morton, and Thomas Rietz. 1998. "Minority Representation in Multi-member Districts." *American Political Science Review* 92, no. 1: 137–44.

Guinier, Lani. 1994. *Tyranny of the Majority*. New York: The Free Press.

Hero, Rodney, and Caroline J. Tolbert. 1995. "Latinos and Substantive Representation in the U.S. House of Representatives: Direct, Indirect, or Non-existent?" *American Journal of Political Science* 39: 640–52.

Jacobson, Gary. 1997. *The Politics of Congressional Elections*, 4th ed. New York: Longman.

Kathlene, Lyn. 1998. "In a Different Voice." In *Women and Elective Office*, ed. S. Thomas and C. Wilcox, 188–202. New York: Oxford University Press.

Mill, John Stuart. 1969. "On Representative Government." In *Representation*, ed. H. Pitkin, 177–97. New York: Atherton Press.

Pateman, Carole. 1989. *The Disorder of Women*. Cambridge, UK: Polity Press.

Phillips, Anne. 1991. *Engendering Democracy*. University Park: Pennsylvania State University Press.

———. 1995. *The Politics of Presence*. New York: Oxford University Press.

Pitkin, Hanna, ed. 1969a. *Representation*. New York: Atherton Press.

———. 1969b. "The Concept of Representation." In *Representation*, ed. Hanna Pitkin, 1–23. New York: Atherton Press.

Rule, Wilma. 1992. "Multimember Legislative Districts: Minority and Anglo Women's and Men's Recruitment Opportunity." In *United States Electoral Systems: Their Impact on Women and Minorities,* ed. Wilma Rule and Joseph Zimmerman, 57–72. New York: Greenwood Press.

Rule, Wilma, and Pippa Norris. 1992. "Anglo and Minority Women's Underrepresentation in Congress: Is the Electoral System the Culprit?" In *United States Electoral Systems: Their Impact on Women and Minorities,* ed. Wilma Rule and Joseph Zimmerman, 41–54. New York: Greenwood Press.

Schroedel, Jean Reith, and Nicola Mazumdar. 1998. "Into the Twenty-First Century." In *Women and Elective Office*, ed. S. Thomas and C. Wilcox, 203–19. New York: Oxford University Press.

Still, Edward. 1992. "Cumulative Voting and Limited Voting in Alabama." In *United States Electoral Systems: Their Impact on Women and Minorities,* ed. Wilma Rule and Joseph Zimmerman, 183–96. New York: Greenwood Press.

Swabey, Marie Collins. 1969. "A Quantitative View." In *Representation*, ed. Hanna Pitkin, 83–97. New York: Atherton Press.

Swain, Carol. 1995. *Black Faces, Black Interests: The Representation of African Americans in Congress.* Cambridge, Mass.: Harvard University Press.

Thomas, Sue. 1994. *How Women Legislate.* New York: Oxford University Press.

U.S. Census Bureau. 2003. *Profile of General Demographic Characteristics: 2000.* Fact sheet. Available at www.factfinder.census. gov.

Weissberg, Robert. 1978. "Collective Versus Dyadic Representation in Congress." *American Political Science Review* 72: 535–47.

Welch, Susan. 1990. "The Impact of At-large Elections on the Representation of Blacks and Hispanics." *Journal of Politics* 52, no. 4: 1050–76.

Welch, Susan, and Donley Studlar. 1990. "Multi-member Districts and the Representation of Women: Evidence from Britain and the United States." *Journal of Politics* 52, no. 2: 391–412.

Zimmerman, Joseph. 1992. "Enhancing Representational Equity in Cities." In *United States Electoral Systems: Their Impact on Women and Minorities,* ed. Wilma Rule and Joseph Zimmerman, 209–20. New York: Greenwood Press.

Part III

A DEMOCRATIC EXECUTIVE?

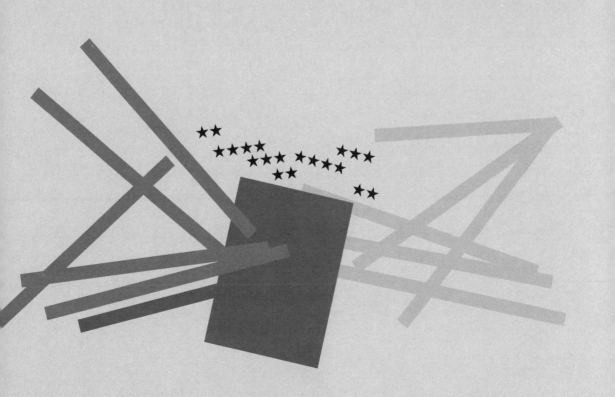

★★★

Chapter 6

A Government That Looks Like America?

Joseph A. Ferrara

itizens and scholars alike have long perceived a natural tension between democracy and bureaucracy—a tension that exists because the foundations and assumptions of democracy and bureaucracy appear to conflict very strongly (Krislov and Rosenbloom 1981). Democratic legitimacy flows from popular elections, but bureaucratic legitimacy flows from specialized knowledge. Democracy is based on—indeed, requires—openness, transparency, and pluralism. Bureaucracy, however, often thrives on secrecy, compartmented information structures, and unity of command. Democracy disperses power; bureaucracy centralizes it.

Yet in the modern American administrative state, democracy and bureaucracy must be reconciled because each depends on the other. Bureaucracy depends on democracy to give it shape and direction, as new political leaders come into office and propose new policy agendas. In turn, democracy depends on bureaucracy to implement the policy outcomes of the governing process and evaluate the performance of public programs.

In this chapter I explore the relationship between democracy and bureaucracy by focusing on three key issues:

- What is the demographic profile of the federal bureaucracy in terms of race, gender, and national origin, and how does it compare with the overall U.S. civilian labor force? Does the bureaucracy look like America?

- How do the political and social attitudes of government employees compare with those of the general U.S. population? Does the bureaucracy think like America?

- What are the recent trends with respect to public trust in government and specifically in public administration? Does America trust its bureaucracy?

Having a representative bureaucracy has long been a concern of American policymakers. Both Thomas Jefferson and Andrew Jackson worked to make administrative appointments that were representative—Jefferson's in partisan terms and Jackson's in social terms (Rosenbloom 1971). Later in the nineteenth century, Congress passed the Pendleton Act, which professionalized the civil service—in part to democratize government employment by basing it on merit and not politics (Rosenbloom 1977; Naff 2001). Today, numerous federal agencies manage diversity programs to ensure a more representative workforce (Naff and Kellough 2001).

Hanna Pitkin's (1967) distinction between "representativeness" and "representing" is pertinent here. Pitkin described representativeness as a passive type of representation that focuses on the characteristics of the representatives themselves, whereas representing is a more active form that emphasizes the actual choices that representatives make in pursuing certain programs and policies. Some scholars have argued that a bureaucracy that exhibits characteristics of "representativeness" has a far greater chance of also being a bureaucracy that also engages in "representing" (Hindera 1993).

Moreover, a bureaucracy that looks like America gains an important measure of credibility and legitimacy with the American public. As one writer put it, "If government employees are representative of their citizenry, sharing their values, beliefs, and attitudes, the public is more likely to feel comfortable with the policies, practices, and power of the bureaucracy" (Lewis 1990, 220). If bureaucrats are perceived as "ordinary people," the public is more likely to trust their decisions and be sympathetic to the challenges they face in their everyday jobs (Goodsell 1994). Given the fact that today's federal agencies wield substantial administrative discretion over policymaking and program implementation, a representative bureaucracy also reassures Americans that all members of society—regardless of race, gender, or national origin—have equal opportunities to become civil servants and rise through the ranks.

Public attitudes about government exert an important influence on what government does (Hibbing and Thiess-Moore 2001). In the early 1960s public trust in government, as measured by Americans' responses to various national surveys, was very high, but starting later in that decade and continuing through the 1990s, trust in government declined. Politicians and scholars have worried about this overall trend and the implications it poses for civic life (Putnam 1995), public service (Light 1999), and governmental effectiveness (Bradley 1999).

Does the Bureaucracy Look Like America?

The notion of examining the social representativeness of the bureaucracy originated with Donald Kingsley's 1944 study of the British civil service. Kingsley argued that by and large the British bureaucracy had faithfully implemented the executive mandates of the party in power because the civil servants shared the middle-class values and beliefs of the ruling party. Kingsley concluded that formal controls on bureaucratic power were not enough to ensure representative outcomes; a professional civil service also must be socially representative: "No group can be safely entrusted with power who do not themselves mirror the dominant forces in society" (Kingsley 1944, 283).

Commenting on American bureaucracy, Norton Long (1952) took the next step in arguing that bureaucracy in fact could be a *more* representative political institution than Congress—which, in Long's view, suffered from institutional deficiencies such as seniority rule and committee-dominated decision making that made it profoundly antidemocratic and unrepresentative of the American people. Today, many studies focus on equal opportunity in federal employment and potential barriers to the advancement of women and people of color to senior management positions (Selden 1997).

How representative is the federal bureaucracy in terms of race, gender, and national origin? The federal government did not begin actively addressing diversity in the bureaucratic ranks until the mid-1990s. In 1993, for example, the U.S. Merit Systems Protection Board (MSPB) issued a report that concluded that most agencies had done little to respond to emerging demographic changes in the U.S. labor force (MSPB 1993). These changes included a projected steady increase in the number of women and minorities in the U.S. workforce. Between 1980 and 1997, the proportion of women in the civilian labor force had increased from 42 percent to 46 percent, and the proportion of minorities had increased from 18 percent to 26 percent— and projections called for continued increases through the year 2025 (Judy and D'Amico 1997).

By the end of the 1990s, however, most federal agencies had become much more proactive about personnel diversity, and that

Table 6.1 Diversity in the Federal Workforce: Percentages of Federal Workforce and U.S. Labor Force

Group	Federal Government (%)	U.S. Workforce (%)
Total minority	30.4	27.6
Asian/Pacific Islanders	4.3	3.8
Blacks	17.6	11.2
Hispanics	6.6	11.8
Native Americans	2.0	0.9
Women	43.8	46.6

Source: Office of Personnel Management Demographic Profile, September 2000; available at www.opm.gov/feddata/demograp/demograp.asp.

trend continues to the present day, although the quality and comprehensiveness of agency efforts are uneven. As one recent report put it, "While many [agencies] had adopted most of the components that the literature prescribes, there is wide variation in that respect. Some had done little more than rename their traditional EEO [equal employment opportunity] efforts while others expanded the demographic characteristics recognized by the [federal government's diversity] program, linked diversity with the organization's strategic plan, and/or issued specific diversity policies or orders" (Naff and Kellough 2001).

Today the federal government has a diverse workforce—in many cases, more diverse and representative than the overall U.S. labor force. As table 6.1 indicates, the proportion of minorities in the federal workforce exceeds the proportion in the overall U.S. civilian labor force, specifically in terms of African Americans, Asian and Pacific Islanders, and Native Americans.

Moreover, agencies are continuing to improve the representation of historically underrepresented groups, especially women and minorities, in the workforce. Although federal employment has declined in the past several years, the proportion of federal workers who are minorities has increased. As table 6.1 indicates, however, Hispanics and women

continue to be underrepresented—prompting the federal government to launch a series of outreach and recruitment programs, such as the Hispanic Initiative, which was launched in 2000 to recruit more Hispanics to federal service.

Even though in the aggregate the federal government is a representative employer, it is not representative of race, gender, and national origin at all ranks. As table 6.2 shows, the top levels of the federal civil service are dominated by people of Euro-American descent (88 percent) and men (79 percent).[1] For example, whereas men occupy only 29 percent of the lowest graded positions (GS 1–8), women occupy more than 70 percent of these jobs.

In addition, there is a gender gap with respect to the types of occupations. As table 6.3 shows, women dominate clerical and administrative positions, whereas men are overrepresented in engineering, mathematics, and statistics positions.

Finally, although there is some evidence that more federal managers have been raised in households where the father was employed in a lower-status job (such as manual labor positions) in the 1990s than in the two previous decades, the changes are modest (Aberbach and Rockman 2000). Table 6.4 shows these trends.

Table 6.2 Diversity in the Federal Workforce: Percentages of Positions Held in Rank Grouping, by Gender and Race/Ethnicity

Group	GS 1–8	GS 9–12	GS 13–15	Senior Ranks
Men	29	57	73	79
Women	70	43	26	21
Black	26	13	8	6
Hispanic	7	6	4	3
Asian Pacific	4	4	4	2
Native American	3	2	1	1
Euro-American	60	75	83	88

Note: Percentages may not total 100 because of rounding.

Source: Equal Employment Opportunity Commission's 1997 *Report on the Employment of Minorities, Women, and People with Disabilities in the Federal Government.*

Table 6.3 Selected White Collar Occupations, by Gender (%)

Occupation	Men	Women
All groups	51.3	48.7
Personnel management	28.7	71.3
Medical and public health	32.1	67.9
Library and archives	33.8	66.2
General administrative and clerical	35.5	64.5
Mathematics and statistics	62.4	37.6
Investigation	75.6	24.4
Equipment and facilities	87.6	12.4
Engineering and architecture	89.8	10.2

Source: Office of Personnel Management Occupational Surveys, September 1999, available at www.opm.gov/feddata/html/occ.asp.

Table 6.4 Occupational Status of Federal Executives' Fathers, by Year (percentage of federal executives who report to political appointees)

Father's Occupation Status	1970	1986–87	1991–92
High management or professional	39	37	49
Low management or professional	30	12	10
Skilled nonmanual	11	12	16
Lower nonmanual	7	9	6
Skilled manual	7	19	2
Semiskilled or unskilled	7	10	16

Source: Aberbach and Rockman 2000.

Does the Bureaucracy Think Like America?

Although surprisingly few studies have addressed this question, the research that has been done tends to support the thesis that bureaucrats are "ordinary people," although there are some important exceptions. For example, Steven Seitz (1978), using data from the National Opinion Research Center's *General Social Surveys* (GSS), showed that respondents employed in public administration did not differ significantly from all respondents when compared across a wide range of demographic data, such as education, religious affiliation, income, and party identification.

Gregory Lewis (1990) reviewed the attitudes of government employees on public policy issues and commitment to traditional values and compared them with the overall U.S. public. Also using the GSS surveys, Lewis found substantial similarity between the two groups. Government employees were about as religious as the overall U.S. population; were just as satisfied with their jobs as the average private sector worker; and were no more likely than the general public to favor more government spending or to have confidence in governmental institutions.

Lewis did uncover some differences in opinion between bureaucrats and citizens, but overall these differences tended to be of degree, not of kind; moreover, if anything, they tended to portray bureaucrats as more tolerant and open-minded than the general public. For example, whereas 81 percent of the American public would not object to having a member of another race to their homes for dinner, 88 percent of government employees felt the same way. Whereas 86 percent of the public say they would vote for an African American for president, 90 percent of bureaucrats feel the same way.

Lewis concludes:

In general, bureaucrats are "ordinary people" when it comes to their attitudes toward government. They are no more or no less cynical than other people in their attitudes toward major institutions of society. Like other people, they would like government to do more to fight crime, improve schools and health care, and combat drug addiction. Also, like ordinary people, they want government to do it without raising their own taxes (Lewis 1990, 226).

Other studies have reached similar conclusions. For example, using data from the American National Election Studies, William Blair and James Garand (1995) compared public-sector and private-sector employees regarding adherence to the general tenets of constitutional and representative democracy. They found that in general the attitudes of government employees were not very different from those of other citizens, although public-sector employees were more likely than other citizens to be knowledgeable about politics and to participate in a wide range of political activities. They also concluded, however, that it was not necessarily government employment per se that was affecting these attitudes. Instead, people who eventually become government employees may enter public service with somewhat different political attitudes than individuals who go to work in the private sector.[2]

Political Attitudes

Indeed, the cumulative data (1972–2000) from the *General Social Surveys* indicate that over time, bureaucrats and citizens have been and continue to be very much alike in their political opinions. The GSS questionnaire asked respondents to identify their occupation ("What kind of place do you work for?"). The responses were then grouped into various industry codes (e.g., manufacturing, agricultural, retail). One of these broad employment categories was public administration. I recoded the employment variable to sort the GSS respondents into government workers and nongovernment workers and then compared the opinions of these two groups on a series of political questions (see table 6.5).[3]

Table 6.5 Comparing Bureaucrats and Citizens (%)

Item	Bureaucrats	Citizens
Lean Democratic	47	46
Lean Republican	41	38
Lean Independent	11	15
Identify with liberals	30	27
Identify with conservatives	37	35
Identify with moderates	34	38
Government has too much power	44	60
Government has too little power	3	4
Government has right amount of power	51	37
Bureaucrats can be trusted	23	20
Bureaucrats cannot be trusted	59	55
Public does control politicians	44	38
Public does not control politicians	56	62
Government is responsive	63	48
Government is not responsive	37	52

Source: National Opinion Research Center, University of Chicago, 1972–2000.

My findings are consistent with earlier research showing that bureaucrats and citizens tend to be fairly similar in their opinions, although there are some striking variations of opinion.

First the similarities. With regard to identification with the major political parties, bureaucrats and citizens are not discernibly different. For example, over the past two decades, 46 percent of Americans have identified themselves as Democrats, whereas 47 percent of bureaucrats have identified themselves as such. Slightly more bureaucrats than nongovernment workers, 41 percent to 38 percent, have identified themselves as Republicans.

There are similarly close results when one compares government and nongovernment responses to questions about ideological persuasion. There is virtually no difference between the percentage of bureaucrats and citizens who identify themselves as conservative (37 percent to 35 percent). Slightly more bureaucrats identify themselves as liberal (30 percent to 27 percent) and slightly fewer identify themselves as moderate (34 percent to 38 percent).

When we move from questions of political and ideological persuasion, some interesting differences emerge. Fully 60 percent of nongovernment workers agree or strongly agree with the statement, "Government has too much power," whereas only 44 percent of bureaucrats feel this way. When presented with the statement, "Government has about the right amount of power," a majority of bureaucrats—51 percent—agree, but only 37 percent of nongovernment respondents feel this way.

A similarly striking opinion gap appears around the question of governmental responsiveness. When respondents were asked whether they believe government is responsive to the people's interests, a strong majority (63 percent) of government employees said they believe it is. Only 48 percent of their fellow citizens share this opinion, however. When respondents were asked whether they think government is *not* responsive to the public's interests, a clear majority (51 percent) of nongovernment workers agreed, whereas only 37 percent of public administration employees felt the same way.

Finally, there are differences of opinion regarding political power and trust in public servants, although they are not as pronounced. For example, slightly more government respondents think that bureaucrats can be trusted (23 percent to 20 percent) and people can control the politicians (44 percent to 38 percent). Interestingly, when respondents were asked whether they believe that public administrators *cannot* be trusted, *more* government than nongovernment respondents agreed (59 percent to 55 percent).

What can we make of these findings? Although it is always difficult (and dangerous) to generalize too broadly from survey research results, it is possible to draw a few tentative conclusions. First, bureaucrats and citizens alike distinguish their ideological and political affiliations from their specific opinions about governmental power and political efficacy. Just because nearly identical proportions of bureaucrats and citizens identify themselves as Democrats or Republicans, as liberals or conservatives, or as independents or moderates does not mean that similar proportions agree on other issues—particularly issues of governmental power and trust.

Not surprisingly, bureaucrats have a more sanguine view of governmental authority and popular control over the political process than does the general public. Knowing and appreciating the nature of the policy process may contribute to the bureaucrat's greater tolerance of the inefficiencies of that process and the constant revisiting of prior decisions.

Attitudes on Government Employment and Quality

One also can compare bureaucrats with the general population on specific questions of government employment and quality. The Council for Excellence in Government (1999) published the results of a survey comparing the views of federal employees with non-government workers. The survey found that 26 percent of federal employees feel that federal workers are of higher quality than workers in the private sector, whereas only 14 percent of private-sector employees share this opinion. Similarly, 31 percent of federal employees believe that government employees work harder than private-sector workers; only 5 percent of nonfederal employees feel this way.

When respondents were asked about working for the federal government, government and nongovernment employees evidenced much agreement, as indicated in table 6.6.

It is interesting to note that more government respondents cited bureaucracy and red tape as a concern than did nongovernment respondents. More government employees also mentioned low pay and a lack of opportunities for advancement.

Finally, government and nongovernment employees diverge with regard to the relative value of public-sector institutions versus nonprofit, public service institutions. Federal workers perceive a greater contribution to

Table 6.6 Comparing Bureaucrats and Citizens: Concerns about Working for the Federal Government (%)

Item	Bureaucrats	Citizens
Too much bureaucracy	46	37
Decisions made on politics not merit	37	47
Poor performers not being dismissed	29	24
Low pay	21	13
Few opportunities for advancement	14	9
Not appreciated/respected by the public	10	9
Work that is not interesting	2	7

Source: Council for Excellence in Government 1999.

society from government than those who work in the private sector.

Responsiveness

Other work in this area has focused on federal executives and their responsiveness to the political system. Joel Aberbach and Bert Rockman (2000), for example, interviewed representative samples of senior federal career executives and presidential appointees in the Washington, D.C., metropolitan area at three points in time—1970, 1986–87, and 1991–92. All of their interviewees came from agencies concerned with domestic policy.

Aberbach and Rockman found that the political attitudes of senior career civil servants reflected changes in the political environment. Whereas only 17 percent of career interviewees identified themselves as Republicans in 1970, by the mid-1980s 45 percent did so. The 1991–92 sample shows a senior federal career civil service almost evenly split in terms of party identification—much like the general population. Similarly, Aberbach and Rockman find that career executives' views on the role of the government in managing the U.S. economy have drifted rightward since 1970, reflecting the change in party control of the executive branch during the 1980s and early 1990s.

Does America Trust the Bureaucracy?

In the American system of democracy, the people delegate power to their elected representatives, who in turn delegate power to government departments and agencies to implement public programs. Implicit in all of this delegation is trust. Why give government more power if you believe it will not exercise that power properly?

Since the ratification of the Constitution, Americans have delegated more and more power to the federal government. From its origins as a tiny administrative apparatus that performed only the most basic public functions, the federal government has grown dramatically—in terms of the number of people it employs, the dollars it spends, the policies it makes and enforces, and the range of public and private behavior it regulates. This growth suggests that Americans have—at least implicitly—trusted the government to do the right thing.

In this sense, trust is essential to a well-functioning democratic system. As recent research has shown, the more trusting the citizenry, the more likely government will be productive and effective in taking bold action to address social and economic problems (Uslaner 2002). Declining trust has translated into a more contentious legislative process characterized by obstructionism and delay (Binder 1999; Uslaner 2002). Trust encourages cooperation, which makes it easier to take collective action to address major policy issues.

Long-Term Trends

Nevertheless, the American people have always been very ambivalent in their attitudes toward government (Craig 1996; Hibbing and Theiss-Morse 2001). Crises of confidence have erupted periodically in response to policy and political scandals. For example, domestic strife over controversial issues such as the Vietnam War, civil rights for African Americans, and the Watergate scandal caused massive political turmoil in the 1960s and 1970s (Citrin and Luks 2001), with corresponding declines in public trust. Yet Americans are very vocal in pressing for new government programs that they believe will benefit them. Paradoxically, trust in government has declined while the desire for specific government programs and services remains strong. The decline in trust began in the late 1960s and continued throughout the remainder of the twentieth century as indicated in figure 6.1.

The Council for Excellence in Government also has conducted a series of studies examining confidence in government. The Council's findings show disparities across age groups: Each successive generation of Ameri-

Figure 6.1 Trust Government in Washington Most or All of the Time (percentage of respondents saying they do)

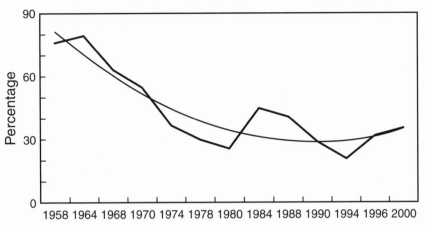

Source: American National Election Studies, 1958–2000.

cans reports higher levels of disconnection from the government than the previous generation. A 1999 survey revealed that 56 percent of seniors (ages sixty-five and older) feel "very or fairly connected" to the government, but only 31 percent of young adults (ages eighteen to thirty-four) feel connected (Council for Excellence in Government 1999).[4]

The Council studies suggest that as people get older and take on more responsibility, they tend to interact with government more frequently. This interaction sustains feelings of connection to the government and higher levels of political participation.

Trust in Agencies

Ambivalence toward government extends to specific agencies. A survey conducted for the Pew Center for the People and the Press about five federal agencies—the Social Security Administration (SSA), Environmental Protection Agency (EPA), Food and Drug Administration (FDA), Internal Revenue Service (IRS), and Federal Aviation Administration (FAA)—found that constituents rated these agencies fairly high in terms of performance and customer service. The ratings appear to be more a function of people's

overall impression of the agency mission than their specific encounters with agency personnel or programs. The one exception to the generally high favorability ratings is the IRS; has any society in all of history ever *liked* the tax collector? People who support tough environmental regulations think the EPA is doing a good job, whereas those who think such regulations are detrimental to economic performance do not rate the agency as highly. Tables 6.7 and 6.8 display some of the results.

In addition to the connection between a respondent's impression of an agency's mission and his or her evaluation of its performance, several other factors also contribute to a person's evaluation. First, the more familiar a person is with a particular government agency, the more likely that person is to rate it favorably—even if that familiarity derives from a relationship that might be more conflictual than congenial. Thus, even business regulatory officers rate the EPA higher than they do the rest of the federal government. Medical professionals and drug advocates rate the FDA higher. This pattern holds true even for the IRS: Professional tax preparers and business tax officers both rate the IRS more favorably than they do the federal government in general. Contrary to the

Table 6.7 Favorability Ratings toward Selected Government Agencies: Percentage of Respondents Who View the Agency Favorably

Agency (by rating group)	Agency	Federal Government
Internal Revenue Service		
Taxpayers	43	42
Business tax officers	40	36
Professional tax preparers	60	41
Social Security Administration		
Recipients	82	44
Payroll taxpayers	57	47
Business payroll officers	77	32
Environmental Protection Agency		
General public	68	48
Business regulatory	52	35
Environment advocates	84	68
Federal Aviation Administration		
Frequent fliers	80	46
Pilots	65	25
Air traffic controllers	61	41
Business regulatory officers	71	39
Food and Drug Administration		
Business regulatory officers	84	43
Medical professionals	84	45
Advocates	88	44
Chronically ill	82	58

Source: Pew Research Center for the People and the Press 2000.

proverbial wisdom, familiarity with public agencies seems to breed admiration, not contempt. Indeed, there is even evidence to suggest that the public trusts federal employees more than members of Congress to do the right thing (Barr 1998).

Second—and not so surprisingly—beneficiaries of the agency's programs and policies rate the agency much more favorably than they rate the overall federal government. Social Security recipients rate the SSA far higher than they rate the federal government—82 percent to 44 percent. Chronically ill respondents have a more favorable view of the FDA. Frequent fliers like the FAA much more than they like the rest of the federal government.

Trust and Devolution

As we have seen, many observers have linked the long-term decline in trust in government to major political scandals and public turmoil. Others, however, have argued that the decline in trust has to do with the growth of government—particularly the federal government—over the past forty years (Peterson 1984). The way to restore some measure of trust in government, these observers maintain, is through an aggressive program of devolution, under which state and local governments would assume more responsibility for programs and policies. This philosophy was a major underpinning of the Republicans' 1994 "Contract

Table 6.8 Favorability Ratings toward Selected Government Agencies: Percentage of Respondents Who View the Agency Favorably, Sorted by Support or Rejection of Agency Mission

Agency (by rating group)	Support Mission	Reject Mission
Internal Revenue Service		
Taxpayers	59	35
Business tax officers	73	27
Professional tax preparers	79	49
Social Security Administration		
Recipients	79	86
Payroll taxpayers	64	42
Environmental Protection Agency		
General public	77	55
Business regulatory	82	25
Environment advocates	84	a
Federal Aviation Administration		
Frequent fliers	80	a
Pilots	73	48
Air traffic controllers	63	a
Business regulatory officers	81	51
Food and Drug Administration		
Business regulatory officers	91	60
Medical professionals	90	a
Advocates	88	a
Chronically ill	89	a

a Numbers omitted by Pew because of small sample sizes.

Source: Pew Research Center for the People and the Press 2000.

with America" and several subsequent laws, including the Unfunded Mandates Act of 1995, the welfare reform legislation of 1996, and the distribution of federal funds in the form of block grants.

When we examine this thesis more closely, however, it does not appear to hold together. As Eric Uslaner put it, "Washington is not the problem. Government is the problem. People who do not like the federal government do not like their state government either" (Uslaner 2001, 133). Uslaner used data from the *Washington Post*–Kaiser Family Foundation–Harvard University joint survey conducted in late 1995. These data

suggest that most people do not discriminate between Washington and their state governments. If a person has a favorable view of the federal government, he or she is most likely to be positive about state government. Moreover, people liked or disliked their state governments for much the same reasons they liked or disliked the federal government. These data lead Uslaner to conclude that "shifting the locus of power will not solve the problem of trust in government" (Uslaner 2001, 133).

Summary

Representativeness

The U.S. federal bureaucracy looks like America. In general, it employs minorities in larger proportions than in the overall civilian labor force. Where diversity goals are not being met, programs are being put in place to achieve them.

Viewed within the hierarchy of government, however, representation is skewed toward Euro-American men, who dominate the senior ranks by a substantial margin. There is a gender gap in occupational specialties as well. Clerical and lower-level administrative positions are disproportionately held by women, whereas higher-paying, higher-status math and science occupational positions are disproportionately held by men.

Moreover, most top federal executives have come from upper-status families (Aberbach and Rockman 2000). Their fathers typically were employed in senior-level professional or managerial jobs. Although there are some signs of change, the top ranks of the federal bureaucracy continue to be recruited primarily from the upper rungs of American society.

Attitudes

Bureaucrats and citizens do not differ much in political opinions, party identification, and political ideology. There are important differences, however, particularly with respect to perceptions of governmental responsiveness and government power. Bureaucrats appear less likely than citizens to think that government is too powerful and more likely to regard it as responsive. In addition, federal workers also rate their colleagues' work quality more highly than do private-sector respondents. Federal employees also have a more positive opinion of government's contributions to society than do nongovernment workers. The two groups are fairly similar, however, in their assessments of the drawbacks of government employment.

Finally, there is evidence to suggest that, contrary to the conventional wisdom, career federal executives respond to shifts in the prevailing political culture. Whereas few career executives identified themselves as Republicans in 1970, nearly half do today.

Trust

At the macro level, there has been a clear and steady decline in popular trust of the federal government to do the right thing most or all of the time. The data indicate a general relationship between external macropolitical events and levels of popular trust. The sharp decline during the late 1960s and early 1970s came amidst a failed war overseas and turbulent political conditions at home. The short-lived increases during the early 1980s coincided with the resolution of the Iranian hostage crisis, a newly assertive U.S. foreign policy, and improving economic conditions. The more recent increase in levels of trust since 1994 also occurred in an environment of economic good times and relative political stability. Finally, trust in government rose sharply after the September 11 terrorist attacks. Americans rallied around the flag in the weeks after the attack, but this rally effect was short-lived; surveys conducted in 2002 showed that public trust had faded to pre–September 11 levels (Deane 2002; Light 2002; Smith, Rasinski, and Toce 2001).

Although Americans do not show a great deal of faith in the federal government, they have more favorable impressions of individual agencies, particularly when their professional or personal lives bring them into close contact with agency programs and personnel. In general, the more favorably a person is disposed toward the mission of an agency, the more likely it is that he or she will have a positive opinion of the agency itself.

Conclusion

As I argued at the beginning of this chapter, there is a natural tension between bureaucracy and democracy. Yet although we are right to be concerned about bureaucratic power in a democratic system, we must recognize that bureaucracy helps make democracy work. After the elections and the swearing-in ceremonies, after the congressional committees have held oversight hearings and passed laws, after presidents have held summits and issued proclamations, after the interest groups have drafted legislation and citizen panels have issued recommendations, and after the courts have issued their orders and inspectors general have published their audits—after all this, someone must actually implement public policy. It falls to the bureaucracy to read the hearing transcripts, the summit proclamations, the laws, the court orders, and the blue-ribbon reports and make all the words a reality.

It turns out that to do so fairly and efficiently, bureaucracies must write rules—lots of them—and do much of their work out of public view. Arcane rules and hidden proceedings rightly stir democratic concerns, but American bureaucracy is remarkably open to inspection—by political executives, legislators, judges, and average citizens. In a sense, the bureaucracy falls squarely into the constitutional tradition of limited and responsible government—a public institution to which busy citizens delegate power so that the public's business can get done. Is this not exactly what the people are doing when they elect a president or a new Congress?

In a sense, yes, but it also is true that the people do not elect their bureaucratic administrators and that the work of the bureaucracy often is more sheltered from public view than is the work of the elected political institutions. These distinctions give rise to the important questions that have been the subject of this chapter. Bureaucracy and democracy are different in key respects, but that does not mean that we should not work to make them as compatible as possible. A bureaucracy that looks like America is more likely to be an effective and representative instrument of American public policy. A bureaucracy that thinks like America is more likely to inspire

confidence. And a bureaucracy that is trusted by America is more likely to take strong and effective action when circumstances dictate.

Even some of the earliest observers of the American political system recognized that although bureaucracy and democracy conflicted in some ways, they also very much depended on one other. John Stuart Mill argued that "every branch of public administration is a skilled business, which has its own peculiar principles and traditional rules" and that skilled administrators were necessary as the "permanent strength of the public service" (Warner 2001). Thus, a professional bureaucracy helps to ensure that representative government is well administered. Professional public administration, rather than necessarily being the natural enemy of democracy, helps support representative government and make it workable.

An important conclusion to be drawn from these findings is that efforts to enhance civic participation in public policy and administration should continue to be supported. Such efforts have at least a reasonable chance of helping Americans achieve a more mature and balanced understanding of both the potential and the limitations of the government that serves them. The findings reported here suggest that when Americans come into closer contact with government—through voting, through professional interactions, or as program beneficiaries—they tend to form more realistic and positive impressions of public administration.

Efforts to maintain and extend participation are particularly important. Although civic participation in the United States has not always been meaningful, it often is "loud" and sometimes "clear," but rarely "equal" (Verba, Schlozman, and Brady 1995). The seeds of future political participation are planted by society's basic institutions, including families, schools, and jobs; individuals who are lucky enough to start their political socialization with plentiful resources are far more likely to become and remain active democratic participants.

Moreover, when levels of participation increase, so does trust in government (Berman 1997). Many agencies, at all levels of government, have been engaged in a variety of programs to enhance citizen participation (King and Stivers 1998). As polls taken in the immediate aftermath of the September 11 terrorist attacks showed, Americans also instinctively rally around public-sector institutions—the presidency, the Congress, the military, emergency managers—in times of crisis (Deane 2002). Higher levels of trust among the citizenry helps make government more productive and effective (Uslaner 2002); as one observer has said, "when government is trusted, it has broad latitude to take bold actions" (Deane 2002). Therefore, any project of rebuilding civic capital should not treat public administration as an afterthought, although many such projects often do (Durant 1998).

The federal government also must do more to ensure equal opportunity in federal employment, particularly in advancement to senior positions. Although the federal workplace is one of the most diverse in the country, this diversity ends at the upper reaches of the bureaucracy. There appears to be not only a glass ceiling but a class ceiling—both of which hinder the greater democratization of the federal service. As long as such inequities exist, the potential for a truly representative bureaucracy will remain unrealized.

The relationship between citizens and bureaucrats is complex and evolving. Federal employment has been slowly democratized since the late nineteenth century, but a truly representative bureaucracy does not yet exist. Bureaucrats and citizens are closer in their political opinions than the conventional wisdom might suggest, but they seem to have different views of governmental power and responsiveness. General levels of trust in government have declined over time, but there is strong evidence to indicate that familiarity and interaction with the federal bureaucracy breeds admiration, not contempt.

In the long run, improving the relationship between citizens and their government is most likely to result from an ongoing effort to build civic capital that emphasizes—not minimizes—the role of public administration. Both sides of the civic transaction must contribute to this effort. Government, for its part, must continue its initiative to expand the diversity and representativeness of the federal service. Citizens, through more direct engagement in the political process, must improve their understanding of the complexity of policy problems. Doing this will make it more likely that we can achieve a government that looks and thinks like America and is trusted by the American people.

Notes

1. The term "Euro-American" has been used in diversity research because it connotes more precision than the more traditional "white," which can be problematic in distinguishing various groups. For example, one might consider Hispanics to be "white." Senior ranks are the Senior Executive Service levels.
2. In a more recent article, however, Corey and Garand (2002) analyze voting in the 1996 U.S. national election and conclude, tentatively, that government employment itself may have some effect on political participation, particularly voting.
3. This recoding from the GSS cumulative files yielded 1,100 government worker respondents and 16,851 nongovernment worker respondents.
4. Respondents reporting high levels of connection also report being more politically active. For example, 50 percent of connected respondents vote regularly, but only 28 percent of disconnected respondents do. Nearly 60 percent of connected respondents reported having attended a public hearing in the past year, whereas only 39 percent of disconnected respondents did so.

References

Aberbach, Joel, and Bert Rockman. 2000. *In the Web of Politics: Three Decades of the Federal Executive.* Washington, D.C.: Brookings Institution Press.

Barr, Stephen. 1998. "Vote of Support for Employees: Civil Servants Favored over Politicians." *Washington Post,* March 10, A15.

Berman, Evan. 1997. "Dealing with Cynical Citizens." *Public Administration Review* 57: 105–12.

Binder, Sarah. 1999. "The Dynamics of American Gridlock: 1947–1996." *American Political Science Review* 93: 519–34.

Blair, William, and James C. Garand. 1995. "Are Bureaucrats Different? Democratic Values, Political Tolerance, and Support for the Political System among Government Employees and Other Citizens, 1982–1992." Paper presented at annual meeting of American Political Science Association, Chicago.

Bradley, Bill. 1999. "Trust and Democracy: Causes and Consequences of Mistrust in Government." In *Congress and the Decline of Public Trust*, ed. Joseph Cooper. Boulder, Colo.: Westview Press.

Citrin, Jack, and Samantha Luks. 2001. "Political Trust Revisited: Déjà vu All Over Again?" In *What Is It about Government that Americans Dislike?* ed. John R. Hibbing and Elizabeth Theiss-Morse. Cambridge, UK: Cambridge University Press.

Corey, Elizabeth, and James Garand. 2002. "Are Government Employees More Likely to Vote?: An Analysis of Turnout in the 1996 U.S. National Election." *Public Choice* 111: 259–83.

Council for Excellence in Government. 1999. "Americans Unplugged: Citizens and Their Government." Survey conducted by Peter Hart and Robert Teeter.

Craig, Stephen C., ed. 1996. *Broken Contract: Changing Relationships between Americans and Their Government.* Boulder, Colo.: Westview Press.

Deane, Claudia. 2002. "Trust in Government Declines: Post-9/11 Jump in Americans' Confidence in Washington Is Fading." *Washington Post*, May 31, A29.

Durant, Robert. 1998. "Missing Links: Civic Trust, Civic Capital, and Public Administration." Included in report of American Political Science Association (APSA)-National Association of Schools of Public Affairs and Administration (NASPAA) Committee on the Advancement of Public Administration, presented at annual meeting of APSA, Boston.

Goodsell, Charles. 1994. *The Case for Bureaucracy*, 3d ed. Chatham, N.J.: Chatham House.

Hibbing, John R., and Elizabeth Theiss-Morse, eds. 2001. *What Is It about Government that Americans Dislike?* Cambridge, UK: Cambridge University Press.

Hindera, John. 1993. "Representative Bureaucracy: Further Evidence of Active Representation in the EEOC District Office." *Journal of Public Administration Research and Theory* 3 (October): 415–42.

Judy, Richard, and Carol D'Amico. 1997. *Workforce 2020.* Indianapolis: Hudson Institute.

King, Cheryl, and Camilla Stivers, eds. 1998. *Government Is Us: Public Administration in an Anti-Government Age.* Thousand Oaks, Calif.: Sage Publications.

Kingsley, Donald J. 1944. *Representative Bureaucracy: An Interpretation of the British Civil Service.* Yellow Springs, Ohio: Antioch Press.

Krislov, Samuel, and David Rosenbloom. 1981. *Representative Bureaucracy and the American Political System.* New York: Praeger Publishers.

Lewis, Gregory. 1990. "In Search of the Machiavellian Milquetoasts: Comparing Attitudes of Bureaucrats and Ordinary People." *Public Administration Review* 50: 220–27.

Light, Paul. 2002. "The Troubled State of the Federal Public Service." Washington, D.C.: Brookings Institution.

———. 1999. *The New Public Service.* Washington, D.C.: Brookings Institution.

Long, Norton. 1952. "Bureaucracy and Constitutionalism." *American Political Science Review* 46: 808–18.

Naff, Katherine. 2001. *To Look Like America: Dismantling Barriers for Women and Minorities in Government.* Boulder, Colo.: Westview Press.

Naff, Katherine, and J. Edward Kellough. 2001. "A Changing Workforce: Understanding Diversity Programs in the Federal Government." Washington, D.C.: PricewaterhouseCoopers Endowment for the Business of Government.

National Opinion Research Center, University of Chicago. 1972–2000. *General Social Surveys.*

Peterson, George E. 1984. "Federalism and the States: An Experiment in Decentralization." In *The Reagan Record,* ed. John Palmer and Isabel V. Sawhill. Cambridge, Mass.: Ballinger Press.

Pew Research Center for the People and the Press. 2000. *Performance and Purpose: Constituents Rate Government Agencies.* Washington, D.C.: Pew Research Center Survey Reports.

Pitkin, Hanna. 1967. *Representation.* New York: Atherton Press.

Putnam, Robert. 1995. "Bowling Alone: America's Declining Social Capital." *Journal of Democracy* 6: 65–78.

Rosenbloom, David. 1971. *Federal Service and the Constitution.* Ithaca, N.Y.: Cornell University Press.

———. 1977. *Federal Equal Employment Opportunity: Politics and Personnel Administration.* New York: Praeger Publishers.

Seitz, Steven Thomas. 1978. *Bureaucracy, Policy, and the Public.* St. Louis: C. V. Mosby Co.

Selden, Sally Coleman. 1997. *The Promise of Representative Bureaucracy.* Armonk, N.Y.: M. E. Sharpe.

Smith, Tom, Kenneth Rasinski, and Marianne Toce. 2001. "America Rebounds: A National Study of Public Response to the September 11th Terrorist Attacks: Preliminary Findings." Chicago: National Opinion Research Center, University of Chicago.

Thompson, Frank J., Michael Brentnell, Robert Durant, Donald F. Kettl, Beryl A. Radin, and Lois R. Wise. 1998. "Report of the American Political Science Association-National Association of Schools of Public Affairs and Administration." Paper presented at annual meeting of American Political Science Association, Boston.

Uslaner, Eric M. 2001. "Is Washington Really the Problem?" In *What Is It about Government that Americans Dislike?* ed. John R. Hibbing and Elizabeth Theiss-Morse. Cambridge, UK: Cambridge University Press.

———. 2002. *The Moral Foundations of Trust.* Cambridge, UK: Cambridge University Press.

U.S. Merit Systems Protection Board (MSPB). 1993. "Evolving Workforce Demographics: Federal Agency Action and Reaction." Washington, D.C.: U.S. Merit Systems Protection Board.

Verba, Sidney, Kay Schlozman, and Henry Brady. 1995. *Voice and Equality: Civic Voluntarism in American Politics.* Cambridge, Mass.: Harvard University Press.

Warner, Beth E. 2001. "John Stuart Mill's Theory of Bureaucracy within Representative Government: Balancing Competence and Participation." *Public Administration Review* 61, no. 4: 403–13.

Further Reading

Alford, John. 2001. "We're All in This Together: The Decline of Public Trust in Government, 1958–1996." In *What Is It about Government that Americans Dislike?* ed. John R. Hibbing and Elizabeth Theiss-Morse. Cambridge, UK: Cambridge University Press.

Center for Political Studies, University of Michigan. 1995–2000. *The National Election Studies Guide to Public Opinion and Electoral Behavior.*

Chapter 7

The Promise and Peril of Presidential Polling: Between Gallup's Dream and the Morris Nightmare

Jeremy D. Mayer and Lynn Kirby

> If we know the collective will of the people at all times the efficiency of democracy can be increased, because we can substitute specific knowledge for blind groping and guesswork.
>
> —Pollster George Gallup

> Morris would simply look at his polls, tap a question on his handheld computer and announce, "The president should come out for a balanced budget."
>
> —Clinton staffer Michael Waldman, on presidential pollster Dick Morris

In 1939 pioneering pollster George Gallup believed that surveying would solve many of the problems of American government, specifically by allowing public opinion to guide the nation's leaders. He hoped that politicians would embrace polling as a way to restore direct democracy to America—lost since the decline of the New England town meeting. In the years since he wrote, politicians, media critics, and political scientists have worried that polls actually have played too great a role in presidential decision making. Moreover, some observers—notably political scientist Benjamin Ginsberg—have worried that public opinion polling has made possible new forms of elite manipulation of popular opinion. In this chapter, we discuss the theoretical questions polling poses for American presidents as they make decisions. Can polling do what Gallup dreamed it could and help make American democracy more participatory? What are the limitations and dangers of polls as influences on presidential policymaking? Next we trace the rise of the pollster from an outsider providing data to an insider playing an influential—indeed, sometimes dominant—role as presidential advisor. In two case studies, we look at how polls played a role in specific instances. We conclude by exploring how polling seems to play a part in the decision making of George W. Bush, who as a candidate for the presidency was openly disdainful of politicians who rely on polls.

Gallup's Dream and the Reality of Polls' Limits

George Gallup, the preeminent pollster of his day, argued that polling would allow our leaders to assess more accurately the wishes of their constituents. Elections were too infrequent and too difficult to interpret to provide guidance to the popular will. Gallup's faith in polling was shared by leading political scientists. In his seminal text, *The Responsible Electorate*, V. O. Key pointed out that elections were limited perhaps most critically by the paucity of choices presented to the electorate. "If the people can choose only from among rascals, they are certain to choose a rascal" (Key 1966, 3). Key, like Gallup, placed faith in public opinion surveying to provide a better clue than elections about why the public embraced one politician or position and not another.

To what use would polls be put? Not even Gallup wanted presidents to blindly follow polls. Instead, he hoped to replace the then-current and flawed means of assessing the popular will—such as tallies of letters to politicians, newspaper editorials, and assessing crowd reactions on the stump—with scientific surveys that would enable leaders to assess the nature of the public's mood, the cost of resisting it, and the best way to persuade. They could then plan their agendas around the public's concerns and fight off the power of special interests with the use of polls, while still holding ultimate authority. Moreover, they would understand public opinion on issues on which they had decided to focus.

Gallup also was aware of limitations in the use of surveys; he believed that the public could never be expected to "express judgment on technical questions of administration and government" because of their limited information. Furthermore, the elite of the country would still be required to present an agenda to the public because the public could not do so. "National policies do not spring full-blown from the common people. Leaders, knowing the general will of the people, must take the initiative in forming policies that will carry out the general will and must put them into effect" (Gallup [1939] 2000, 221).

As many subsequent students of survey research have observed, however, polls as guides to governance are even more limited than Gallup imagined. First, and perhaps most important, polls may not be accurate. Gallup hoped that polls would become increasingly accurate, and surely they have. But every poll comes with the potential for error, from myriad sources. We are much more aware today of how easily unintentional error may be introduced into a poll, through question wording or even question ordering. Polls also may be subject to intentional manipulation and biased interpretation. Most polls fail

to measure the intensity of opinion. Writing a letter to a president, taking part in a demonstration, even getting to the polls to vote require much more initiative and effort than answering a survey at home. As political scientist Benjamin Ginsberg argued, the poll is a measure of passive opinions and may, "in effect, submerge individuals with strongly held views in a more apathetic mass public" (Ginsberg 1986, 65). The weighting of each opinion equally—a core democratic value—may have a perverse effect in polls.

Another effect unanticipated by Gallup is that polls have become so influential that they now have "observer effects" on presidential decision making and the president's prestige. In other words, as pollsters seek to measure the public's esteem of the president, they change what they seek to measure. No president before George H. W. Bush rose as high as he did in 1991 following the allied victory in the Gulf War—or fell as quickly as the economy soured. The extreme volatility in that period surely was a product of events, but constant reporting of changes in public opinion also may produce a "bandwagon" effect, exacerbating the pace of change. Minor changes in a president's approval rating that would not even have been measured in 1950 because of the infrequency or inexactness of polling are now headline stories in major newspapers. Moreover, the existence of frequent public and private polling also changes the way presidents behave; they now have an incentive to maintain consistently high approval ratings and may choose policies in pursuit of minor bounces in the polls.

The frequency of modern polling also has affected how presidents interact with other institutions. Consider the change since political scientist Richard Neustadt wrote *Presidential Power*—the foundational text for the modern study of the presidency. Writing a few decades after Gallup, Neustadt felt that the public prestige of the presidency was such a central component of the president's power that it merited an entire chapter. When Neustadt wrote in 1960, however, prestige was only partially measured by polls:

How do members of the Washington community assess a president's prestige with the American public? They talk to one another and to taxi drivers. They read the columnists and polls and news reports. They sample the opinions of their visitors and friends. They travel in the country and they listen as they go. Above all, they watch Congress.... Congressional sentiment tends to be officialdom's pragmatic substitute for "public opinion" (Neustadt 1976 [1960], 157).

Today, although success in Congress may be considered a cause of a president's public prestige, rare is the Washington insider who would look to prestige, rather than to polls, as a measure of the public's approval. Neustadt (1960) wrote, "A president's prestige is not a very precise thing to keep in view." Modern polling makes that statement seem much less true today, altering presidential power and increasing the influence of polls.

Although Gallup was aware of polls' limitations, he was insufficiently fearful of their negative consequences, which should draw the attention of scholars of American government today. Even if polls were accurate and the intensity problem did not exist, the extraordinary low levels of information that Americans possess about politics may make them poor judges of appropriate policy choices. The ignorance and shortsightedness of the American public is nothing new. In the midst of World War II, more than half the U.S. public believed that America had joined the League of Nations in the interwar period. After the war was over, most Americans initially opposed assistance to western Europe— even financial aid to our closest ally, Great Britain, as it was on the verge of debt default (Leebaert 2002, 7, 25).

Nor have leaps in education produced more knowledge about governmental issues. A comprehensive comparison of political knowledge in the 1930s and 1940s to what is known today indicates a broad and relatively stable level of ignorance (Samuelson 2002). What has changed since the presidencies of Franklin Roosevelt and Truman is that the American public today is being asked to do exactly the things that Gallup thought would remain in elite hands: decide technical questions and set the nation's agenda. The role of the pollster has become institutionalized in the modern White House; thus, the public opinion poll today has the potential to influence presidential decision making to a much greater degree than in the past.

Institutionalization of the Pollster's Role in White House Policymaking

The first president to use public opinion polls with any regularity was Franklin Roosevelt (Edwards and Wayne 1999, 97). This observation is not surprising because the Gallup Poll began in 1935 and made its first election prediction about Roosevelt's 1936 reelection. By 1940 Roosevelt had begun to consult with pollsters about some of the most important issues of the day, including aid to Britain (Roper 1957, 71). Roosevelt was so intrigued by the possibilities of polling that he had a privately funded arrangement with Hadley Cantril, a pollster headquartered in Princeton, New Jersey, to do both long-term "trend" polling and same-day quick responses to new issues (Steele 1974; Cantril 1967). There was even the appearance, in embryonic form, of an official, government-sponsored poll run out of the Agriculture Department (Jensen 1980, 53).

Roosevelt's early enthusiasm for surveying was not emulated by his successor, Harry Truman. "It isn't the poll or public opinion at the moment that counts, it's right or wrong," said the man who had famously watched the polls erroneously declare him the loser of the 1948 campaign (McCullough 1992, 194). Indeed, Truman is regarded today as a president who stood up to public opinion at several crucial points in his presidency, from his firing of popular general Douglas

MacArthur to his decisive role in forcing a reluctant public to go along with support for threatened democracies in western and southern Europe.

Although Eisenhower used polls more than Truman did, the president who returned to the kind of intimate relationship with pollsters that FDR had cultivated was John F. Kennedy. Some scholars have even found a strong statistical relationship between poll results from JFK's pollster and Kennedy's later policy positions (Jacobs and Shapiro 1992, 161). Like many prior and subsequent pollsters to presidents, Kennedy's pollster averred that the president used polls only to package his policies, to aid in the selling of his plans for America—not in the creation of those plans (Harris 1973, 26).

Kennedy's successor, Lyndon Johnson, intensified the frequency of polling for the White House, commissioning more than four times as many polls as Kennedy in the same period (Jacobs and Shapiro 1995, 167). Johnson even carried his poll results around in his pocket, for use in debates over his standing with the American people (Goldman 1969, 192). In addition to having more polls done, Johnson continued the institutionalization of the polling process by tasking one staff member with analysis of all polls.

Richard Nixon further institutionalized the use of polls during his time in office by making them the focus of weekly meetings. Like LBJ, Nixon had one staffer who became the point person for polling (Wheeler 1976, 8). The president also sought new access to public pollsters: He had staffers assigned to interact with the Harris and Gallup surveys— to get prepublication data from them, influence their questions, and even attempt to influence their public interpretations (Wheeler 1976, 2–4). Thus, Nixon had insights gleaned not only from the commissioned polls that were specifically designed for his needs but also from the best minds in public polling.

During the Carter administration an important barrier came down: Pollsters moved from the outside to the inside. Prior to Carter pollsters had grown in influence, but their advice had always come, to a lesser or greater degree, from outside the White House's direct control (except briefly during the Roosevelt years). It was significant that men such as Louis Harris (pollster for Kennedy) and Oliver Quayle (pollster for LBJ) were only occasional visitors to the White House, not indistinguishable from White House aides as pollsters seem to be today.

Although Carter brought polling into the White House in a way that no previous president had, it seems that by some measures Carter was less influenced by polling than other presidents had been (Kirby 2002). The president seemed to follow his own moral compass, even in the face of widespread popular opposition to policies such as the return of the Panama Canal. Carter made conservation his most prominent response to the energy crisis, even though most Americans did not support turning the lights down or the air conditioning off. Carter also resisted public opinion on taking stronger action toward Iran during the hostage crisis. The fact that Carter left the presidency as an extraordinarily unpopular president did not escape the notice of his successor, Ronald Reagan, and Reagan's public relations advisors.

Case Study: Ronald Reagan and Central American Policy

Ronald Reagan came to office with a relationship of long standing with Richard Wirthlin, an economist who had worked on his campaigns for governor and president. Wirthlin— perhaps mindful of the criticism that Caddell's close relationship with Carter had attracted—opted to remain outside the official White House staff. Nevertheless, a small White House staff was created to keep atop Wirthlin's reports and other public polling data. Wirthlin had helped select the staffers and therefore, according to some observers, had even more influence than Caddell (Bonefede 1981, 2185; Wirthlin 2001). Wirthlin directly provided the president with polling interpretations and data more than thirty times in the first year of the Reagan presidency (Wirthlin 1993, 29).

Among the issues that Reagan had put high on his foreign policy agenda were the related problems of the left-wing Sandinista government in Nicaragua and the powerful Marxist rebel forces in neighboring El Salvador. Reagan's very first briefing as president addressed the potential shipment of destabilizing Soviet MIG aircraft to Central America (Wirthlin 2001), and throughout his presidency Reagan urged the public and the Congress to be more vigilant about Communist infiltration of Central America.

Reagan's appeals, however, fell on deaf ears. Early in his presidency majorities of Americans opposed sending U.S. military advisors, large military aid packages, and even enhanced economic assistance to El Salvador (Editor's Report 1982, 16). Much of the public seemed to be in the grip of what pollsters called "Vietnam syndrome": the fear of injecting U.S. troops into a bitter civil war with no fixed exit strategy. They were not interested in taking the side of the pro-American rebels (the "contras") in Nicaragua or the pro-American government in El Salvador.

Reagan was still constrained by this popular attitude and by opposition from House Democrats as he ran for reelection in 1984. Wirthlin, as pollster, advised the president against mentioning Central America during the campaign because it was such an unpopular issue. Only 37 percent of the public had heard of Nicaragua, and of those only 18 percent agreed with Reagan's position. So convinced was Wirthlin that the public's views on Central America had to be respected that Wirthlin went "bananas at just the mention of the word 'contra,'" according to one Reagan official (Mayer and McManus 1988, 15).

The president began to talk more about the need to oppose Communist infiltration of Central America in his second term, despite the continued public opposition to U.S. military aid (Sobel 1989, 123–24). Awareness of the region's conflict increased, and by March 1986, 78 percent of the public knew that there was fighting in Nicaragua. As late as 1987, however—after six years of fairly substantial coverage of the problems in Nicaragua—only 32 percent of the populace knew what continent it was on (Sobel 1989, 114–15). Nevertheless, Americans remained resolute in their opposition to greater U.S. involvement.[1] Reagan was never able to get a full package of military aid through Congress, although he never stopped trying until his administration's extraconstitutional policies of financing the contras were revealed in the Iran-Contra scandal.

Several insights can be gleaned from the role public opinion played in Central American policy during the Reagan presidency. First, there is no evidence that Reagan behaved in a slavish fashion towards public opinion; in the face of sustained and firm opposition to his policies, Reagan's position was unchanged. It does seem clear, however, that—particularly during the 1984 reelection campaign—polling data did influence the degree of emphasis Central America received from the president. Second, and perhaps most important, public opinion served as an indirect constraint on presidential decision making, through the intervention of Congress. Reagan, who was so popular during much of this period that he became known as the "Teflon president" and "the Great Communicator," was unable to get Congress to consistently support one of his highest priorities. Democrats in Congress, buoyed by the polls on Central America, passed several measures that obstructed (and, absent illegal acts, would have prevented) aid to the contras. Despite the fact that a popular and persuasive president remained determined to change public opinion, public opinion acted as a blunt veto on his policies.

Case Study: Bill Clinton and Welfare Policy

From its earliest days, the Clinton White House was perceived as suffused with pollsters and polling (Drew 1994, 124). Clinton polled more frequently than any of his predecessors. Meeting alone with his pollster at least once a week, Clinton studied focus group results, multivariate regression analysis, time series data, and factor analysis (Jacobs and Shapiro 2000, 95). It is unlikely that any previous president would have been able to grasp the meaning of many of these statistical techniques.

Clinton's first pollster, Stan Greenberg, wrote the memos that became the basis for the long-term planning meetings. Greenberg was a presence in the West Wing on an almost daily basis (Gergen 2000, 330; Berke 1993). Following the massive defeat of the Democratic Party at almost all levels of government during the Republican Revolution of 1994, Clinton turned to a political strategist with strong Republican ties, Dick Morris, who secretly had polls conducted for the president on nearly every aspect of his presidency. Top presidential advisor George Stephanopoulos contended that from December 1994 to August 1996, "no single person more influenced the president of the United States than Dick Morris" (Stephanopoulos 1999, 330). Unlike nearly all previous pollsters, who usually had claimed that their advice was about packaging issues and helping the president select items to emphasize from an existing agenda, Morris bluntly took credit for creating policies and pushing presidential decision making in an aggressive fashion. Clinton later expressed a preference for pollsters who did not just analyze data but told him what to do on the basis of their polling (Harris 2000). This preference is well displayed in Clinton's decision making on welfare policy.

Clinton had campaigned on a pledge to "end welfare was as we know it"—part of his New Democrat appeal. Welfare reform was put on the back burner for the first two years of his presidency, however, while other issues—notably the economy, the budget deficit, and health care—took center stage. The Republican revolution of 1994 brought congressional majorities intent on changing welfare and gave Clinton new incentives to return to his centrist campaign pledges of 1992. Polling also showed that vast majorities of

Americans supported some version of welfare reform (Burns and Sorenson 1999, 234).

The first two iterations of welfare reform passed by the new Republican majorities contained cuts in Medicaid and welfare benefits. Clinton vetoed them. In the summer of 1996, Clinton received a third welfare bill, this time without the Medicaid elements to which he had objected previously.

Clinton and his aides were deeply conflicted about what to do. There was much Democratic opposition to the legislation in its current form. Personal friends inside and outside the administration felt that signing the bill would be a betrayal of sixty years of Democratic beliefs and might lead to the suffering of millions of innocent children. Half of the Democrats in Congress were opposed to the bill, some using extraordinarily impassioned rhetoric in their floor speeches. Several elements in the third bill were directly opposed to positions Clinton had publicly espoused.

The White House staff had debated the issue for months, and the debate was well known to the Washington establishment. Morris, however, advised the president to sign the bill: "I told him flatly that a welfare veto would cost him the election . . . a welfare veto by itself would transform a fifteen-point win into a three-point loss" (Morris 1997, 300). Morris had polled in 1995 and found that the populace would accept almost no excuse for a presidential veto of a welfare bill (Morris 1997, 465). After Clinton made perhaps the most difficult domestic decision of his presidency and signed the welfare reform legislation, he called his pollster. "I want you to know I signed that bill because I trust you," said the president (Morris 1997, 304).

It is clear that Morris' polling on welfare reform was a crucial—indeed, decisive—influence on the president's choices in the welfare reform debate of 1995–96. Supporting this version of welfare reform put Clinton in opposition to many of his staff members, key Cabinet members, Democrats in Congress, and, to some extent, his own conscience. Why was public opinion so influential on Clinton, in contrast to Reagan and Central America?

Several plausible explanations are apparent. First, Clinton was presented with a single, high-profile decision on welfare reform at a crucial moment in his reelection drive. By contrast, Reagan's Central American policy was simply maintained over six years without any single moment of high drama or confrontation with Congress. Second, welfare reform was a domestic issue, on which the public may have felt more confident in expressing its opinions. Americans have much less information about foreign policy matters and therefore have less resistance to attempts by elites to shape their opinion on those questions (Zaller 1992, 44–46). The most important reasons, however, may have been the president's own attitude toward polling and the type of polling that was done. Clinton trusted and understood polls in a way that Reagan never did.

Moreover, Morris was using hypothetical questions to drive his point home. Voters were asked what they would do in the election if the president vetoed welfare reform. This prospective polling, if it is believed by the president, makes the pollster's advice far more powerful. Rather than merely telling the president about the existing attitudes of the public, he was able to tell the president how public opinion and behavior might change if he made a certain decision.

Comparison of these two case studies suggests that changes in the way polling is conducted and the level of trust presidents put in their pollsters altered decision making in the modern White House. Other explanations are possible, of course. They also illustrate that the varying influence of public opinion depends on the conviction with which presidents adhere to a particular policy position. Finally, they show how hypothetical public responses affect ongoing presidential decisions.

Four Aspects of Modern Presidential Polling

With Morris, polling reached its most influential moment in the history of the American presidency. The historical forces that produced the Morris moment may seem to be an aberration, unlikely to be repeated. Clinton had a particularly deep understanding of polling, grasping the intricacies of sampling and statistics better than any previous occupant of the White House. He absorbed himself in the details of polls and was the first to see the latest numbers. Moreover, Morris' ascendancy followed the historic collapse of Clinton's party and popularity in late 1994. The "triangulation" that Morris prescribed, based on his polling, was strong medicine, but Clinton's presidency was quite sick at the time. Morris' alterations in the nature of polling represent a culmination in the evolution of public opinion surveying; the great success that Morris and Clinton experienced in resurrecting Clinton's electoral chances from 1995 to 1996 suggests that this pattern may be emulated by future politicians.

As shown in figure 7.1, the relationship between the president, the pollster, policy, and the public is now exceedingly complex. As with pollsters since FDR, a modern pollster provides the president with a *base* reading of the public's mood. This base reading would include the popularity of the president, as well as the parties and key political figures. Most presidential polls now, however, also include a *"predictive"* element. An example is the now-famous poll that Clinton commissioned from Morris in the early days of the Monica Lewinsky scandal.[2] Citizens were asked how they would feel if it were revealed that the president had had a consensual sexual relationship with an intern. Next they were asked how they would feel about Clinton if he had perjured himself or obstructed justice in addition. The poll results told Clinton that he could get away with the first but would not survive the second, and eventually this was the story that the president adopted. Such predictive questions also were used extensively in putting issues on Clinton's reelection agenda.

Today Americans are asked numerous hypothetical questions about their leaders and their policies, in an attempt to discern

Figure 7.1 The Complex Role of the Modern Pollster

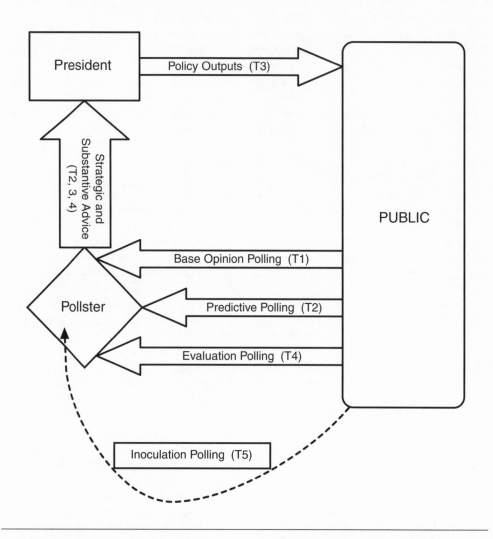

T1: **Base Opinion Polling:** The pollster measures the basic attitudes and preferences of the American public.

T2: **Predictive Polling:** Simultaneously or based on the earlier poll, the pollster assesses how the public would respond to various measures and the packaging of the president's upcoming policy moves.

T2,3,4: **Strategic and Substantive Advice:** The pollster interprets the public's responses for the president.

T3: **Policy Outputs:** The president's decisions are experienced, either directly or through the media, by the public.

T4: **Evaluation Polling:** The pollster measures how the public responded to the policy output.

T5: **Inoculation Polling:** The pollster assesses how effective various tactics and policy moves by the opposition party or candidate would be and how best to combat them.

Note: "Polling" can include random sample surveying, focus groups, and panel studies.

which policies would attract more support. This technique is quite different from finding out whether the president's policies are popular or how they might be better packaged. This hypothetical poll is prospective and substantive, but it also may be based on an epistemological impossibility. Can a citizen answer accurately how he or she will feel about a policy proposal in a vacuum, without hearing from the opposition that might emerge or perceiving the media framing of the policy? Regardless, such questions are now part and parcel of the modern polling operation. Numerous Clinton policies, from school uniforms to television V-chips, were chosen on the basis of predictive polling (Morris 1997). Today a president finds out not only how he is doing but how he might do if he took step X, used phrase Y, or enacted policy Z.

The results of predictive polling and those of base opinion polling are given to the president to aid him in the policymaking process. When a policy output is finally implemented, the pollster then assesses the public's reaction with *evaluation* polling. Did the prediction work? Did the policy actually provide the popularity boost that was expected? Morris conducted exactly this type of polling following the welfare reform decision:

> After the welfare announcement, I began to see large shifts in public opinion that our polling had predicted. Voters were willing to open their hearts and their government's checkbook to be sure that welfare reform succeeded.... The president was thrilled with the news (Morris 1997, 304).

If evaluation polling confirms the pollster's predictive advice, the president will be even more likely to trust the pollster in the next substantive debate.

A final type of polling that modern pollsters undertake is the most subtle and unusual of all. In preparation for the 1996 presidential election, Morris wanted not only to see where the Republicans and Clinton were weak or strong, he wanted to see how various Republican messages would work against his candidate. Morris had his associates make several anti-Clinton TV ads and showed them to focus group participants, to gauge which attacks drew blood and caused Clinton's support to drop. Next he tried to divine what countermeasures might work. This *"inoculation"* polling served Clinton, and surely will be emulated by future pollsters. Before Republican candidate Robert Dole had even begun his campaign, Morris had a fairly good idea which attacks would work and how they could be defeated (Morris 1997, 272), thereby giving Clinton a sustainable tactical advantage.

The growth in the types of polls and the frequency with which they are used also has been part of the extraordinary increase in the costs associated with running for president in the United States. All four types of polling also look at subgroups, allowing presidents to target demographic groups by age, occupation, race, religion, or even more rarefied characteristics. Subgroup analysis often requires larger surveys, adding to the expense.

With base, predictive, evaluative, and inoculation polls and focus groups to conduct, Morris' combined tab during the 1995–96 election cycle was well in excess of $2 million—paid for by soft money raised by the Democratic National Committee. The targeted television campaign that resulted from his insights was even more expensive. When Clinton invited Chinese arms dealers for tea at the White House; when Al Gore illegally raised money at a Buddhist temple or through phone calls from his office; whenever the campaign finance laws were stretched and indeed torn, one of the proximate causes was the high cost of polls and the president's reliance on them. The Republican party, with an even bigger bankroll, was conducting its own expensive polling. It remains to be seen if the McCain-Feingold campaign finance legislation banning soft money at the federal level will lead to a reduction in the pervasive nature of polling in American politics. If history is any guide, the political appetite for expert readings of public opinion will be satiated, regardless of how many legal loopholes will have to be devised.

Toward a Conclusion: *Vox Populi, Vox Dei*?

As we have seen, polling has come to occupy an increasingly prominent role in White House staffing. The pollster has moved from a distant outsider to a daily insider, and polling data are widely distributed among top staff. At some points, for some presidents, polling results have been used as deciding factors on policy matters, much as less accurate measures of public opinion were used in the past. "Politicians have been good at public opinion forever, and the best politicians are the best at it, long before polls" (Teeter 2001). Yet some contemporary uses of polling do raise troubling questions about presidential decision making—questions that are different from those raised in the past.

First, if polls are truly more influential today than in 1940, 1960, or 1980, then we face the problem of low information content on the part of the citizenry. Polling has grown far beyond what some observers regard as natural limits to its influence. Recall that Gallup—polling's strongest advocate in its early years—had believed that polls should not become guides on "technical" questions because of the limitations of public knowledge. In March 1995 Clinton was conducting negotiations with Boris Yeltsin about U.S. aid to Russia and the American desire for Russia to stop aiding the construction of an Iranian nuclear plant. As Morris remembers it:

> I conducted a poll to see how people felt about the Iranian deal and about a cutoff in aid to Russia. The poll revealed that voters were tremendously concerned about the sale of reactors to Iran but also were sympathetic to the complexities of U.S.-Russian relations, and they wished to see the diplomatic discussions continue (Morris 1997, 251).

The idea that the public understood "the complexities of U.S.-Russian relations" or the question of nuclear reactors in Iran strains credulity to the breaking point. The public's attitude toward nuclear reactors in Iran or security in the Persian Gulf may reflect little more than xenophobia and prejudice. Moreover, even assuming that the public has accurate information on a topic, they may still make poor policy judgments.

Of course, it is entirely possible that—Morris' claims notwithstanding—the polling Morris did on Iran's nuclear program and relations with Russia played no part in the president's policies, or at best set broad parameters for the decision making. It is unlikely, however, that presidents who receive frequent updates on their approval ratings and are jubilant over five-point rises in the public's esteem remain unaffected if they know the popularity or unpopularity of various courses of action.

The United States was founded by men who distrusted democracy; they constructed a government designed to distance the passions of the people from day-to-day decision making. Unlike Rousseau, James Madison feared that a united citizenry would become the source of tyrannical demagogues and factitious leaders. A United States in the grip of public opinion would not have paid for a Marshall plan or armed Britain in 1940.

Finally, there is the danger that by using the predictive data provided by the Dick Morrises of future White Houses, presidents may become supremely adept at manipulating public opinion and using it as a battering ram to defeat the less-skilled competing institutions of American government. It was the intent of the founders that the House of Representatives should be the voice of the people, but today the president monitors that opinion directly—not through the prism of the House. Thus, polling represents a potential challenge to two fundamental issues in American government: which institution should represent the people's will and how that will should be determined.

Polling also may have gained in influence because of a vacuum at the core of American politics. Pollster Stanley Greenberg argued that the decline of the political parties and the lower levels of trust Americans have in the institutions of government have made polls more important to governing (Greenberg 1993, 37; Rosenstiel 1993). It may be no accident that the greatest modern advocate of Gallup's dream was Ross Perot, the antipartisan candidate of 1992 and 1996. Echoing Gallup's endorsement of polling as a restoration of New England town democracy on a national scale, Perot put forth an impassioned proposal for an "electronic town hall" in which major issues such as health care or the deficit would be explained to the nation in detail, and then the voters would call toll-free telephone numbers (or, later, log onto a website) to register their opinions. Perot prescribed this instant opinion polling as a solution to gridlock and promised that it would soon get the White House and Congress "dancing together like Fred Astaire and Ginger Rogers" (Fishkin 1992, 21).

The Internet and broadband technology offer the potential for interactive measurements of public opinion of increasing complexity and depth. Like populists of the pre-polling era, Perot portrayed himself as a spokesperson of the common man against the elite special interests. Unlike those earlier populists, Perot could claim to have proof of the people's preference for him and his positions.

Technology has already altered the role polling plays in presidential decision making. It surely will continue to do so. Improvements in the mathematical modeling of public opinion data, the insights of political psychologists, the cunning of marketing experts, and the intricate design of modern surveys all suggest that the medium of polling may be only in its adolescence. Polling may still be awaiting a master who can do for it what Pericles did for rhetoric—or Goebbels for radio and newspapers. In the appropriate hands, polling could be a tool for ameliorating special interest and elite abuses of an alienated ma-

jority—exactly as Gallup hoped. Yet polling may be at least as likely to make new methods of elite domination possible, behind a facade of democracy (Ginsberg 1986).

There may be a final irony in the comfort some observers take in the anti-poll rhetoric of president George W. Bush. Throughout his campaign for the White House, Bush made his disdain for polling evident, and it was part of his implicit criticism of Clinton. Bush pledged that he would not let polling numbers influence his decisions. "I will not be a president who uses my office as a mirror of public opinion. . . . The most important job in Washington should be the president, not the president's pollster" (Scully 1999). Yet once in office, Bush made extensive, if secretive, use of polls. Great efforts were made to shield the influence of Bush's pollsters from public view, and costs were allocated in a way that made it difficult to compare Bush's outlays against those of previous presidents. Nevertheless, by one estimate the Republican National Committee has spent much more on polling than it did in the administration of George H. W. Bush, although significantly less than the Democratic National Committee spent during Clinton's presidency (Green 2002).

Bush advisors make it clear that the polling that takes place is only about packaging and spin, rather than making policy—echoing the more traditional statements of pre-Morris pollsters. There may be a tactical reason for Bush's stance, however: that voters were sick of a poll-driven president like Clinton and wanted a change. Ironically, the most plausible way that Bush could have known for certain would have been to hear it from a pollster. Suppose, then, that the public begins to feel that Bush is not listening to them? If pollsters receiving hundreds of thousands of dollars to assess the public mood for George W. Bush tell him that the public feels he should listen to them more attentively, will he reject that advice? Some evidence would suggest no. Even as Bush's spokespersons continue to advertise him as a man who is unaffected by polling, they repetitively point to his high approval ratings as proof of support for his policies; note the comment made by former press secretary Ari Fleisher in 2002: "The American people, as shown by all the data, powerfully, continually support the president at record-breaking levels" (Milbank 2002). Even a president who attacks the pollsters employs them and consistently uses their numbers to buttress his authority in Washington and the nation.

Notes

1. This may be an illustration of Elmo Roper's 1942 observation: "A great many of us make two mistakes in our judgment of the common man. We overestimate the amount of information he has; we underestimate his intelligence" (Samuelson 2002).
2. It should not escape note that in the midst of the greatest crisis of Clinton's presidency, one of the first people Clinton called was Morris, and the advice Morris provided was based on predictive polling.

References

An Editor's Report on El Salvador (Editor's Report). 1982. *Public Opinion* 5, no. 2: 16.

Berke, Richard. 1993. "Clinton Adviser Says Polls Had a Role in Health Plan." *New York Times*, December 9, A1.

Bonafede, Dom. 1978. "Carter and the Polls—If You Live By Them, You May Die By Them." *National Journal* 10, no. 33: 1312–15.

———. 1981. "As Pollster to the President, Wirthlin Is Where the Action Is."*National Journal* 13, no. 50: 2184–86.

Burns, James MacGregor, and Georgia J. Sorenson. 1999. *Dead Center: Clinton-Gore Leadership and the Perils of Moderation*. New York: Scribner.

Cantril, Hadley. 1967. *The Human Dimension*. New Brunswick, N.J.: Rutgers University Press.

Drew, Elizabeth. 1994. *On the Edge*. New York: Simon and Schuster.

Edwards, George C., III, and Stephen J. Wayne. 1999. *Presidential Leadership: Politics and Policy Making*, 6th ed. New York: Bedford.

Fishkin, James. 1992. "Talk of the Tube." *The American Prospect* 3, no. 11 (September 1): 46–52.

Gallup, George. [1939] 2000. "Polling the Public." In *Public Opinion in a Democracy*, ed. Charles William Smith. New York: Prentice-Hall.

Gergen, David. 2000. *Eyewitness to Power: The Essence of Leadership*. New York: Simon and Schuster.

Ginsberg, Benjamin. 1986. *The Captive Public: How Mass Opinion Promotes State Power*. New York: Basic Books.

Goldman, Eric. 1969. *The Tragedy of Lyndon Johnson*. New York: Knopf.

Green, Joshua. 2002. "The Other War Room." *Washington Monthly Online*. April. Available at http://washingtonmonthly.com/features/2001/0204.green.html (last accessed October 22, 2003).

Greenberg, Stanley. 1993. Panel discussion, American Enterprise Institute Annual Policy Conference: Pollsters [Transcript]. December 8.

Harris, John F. 2000. "The Clinton Years/Story of a Survivor: Policy and Politics by the Numbers." *Washington Post*, December 31, A1.

Harris, Louis. 1973. *The Anguish of Change*. New York: W. W. Norton.

Jacobs, Lawrence, and Robert Shapiro. 1992. "Public Decisions, Private Polls: John F. Kennedy's Presidency." Paper presented at annual meeting of Midwest Political Science Association, Chicago, April.

———. 1995. "The Rise of Presidential Polling: The Nixon White House in Historical Perspective." *Public Opinion Quarterly* 59: 163–95.

———. 2000. *Politicians Don't Pander*. Chicago: University of Chicago Press.

Jensen, Richard. 1980. "Democracy by the Numbers." *Public Opinion* 3, no. 1A: 53–59.

Key, V. O. 1966. *The Responsible Electorate*. Cambridge, Mass.: Belknap Press.

Kirby, Lynn. 2002. "Public Opinion and Policymaking: The Pollster as Presidential Advisor." Ph.D. diss., Georgetown University.

Leebaert, Derek. 2002. *The Fifty Year Wound*. New York: Little, Brown.

Mayer, Jane, and Doyle McManus. 1988. *Landslide: The Unmaking of the President, 1984–1988*. Boston: Houghton Mifflin.

Mayer, Jeremy D. 2002. *Running on Race: Racial Politics in Presidential Campaigns 1960–2000*. New York: Random House.

McCullough, David. 1992. *Truman*. New York: Simon & Schuster.

Milbank, Dana. 2002. "At the White House, 'The People' Have Spoken—Endlessly." *Washington Post,* June 4, A15.

Morris, Dick. 1997. *Behind the Oval Office*. New York: Random House.

Murray, Shoon, and Peter Howard. 2002. "Variation in White House Polling Operations: Carter to Clinton." Paper presented at annual meeting of International Studies Association, New Orleans, March.

Neustadt, Richard E. 1976. *Presidential Power: The Politics of Leadership*. New York: Wiley.

Roper, Elmo. 1957. *You and Your Leaders*. New York: Morrow.

Rosenstiel, Thomas B. 1993. "President's Pollsters: Who Follows Whom?" *Los Angeles Times*, December 28, A5.

Samuelson, Robert J. 2002. "What We Don't Know Won't Hurt Us." *Washington Post*, May 15, A27.

Scully, Sean. 1999. "Bush Pledges Return of Ideals." *Washington Times*, June 23, A1.

Sobel, Richard. 1989. "Public Opinion about United States Intervention in El Salvador and Nicaragua." *Public Opinion Quarterly* 53: 114–28.

Steele, Richard W. 1974. "The Pulse of the People: FDR and the Gauging of American Public Opinion." *Journal of Contemporary History* 9: 195–216.

Stephanopoulos. George. 1999. *All Too Human*. Boston: Little, Brown.

Teeter, Robert. 2001. Telephone interview with author Kirby. November 20.

Waldman, Michael. 2000. *POTUS Speaks*. New York: Simon & Schuster.

Wheeler, Michael. 1976. *Lies, Damn Lies, and Statistics*. New York: Dell.

Wirthlin, Richard. 1993. American Enterprise Institute. Annual Policy Conference: Pollsters. Transcript. December 8.

———. 2001. Telephone interviews with author Kirby. April 30 and May 14.

Zaller, John R. 1992. *The Nature and Origin of Mass Opinion*. New York: Cambridge University Press.

Chapter 8

Democratic Government and the Unilateral Presidency

Margaret Tseng

In the 1960s, Richard Neustadt argued that separated institutions with shared powers are the hallmarks of American government (Neustadt 1990). Neustadt's paradigm-shifting observation turned attention to the behavioral aspects of the presidency, long neglected in presidential studies. It also questioned the assumption that the expansion of presidential roles and responsibilities produced a very powerful presidency. Neustadt argued against the proposition that presidents are powerful; instead, he urged presidents to use bargaining techniques to overcome the inherent weakness of the institution.

Since the expansion and institutionalization of the presidency during the Franklin D. Roosevelt era, the president has shouldered increasing policymaking expectations. Before Roosevelt, Congress had dominated domestic policymaking, permitting the president to recommend but not dictate the legislative agenda. Growing presidential influence on that agenda has been facilitated by the bully pulpit, magnified by the electronic media. The attention presidents can bring to an issue alerts the public and mobilizes congressional support to achieve their policy priorities.

Setting the agenda and using the persuasion strategy often are not enough, however, for a president to achieve his administration's policy goals. Presidential promises can fall on deaf ears in Congress if they fail to generate broad-based constituency support. Nor can partisan politics always or even usually over-come congressional intransigence. Divided government has reinforced the constitutional divide for much of the past forty years, constraining the president's ability to convert initiatives into legislative output.

Although closed-door bargaining still exists (Conley 2001), it is onerous and has political costs. Moreover, victory is by no means certain. The magnitude of the bargaining effort combined with the time, energy, and psychological constraints provide incentives for presidents to rely on unilateral powers to achieve their political agenda. The exercise of powers such as executive orders, proclamations, rulemaking, and recess appointments is rarely checked or overturned by Congress or the Supreme Court.

The use of these powers has enabled presidents to close the gap between public expectations and their own dispersed resources. The thesis of this chapter is that presidents have increased their use of unilateral powers over time and that the exercise of that authority clashes with the constitutional design—and, during a president's final term, with the "democratic spirit" of American government. By bridging the expectations gap with unilateral action, presidents can thwart checks and balances in the name of efficiency and, in some cases, their historical legacy. That is, they may use unilateral authority to establish new public policy that may continue long after they have left office. In this chapter I attempt to evaluate the "democratic character" of unilateral actions by discussing the parameters of those actions, how often they are used, and whom they benefit. I focus my study on four pillars of the unilateral presidency: recess appointments, executive orders, monument proclamations, and administrative rulemaking.

Recess Appointments

Recess appointments are appointments made by the president during a congressional recess. Although most executive appointments require Senate confirmation, presidents can bypass the Senate by making appointments when the upper chamber is not in session. They may do so because the Senate has not acted on a nomination or because a vacancy has occurred during a congressional recess or adjournment.

Historically presidents have used recess appointments to advance candidates that otherwise might not be confirmed for ideological or other partisan, political reasons. They have used such appointments to address diversity issues—to place women and minorities on the bench, for example. Another illustration of this practice occurred in 1999 when President Clinton appointed James C. Hormel as Ambassador to Luxembourg during a congressional recess. Hormel was the first openly gay ambassador ever appointed. As a consequence of the Hormel appointment, Senator James M. Inhofe (R-Okla.) placed a permanent hold on all of Clinton's nominations, calling Clinton's appointment of Hormel a "flagrant abuse of the recess appointment power" (Shenon 1999).

Recess appointments initially were not envisioned as a way for presidents to circumvent the senatorial confirmation process. The constitutional provision that gave the president the power to make such appointments envisioned a Congress meeting for only a few months of the year. Senators could not easily and quickly assemble to approve a nomination given the state of transportation at the time; thus the contingency provided in Article 2, Clause 3 of the Constitution: "The President shall have Power to fill up all Vacancies that may happen during the Recess of the Senate, by granting Commissions which expire at the End of their next Session."

Times have changed. Although the congressional session has been extended, so have the obstacles to Senate confirmation. Individual senators may put "holds" on nominations, thereby delaying them indefinitely. In Ronald Reagan's first term, the Senate took an average of thirty days to confirm his nominees. In 1993 Clinton's nominees waited an average of forty-one days for confirmation. And both presidents faced "friendly," same-party Senates at the time! By 1999 the confirmation process was taking more than twice as long—averaging eighty-seven days (Loomis 2001)—thereby extending the period during which positions remained vacant. In 1997 fifteen prominent countries did not have an ambassador from the United States, and one-third of the government's senior jobs were open (Mackenzie 2001). Thus, the partisan environment combined with liberal Senate rules provide an incentive to circumvent the process entirely, which may explain why presidents step up the number of recess appointments during election years and during their last year in office (figure 8.1).

Although Clinton was reluctant to make recess appointments early in his administration, he made an unprecedented fifty-three of them in his last year. Because Clinton came into office with a Democratic Senate and left with a Republican Senate, we can speculate that party politics affected his increased use of recess appointments. Reagan also faced an oppositional Senate in his final years in office. He too made a large number of recess appointments (forty-five) during his last year, as did presidents Carter and George H. W. Bush.

Of all the presidents, Ronald Reagan made the most recess appointments: more than 200 during his two terms. He often received criticism for doing so. In 1985, when the president contemplated promoting William Bradford Reynolds to associate attorney general through a recess appointment, Democrats loudly objected. Senator Byrd

Figure 8.1 Recess Appointments, 1964–2001

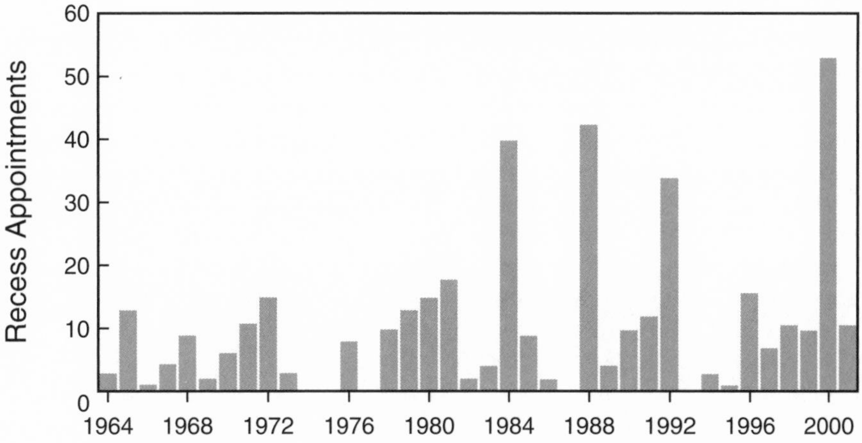

Source: Data compiled by author from *Weekly Compilation of Presidential Documents.*

(D-W.Va.) called the pending appointment an insult to the Senate. He specifically noted, "A recess appointment . . . would be inappropriate and unacceptable. We urge you not to make this recess appointment" (United Press International 1985). Reagan had previously sent Reynolds' nomination to the Senate, but the Senate Judiciary Committee rejected the nomination.

The Senate threatened to hold all nominations if Reagan proceeded with the recess appointment. When he did so, Democrats blocked all other nominations for three months. To release the "holds" that had been placed on these nominations, Reagan had to promise to provide the Senate with prior notice if he intended to make additional recess appointments.

Even George W. Bush—who campaigned on ending Clinton's abuses of presidential power—made fourteen recess appointments during his first months in office. Two of them caught the attention of the Senate: Otto Reich as Assistant Secretary of State for Western Hemisphere affairs and Eugene Scalia, son of the Supreme Court Justice Antonin Scalia, as Solicitor General for the Labor Department. Both nominations had been stalled by political opponents such as

Senator Edward Kennedy (D-Mass.) who claimed that "Scalia's record showed a lack of commitment to the rights of workers. I continue to believe that Mr. Scalia is not the right person for this important Labor Department position" (Gerstenzang 2002).

The framers separated the powers among the three branches of government to prevent one institution from dominating the government. The ability of a president to circumvent the Senate through recess appointments contributes to executive domination. Whether it also undercuts the democratic character of the system, however, depends on one's perspective. The president is nationally elected; senators are responsive to their states. Does it comport with democratic values to allow individual senators to obstruct the administration of government by delaying or denying confirmation to the president's appointees? On the other hand, should presidents—particularly those who are no longer eligible for reelection—be able to unilaterally choose whomever they want to serve in high executive branch position in the absence of Senate action?

Figure 8.2 Symbolic Proclamations, 1929–2000

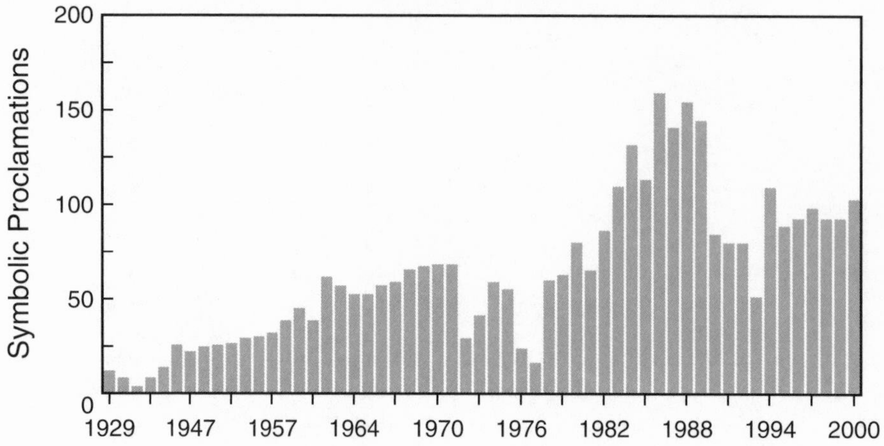

Source: Data compiled by author from *Weekly Compilation of Presidential Documents*.

Presidential Directives

Issuing directives and orders that have the force of law and can establish national policy, often with broad social implications, are other ways that presidents can circumvent constitutional checks and balances. "Stroke of a pen, law of the land. Kind of cool." That is how Clinton strategist Paul Begala described his president's use of executive orders (Bennet 1998). One wonders whether Begala and other Clinton staff members would have regarded George W. Bush's order to prohibit U.S. aid to international groups that preached, promoted, or promulgated information on abortions as "kind of cool."

The bottom line is that presidents have used executive orders and other directives to *initiate* and *implement* policy. Although Congress and the courts can overturn that policy, they rarely have done so (Moe and Howell 1999).

Proclamations

George Washington made the first presidential proclamation, declaring November 26 as Thanksgiving Day (Relyea 2001). Although most proclamations are ceremonious, they also can address issues of national safety. In 1794 President Washington used a proclamation to call forth the military to deal with rebellious citizens from Pennsylvania and Virginia who were protesting certain federal taxes.

Since the beginning of the twentieth century, proclamations have honored or paid tribute to thousands of individuals and groups. One reason these proclamations have proliferated is that they can increase a president's political capital (see figure 8.2). In other words, it is good politics.

Aside from issuing politically symbolic proclamations, presidents also can use proclamations to influence foreign commerce. Although the Constitution gives Congress the authority to regulate commerce, Congress has delegated some of that authority to the president. The Agreement Act of 1934 and the Lend Lease Act of 1941 both gave the president power to make trade decisions.

Using their statutory authority, presidents can end trade agreements or place embargoes on the exportation of certain items. Theodore Roosevelt's termination of arms exports to the Dominican Republic and Dwight Eisenhower's termination of a trade agreement with Iran are two examples of unilateral presidential actions. Clinton used proclamations to limit immigration of individuals from Nigeria and Liberia. More recently, George W. Bush used this power to resume normal trade relations with Afghanistan.

A more controversial dimension of presidential directives entails proclamations used to create, adjust, or enlarge national monuments under the authority of the Antiquities Act of 1906. Created during Theodore Roosevelt's presidency, the Antiquities Act empowers presidents to expediently protect federal lands. In total, presidents have designated more than 100 monuments spanning about 70 million acres.

The Antiquities Act instructs presidents to reserve "the smallest area compatible with the proper care and management of the objects to be protected." The debate over the definition of the "smallest area" has prompted protests and lawsuits such as the one initiated by the Anaconda Copper Company, which challenged three of President Carter's monument proclamations in the state of Alaska. Anaconda claimed that the location of the monuments blocked them from continuing to mine. A federal district court judge disagreed, however, noting that the president had seventy-five years of legal precedent behind him in protecting the nation's lands.

The monument proclamation was not used again until the next Democratic president came to power. In 1996 President Clinton proclaimed the Grand Staircase-Escalante National Monument in Utah protected under the Antiquities Act. Creation of the monument blocked the development of the largest known coal reserve in the country, worth nearly $1 trillion. The Utah congressional delegation unanimously opposed the declaration, but Clinton, recognizing the national popularity of preserving the region, went forward with it anyway.

The opposition Clinton encountered in 1996 was mild compared to the firestorm that erupted when he proclaimed twenty-one new monuments in his last year in office. Mining, timber, and grazing industries cried foul, contending that the real purpose of Clinton's actions was to prevent the development of resources, not to preserve pristine lands. Clinton's large-scale designation did expand the definition of a national monument to include anthropological ecosystems such as the Canyon of the Ancients in Colorado. Did the president misinterpret the intent of the statute? Did he overreach? Did he make a poor policy judgment?

Congress has the authority to rescind presidential proclamations but has done so rarely. Only 5,000 acres of the 70 million designated under the Antiquities Act have been reversed by Congress (see www.npca.org). Moreover, the courts generally have sided with the president in challenges over the scope of proclamations.

Executive Orders

Executive orders, another of the many kinds of presidential directives, technically assist the president in his role as chief executive. Kenneth Mayer, in his book *With the Stroke of a Pen*, has classified these orders into eight categories: civil service, public lands, war and emergency powers, foreign affairs, defense and military policy, executive branch administration, labor policy, and domestic policy (Mayer 2001).

The executive order has gone through an evolution. Lyn Ragsdale (1998) writes that prior to World War II, executive orders were used mostly for "routine administrative matters." Franklin D. Roosevelt accelerated their use during World War II. When Japan declared war on the United States through the attack on Pearl Harbor, Roosevelt issued Executive Order 9066, which allowed military commanders to intern Japanese Americans on the Pacific Coast. The Supreme Court declared this order to be constitutional. President Truman's executive order to seize the steel industry during a labor dispute, however, was deemed unconstitutional by the Supreme Court.

Executive orders are the law of the land unless and until Congress legislates on the matter or the courts rule on them. Both of those branches have shown extreme reluctance to

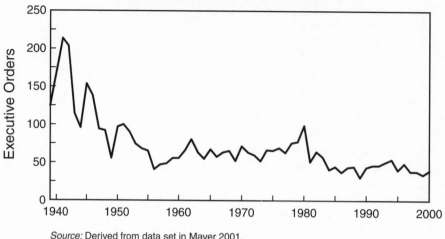

Figure 8.3 Executive Orders, 1939–2000

Source: Derived from data set in Mayer 2001.

revoke executive orders. From 1973 to 1997, U.S. presidents issued a total of 1,400 executive orders. Congress attempted to eliminate thirty-six of those orders but succeeded with only one: President Nixon's order giving a pay raise to federal employees (Moe and Howell 1999).

On the whole, contemporary presidents have used executive orders mostly to oversee the executive branch. In a study of executive orders from 1936 to 1999, Mayer tallied the percentage of presidential executive orders by types. Orders relating to executive branch administration constituted 22.5 percent of all such orders, those relating to civil service were 19.6 percent, orders relating to public lands were 15.6 percent, orders concerning defense and military policy were 11.9 percent, those relating to foreign affairs were 11.3 percent, orders covering war and emergency powers were 7.1 percent, labor policy orders were 5.4 percent, and orders relating to domestic policy were 3.8 percent (Mayer 2001) (see figure 8.3).

Moreover, Mayer discovered certain patterns in presidential use of these orders. Democrats issued executive orders more often than Republicans. Moreover, presidents of both parties tended to issue more executive orders at the end of their terms, espe-

cially before a partisan turnover of the White House. This lame duck effect can have long-term consequences. Although a newly elected president can overturn an executive order with an executive order of his own, he alienates its beneficiaries when he does so. He also brings attention to political controversy at the time he desires a honeymoon from criticism. In his first year in office, George W. Bush issued an executive order to end funding to foreign agencies that promoted or performed abortions. When prochoice senators Barbara Boxer (D-Calif.) and Paul Wellstone (D-Minn.) threatened to debate the order on the floor of the Senate, however, Bush retracted it and issued a memorandum instead—which attracted much less attention.

Rulemaking

During President Clinton's last year in office, he went on a blitzkrieg to get all of his bureaucratic rules in place before the clock struck midnight on January 20, 2001. Through rulemaking, he banned snowmobiles from national forests and ordained certain ergonomic rules for the office. All of Clinton's new rules were suspended by George W. Bush once he took office, but not all of them were termi-

Figure 8.4 Significant Rules, 1981–2000

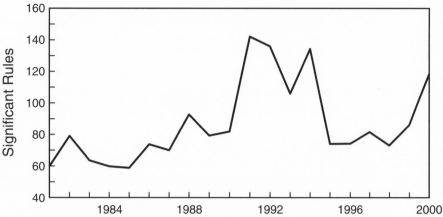

Source: Data compiled by author from monthly and annual tabulation of significant rules posted at www.omb.gov.

nated. Bush successfully reversed the rule on ergonomics and work safety, but most of the other forty-five rules he denoted as "target rules" remained intact because of the administration's sensitivity to its public perception as "antienvironmental."

The past five administrations have shown a pattern of "midnight rulemaking" (see figure 8.4). Despite the almost ritual public pronouncements of outgoing presidents that they will cooperate with the incoming administration in every way possible to facilitate a smooth transition, they have not done so when partisan control of the White House is about to change. Consider Lyndon Johnson, for example. In 1968, when he decided not to run for reelection, the president advised his cabinet not to make it difficult for the incoming administration. Johnson said, "It is neither desirable nor equitable to bind the hands of the next Administration in major program areas unless there is overriding necessity to do so. We should not needlessly foreclose the options of the new Administration to initiate their own program changes. It would be particularly unfair to take actions now which must be implemented over a long period of time" (Pfiffner 1996, 6). Yet although Johnson warned his staff against last-minute actions, he issued more execu-

tive orders and monument proclamations during his final year than in any other year of his presidency.

Similarly, in his last year in office President Carter issued a memo to his staff not to make improper last-minute decisions. Yet his administration issued a record number of regulations in that last year, and Carter himself made a relatively high number of recess appointments.

Bureaucratic rules can have small or large impacts on agencies and their clients. Some of them go virtually ignored by journalists and the public; others gain disproportional attention—such as the ergonomic rules the Clinton administration issued. These rules, which took eleven years to bring to fruition, were intended to help the 1.8 million workers suffering from tendonitis, carpal tunnel syndrome, and lower back pain. The Occupational Safety and Health Administration (OSHA) estimated that businesses would pay $4.5 billion per year for the alterations but would save $9.1 billion per year in compensation claims and lost work days (Haarlander 2001). Business owners and corporate executives were not convinced, however. They put pressure on the Republican Congress to reverse the rules, and Congress did so in 2001, with the active support of the Bush administration.

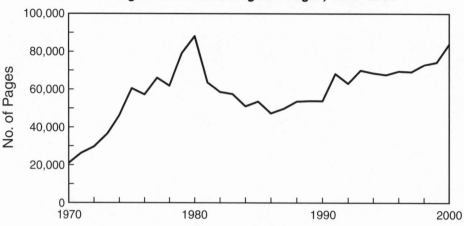

Figure 8.5 *Federal Register* Pages, 1970–2000

Source: Data compiled by author from *Federal Register*.

Critics accused Clinton of abusing his administrative powers by excessive rulemaking at the end of his second term. They pointed to the sizeable increase of the *Federal Register*, the publication in which the new rules are listed, as evidence. Clinton was not alone. According to Cochran (2001), for the past fifty years the postelection quarter experienced a 17 percent increase in the volume of rules issued. Overall, rulemaking has steadily increased in the past three decades (figure 8.5).

More important than the sheer number of pages in the *Federal Register* is the economic impact of the rules issued. In 1981 Ronald Reagan issued Executive Order 12291, which required the Office of Management and Budget (OMB) to review rules and determine which rules would cost more than $100 million. OMB's determination was binding on executive departments and agencies. Through this regulatory review process, OMB has acted as a surrogate for the president, imposing the administration's regulatory perspective on the rest of the executive branch.

Conclusion

Presidents are more likely to use unilateral actions to govern as they near the end of their time in office. They believe that they have

little choice and little to lose. They lack political influence even with their own partisans. With Congress usually in adjournment during the period from the election until the new administration takes over, presidents need to exercise their unilateral powers if they are to exercise power at all. Moreover, they are less able to use their bully pulpit to get the word out because the news media focus almost exclusively on the president-elect, his new appointees, and his policy agenda.

Does this exercise of unilateral powers, particularly during the lame duck period, conflict with the people's judgment as expressed in the election? Many observers believe that it does. They contend that the unilateral exercise of presidential power represents the dying gasp of the old rather than the mandate of the new. Congress—particularly partisans of the party taking over the White House—has complained but not legislated.[1]

The marked increase in the exercise of unilateral authority by the president combined with the persistence of the lame duck effect raises important questions about constitutional balance and democratic government. Has the balance been permanently upset by the unilateral presidency? Have presidents exceeded their constitutional and statutory authority or simply moved into a vacuum created by congressional inaction and reinforced by the electoral calendar and the Twenty-Second Amendment to the Constitution? Why haven't Congress and the courts been more resistant to this exercise of executive authority?

In imposing their personnel and policy judgments, are presidents acting in accordance with democratic principles, or are they engaged in a form of autocratic behavior? Much depends on whether they are eligible for reelection. Presidents who use unilateral powers that Congress does not challenge can still be constrained by judicial decisions and held accountable by the electorate, if and when they run for reelection, but lame duck presidents cannot be held accountable—although they do face the judgment of history. Should additional constraints be placed on lame duck presidents? Should the presidential transition be shorter? Should Congress be required to stay in session? Should statutory discretion that has been given to the president lapse during the final three months in office?

Should the actions of presidents at the end of their administrations be regarded as the completion of the presidency to which they were elected or the imposition of their judgment on voters who have already made their choices and thereby reflected their opinions in the most recent election? Answering this question is difficult enough without the issue of policy agreement or disagreement with the president's actions clouding our own judgment, but it usually does. For example, environmentalists applauded Clinton's monument proclamations, but economic developers protested loudly. Conservatives lauded Bush's recess appointments of Eugene Scalia and Otto Reich, but liberals cried foul. On the other hand, there was almost unanimous disapproval of Clinton's pardon of financier Marc Rich, suggesting that the most capricious decisions—those that are highly personalized, those that circumvent ongoing advisory and decision-making processes—are the most dangerous and thus the most necessary to prevent or discourage.

The exercise of unilateral authority by the president has shifted the power equation in the president's favor. It has made governing possible in periods of divided government and at the end of an administration. But it has done so at the expense of the constitutional design and, in the last three months of a president's term, at the expense of democratic governance.

Note

1. A bill introduced by Representative Ron Paul (R-Texas) would require that the president, in issuing executive orders, cite the specific constitutional or statutory authority upon which the order is based, prohibit delegation of power to a foreign government or international body when no such delegating authority exists under the Constitution, and grant legal standing to individual members of Congress, state officials, and private citizens to challenge a presidential directive they believe is unconstitutional. The legislation would also repeal the War Powers Resolution, end states of national emergency, and make treaties and executive agreements that assign powers not specified in the Constitution nonbinding. The House has not acted on the bill, however.

References

Bennet, James. 1998. "True to Form, Clinton Shifts Energies Back to U.S. Focus." *New York Times,* July 5.

Cochran, Jay, III. 2001. "The Cinderella Constraint: Why Regulations Increase Significantly During Post-Election Quarter." Unpublished manuscript. Available at www.mercatus.org/people.php/23.html.

Conley, Richard. 2001. "George Bush and the Efficacy of Veto Threats in the 102nd Congress: An Archival Analysis." Paper presented at Midwest Political Science Association meeting, Chicago, April.

Gerstenzang, James. 2002. "Contested Bush Nominees Bypass Senate." *Los Angeles Times,* January 12.

Haarlander, Lisa. 2001. "Reducing Injuries through Ergonomics: New OSHA Rules Have Triggered an Intense Battle." *Buffalo News,* January 1.

Loomis, Burdett. 2001. "The Senate as a Black Hole? Lessons Learned from the Judicial Appointments Experience." In *Innocent Until Nominated: The Breakdown of the Presidential Appointments Process*, ed. G. Calvin Mackenzie. Washington, D.C.: Brookings Institution Press.

Mackenzie, G. Calvin. 2001. *Innocent Until Nominated: The Breakdown of the Presidential Appointment Process*. Washington, D.C.: Brookings Institution Press.

Mayer, Kenneth. 2001. *With a Stroke of a Pen: Executive Orders and Presidential Power*. Princeton, N.J.: Princeton University Press.

Moe, Terry, and William G. Howell. 1999. "Unilateral Action and Presidential Power: A Theory." *Presidential Studies Quarterly* 29 (December): 132–79.

Neustadt, Richard. 1990. *Presidential Power and the Modern Presidents: The Politics of Leadership from Roosevelt to Reagan*. New York: Free Press.

Pfiffner, James. 1996. *The Strategic Presidency: Hitting the Ground Running*. Lawrence: University Press of Kansas.

Ragsdale, Lyn. 1998. *Vital Statistics on the Presidency: Washington to Clinton*. Washington, D.C.: Congressional Quarterly Press.

Relyea, Harold C. 2001. "Presidential Directive: Background and Overview." Congressional Research Service document 98-611. November 9.

Shenon, Phillip. 1999. "In Protest, Senator Blocks All Nominations." *New York Times*, June 9.

United Press International. 1985. "Support of Reynolds Elicits Warning from Democrats." *Los Angeles Times*, July 17.

Further Reading

"Clinton's Executive Orders." 2001. www.truepatriot.com/executive_orders.html 2001.

Congressional Universe. 2001. Available at www.lexis-nexis.com/congroup.

Egan, Timothy. 1996. "Clinton Enters Utah over Fate of Wilderness." *New York Times*, September 6.

Eilperin, Juliet. 2001. "GOP Won't Try to Halt Last Rules by Clinton; Hill Power Shift Forces Retreat on Spring Plans." *Washington Post*, July 30.

Federal Register 1970–2002. Washington, D.C.: National Archives.

Garcia, Rogelio. 2001. "Recess Appointments Made by President Clinton." Congressional Research Service document 31112.

Gomez, Brad, and Steven Shull. 1987. "Adoption Versus Implementation: Examining the Policy Context of Executive Orders, 1949–1997." Paper presented at American Political Science Association meeting, Washington, D.C., August.

Judson, David. 2000. "Presidential Land Decrees Seen as Anti-Democratic." *USA Today*, April 3.

Kernell, Samuel. 1997. *Going Public: New Strategies of Presidential Leadership*. Washington, D.C.: CQ Press.

Mackenzie, G. Calvin. 2001. "Nasty and Brutish without Being Short: The State of the Presidential Appointment Process." *Brookings Review* 19 (spring): 4–7.

"National Monument Proclamations under the Antiquities Act." National Park Service document. Available at www.cr.nps.gov.

National Parks Conservation Association website: www.npca.org.

"President Clinton Appoints Roger Gregory to the US Court of Appeals for the Fourth Circuit." White House news release, December 1999. Available at www.whitehouse.gov.

Public Papers of the Presidents of the United States, 1929–2002. Washington, D.C.: National Archives.

"Recess Appointments during an Intrasession Recess." Available at www.doj.gov 2000.

Rivers, Douglas, and Nancy L. Rose. 1985. "Passing the President's Program: Public Opinion and Presidential Influence in Congress." *American Journal of Political Science* 29 (May): 183–96.

Weekly Compilation of Presidential Documents, 1929–2002. Washington, D.C.: National Archives.

★★★

Chapter 9

Can the Federal Budget Be Democratic?
OMB's Invisible Hand

Lynn Ross

Tensions exist in any democratic government. There are tensions between serving special interests and serving the "public" interest. There are tensions between creating open and accessible processes and conducting efficient processes that seek effective outcomes. There are tensions between new and innovative policymaking and routine, bottom-line-oriented program implementation. There are tensions between politics and merit. The Office of Management and Budget (OMB) offers a unique crucible for examining these tensions in the American system of government.

OMB is uniquely involved in designing each administration's blueprint for funding competing interests. Thus, its budget process offers a window into the tensions between those interests. OMB also is charged with overseeing government operations to ensure program efficiency and effectiveness. Thus, its relationship with federal departments and agencies provides a real-world case of clashing demands for open and accessible government and efficient processes that lead to effective programs more broadly defined. OMB's oversight of agency programs points up the tension between designing new and innovative policies that likely require new investment and implementing current programs efficiently, as well as funding new programs within established fiscal targets. Finally, OMB's position within the executive branch—career staff working closely with high-level political appointees within the

president's executive office—brings it face to face with the tension between serving a political agenda and providing analytical and neutral advice that is based on technical merits.

We expect the tensions that arise in democratic systems to be balanced against one another. Specifically, we expect that special interests will have a voice, but not at the expense of the public interest. We expect that political processes will be open, but not to the extent that deliberation paralyzes policymaking. We expect that innovative ideas will spring forth, but not to the demise of good management of ongoing programs. And we expect that legitimately chosen political principals will make critical policy decisions, but not without studying the facts and merits of each case. Political processes and government institutions provide the fulcrum on which such competing demands can balance. For its part, OMB offers a kind of counterbalance to the elements of a system that on their face are democratic (responsive, open, innovative, politically legitimate) but if taken too far can undermine the very system they define.

Methodology

OMB is involved in many varied aspects of the public policymaking process. It coordinates the president's legislative program (Legislative Reference Division); it reviews regulations and government forms, and it develops government statistical policy and information technology policy (Office of Information and

Regulatory Affairs); it is responsible for financial management policy and guidelines to federal agencies (Office of Federal Financial Management); it develops federal procurement policy (Office of Federal Procurement Policy); and it prepares economic models for making economic and fiscal forecasts (Economic Policy Office). These roles make OMB central to the operations of government. The focus of this examination, however, is on the more commonly known aspect of OMB's position in the executive branch—budget office to the president. In particular, the focus here is on the budget formulation process, which tends to be dominated by OMB's resource management offices (RMOs). A focus on RMOs affords a glimpse into the other roles OMB plays because RMOs tend to be involved in most aspects of OMB's work—mostly because RMO program examiners are supposed to be experts in agency programs and, as a result, tend to be involved in most aspects of their agencies' operations. In addition, the budget formulation process, in which RMOs are key players, is the most visible and relevant process through which to explore the democratic nature of government. First, its outcomes represent the public policy priorities of the administration that was elected to represent the people; second, the process itself offers public constituencies the opportunity to weigh in on government priorities, at least during certain key phases—most notably the congressional budget process.

To delve into the particulars of the budget process and OMB's place in it, I conducted several interviews with OMB and agency staff members.[1] Beyond interview data and some of the scholarly literature that considers OMB's culture and historical mindset, I also examined several internal OMB documents: its strategic plan, its training manual, its Management Committee report on workload, its most recent internal "climate" survey (conducted in 1996), and other internal "think pieces." Finally, I have relied heavily on the personal experience that seven years of working at OMB as a program

examiner afforded. Although the particulars of my experience are not the topic of this chapter, and there are notable differences between various examiners' perspectives based on the programs they oversee and other personal factors, seeing the OMB budget process in operation many times, in many variations (under four different directors and two presidents), with a front-row seat, gave me the kind of practical experience that informs much of my understanding of the budget cycle and the dynamics at work inside OMB.

OMB's Historical Context

OMB has remained relatively stable in size and budgetary resources since the middle of the twentieth century. Its staff currently numbers about 520, making it the largest component of the Executive Office of the President (which has about 1,800 employees in total). OMB's mission, power base, and multifarious roles provide an important context for understanding the relationship it has with executive branch agencies, the strategies it uses to get information from those agencies during budget formulation, the power dynamics that ensue within the executive branch, and the extent to which it regards its role as serving the president or the presidency. Following is an abbreviated history, and then a description of some important elements of OMB's culture.

From the nation's beginning until 1921, the Treasury Department gathered executive departments' and agencies' appropriations requests and compiled them, without review, in the "Book of Estimates."[2] Agencies justified their requests separately before Congress, and presidents did not participate in the budget process in any meaningful way. In response to escalating spending and attendant fiscal deficits from World War I, as well as trends in state governments toward improving government economy and efficiency, Congress enacted the Budget and Accounting Act of 1921. This landmark legislation injected discipline (or at least centralization) into the federal budgeting process by making the president responsible for submitting a single budget to the congressional appropriators. The 1921 act also established the Bureau of the Budget (BOB) in the Treasury Department to carry out this new executive responsibility.

Although BOB was housed within the Treasury Department, it was not under the direct authority of that department's secretary. Instead, BOB reported directly to the president. The president appointed the BOB director, but that position was not subject to confirmation by the Senate, which further emphasized the neutrality with which BOB was supposed to operate. Moreover, BOB staff did not traditionally testify before Congress in support of the president's budget because BOB staff were regarded as "neutrally competent," and advocating any position before Congress might give the impression of political involvement. The staff, as well as the director, maintained very low profiles—staying out of the political fray by not appearing at hearings and not meeting with the press. Very few people outside the federal government knew what BOB was.

The 1921 law also set procedures for executive agencies' and departments' roles in budget formulation. Specifically, it prohibited them from lobbying Congress for larger appropriations. "No estimate or request for an appropriation and no request for an increase in an item of any estimate or request . . . shall be submitted to Congress or any committee thereof by any officer or employee of any department or establishment, unless at the request of either House of Congress" (18 U.S.C. 1913). This provision set the stage for BOB/OMB's relationship with the agencies for which it developed those budgets. Because agencies are required to justify the president's budget request—which probably is something less than the agency requests from OMB—it is not surprising that agencies have lobbied Congress now and then for more funding. President Truman, for example, found it necessary to remind agencies and departments that he expected them to support only the White House's estimates at

hearings and in discussions with congressional members. A month after Truman's admonition, BOB issued a circular that outlined what behavior it expected from agencies during the appropriations process (OMB Examiners Handbook 1999, 2),[3] and in 1948 the law was revised to explicitly prohibit departments and agencies from lobbying for appropriations, under penalty of removal from office (18 U.S.C. 1913). Even today the issue of supporting the president's budget still comes up, and agencies are periodically reminded of OMB's requirements. In 2001, for example, Mitch Daniels, George W. Bush's first budget director, sent a memorandum to heads of executive departments and agencies reminding them of this policy after an assistant secretary of the Army violated it while testifying before Congress and was fired by the administration.

Arguably this arrangement created an institutional "us and them" between the agencies and BOB, especially when the president's budget asked for considerably less funding than an agency originally proposed. This arrangement also highlighted the importance for agencies of convincing BOB/OMB that their request was reasonable and should go forward, intact, to Congress.

In July 1970, BOB's successor agency, OMB, was officially established by Executive Order 11541, following the recommendations of the Nixon-appointed Ash Commission. Nixon greatly increased the management arm of OMB—which dealt with program coordination, organization and management systems, and legislative reference—but he also stripped the new organization of some of the policymaking responsibility it had when it was BOB. Nixon preferred to deal with the White House's Domestic Council and other political loyalists on matters related to policy. This preference informed his view about the role the new budget office (dominated by career civil servants) should play. Ironically, Nixon later assigned many of the tasks he had intended for his White House Policy Council to OMB (Tomkin 1998, 50).

Over the succeeding decades, OMB has undergone changes based on who was in the

White House, what the fiscal climate was, and what changes Congress made to its mission. One of the most heated debates spawned by changes in the staff makeup and employment status of OMB leaders was whether the organization was becoming too politicized. In 1973 the OMB director and deputy director were made subject to Senate confirmation, and by 1975 four political program associate directors (PADs) were added to OMB's roster. Before 1968 there had been no more than four political officials in the BOB other than the director and deputy director.

The increase in political positions caused concern among some scholars, who regarded these changes as potentially eroding OMB's analytical capability and the institutional qualities that had allowed it to be "neutrally competent." Hugh Heclo (1975) was one of the first academics to lament these changes. Specifically, he was concerned that PADs would ignore or selectively use "advice on the merits" before it could reach the White House. Shelley Tomkin labels politicization one of the major institutional trends within OMB, and she argues that by the 1970s what had become an "important issue" for OMB became a "potential dilemma" in the 1980s. Specifically, during various presidencies OMB staff members were used to sell particular policies. This development undermined or at least conflicted with BOB/OMB's traditional mission to provide neutral information and advice to the president (Tomkin 1998, 312).

In the 1980s, when David Stockman took over at OMB under President Reagan, OMB underwent an important change in terms of both its operating style and its visibility. Stockman is credited with putting OMB on the map, but he also reopened the perennial neutrality-responsiveness debate. As in the Nixon era, there were concerns during Reagan's presidency that OMB was becoming too political. It was perceived as a strongman for the president more than an unbiased analytical arm—and it didn't help that Stockman admitted to "cooking the books."

There have been eight budget directors and three presidents since David Stockman.

Each director has left a different mark on OMB, based on his or her personal style (e.g., bottom-up versus top-down budget decisions, open interactions with line staff versus hierarchical operations), and each president has used OMB in different ways, with varying degrees of politicization. Yet much remains constant at OMB. As Tomkin argues, "Presidents . . . need OMB to tell them how the public's collective will is being translated into executive governance, with what cost, and with what degree of efficiency. That requirement, most of all, is not likely to change in the future" (Tomkin 1998, 312).

OMB's Abiding Culture

BOB/OMB traditionally has been regarded as an organization that attracts high-quality analytical talent. Even during times when it was charged with becoming politicized, staff members were still almost uniformly perceived as intelligent, hard working, and dedicated (Tomkin 1998, 279–80).

Several scholars attribute the quality standards that OMB has maintained over the past several decades to the "wisdom and foresight" of Harold Smith, Franklin Roosevelt's third budget director (Tomkin 1998, 35).[4] Not only did Smith increase BOB's budget and staff size, he also painstakingly recruited "quality" over "quantity," often leaving slots open for protracted periods until he found the right person for the job. Smith looked for people who had a "balanced outlook and judgment," "planning types of minds," and "social science skills" to fill BOB slots (Berman 1975, 20).[5] Smith highlighted the importance of staff valuing "the good of the organization over their own personal goals" (Berman 1975, 20). He also imbued staff members with the importance of serving the presidency as "institutional career staff, distinct from personal White House aides" (Berman 1975, 22). This culture was firmly implanted within the Bureau, as many of the staff members who "grew up" under Smith remained at BOB for years thereafter. Thus, the norms of excellence, neutral competence, and sense of purpose in serving the presidency became institutionalized within OMB. If Tomkin's in-depth examination of today's OMB is to be believed, these norms still exist.

Another relevant aspect of OMB's culture centers on the short time frames within which OMB operates and the resulting urgency with which it feels it must do its job. While BOB/OMB has remained relatively stable in size, its responsibilities have grown considerably. Just within the past decade, statutes such as the Government Performance Review and Results Act of 1993, the Federal Workforce Restructuring Act of 1994, the Clinger-Cohen Act of 1996, and the reauthorization of the Paperwork Reduction Act of 1995, as well as the year 2000 computer project, have added responsibility to OMB's already full plate. Although OMB tends to pride itself on its heavy workload, long hours, and the stoicism with which it handles its many responsibilities, there is evidence that OMB's operating environment has negative long-term consequences on its capacity. For example, staff turnover in recent years has been exceedingly high—estimated at about 20 percent per year for examiners.[6] This turnover has caused some observers to voice concern about the loss of the very institutional memory for which BOB/OMB has long been valued, especially among those who worry about service to the presidency. In addition, OMB has suffered from low staff morale, which often is attributed to the crisis-management environment in which it operates. In an internal report submitted by branch chiefs, one branch chief described this environment: "One metaphor for working here is that you stand with your tennis racket at one end of the court while a large crowd of agency, White House, and Congressional staff hit tennis balls (each labeled 'problem') at you from all directions. Most balls you return where you want, a few you hit out of bounds, and some you miss."[7]

A final relevant part of OMB's culture emanates from its image as "naysayer." Tomkin says that the "'naysayer' image of BOB/OMB staff has persisted since the creation of the institution in 1921" (Tomkin 1998, 26). This image (and, indeed that part of OMB's culture) is best explained by the role OMB has been set up to play during most administrations, especially when federal budget deficits are large. Specifically, it sees itself as injecting fiscal constraint into the federal budgetary process and, later in its history, with hitting fiscal targets. Because most agencies have incentive to garner financial support for their programs, an organization such as OMB, which considers broader economic implications, often is put in the position of saying no. Of course, not all OMB examiners aim to cut the programs they oversee. Aaron Wildavsky, for example, found great variation among examiners' attitudes toward spending on programs they personally supported (Wildavsky 1964).

Nonetheless, as an institution OMB often is regarded as the people who say no. David Stockman arrived on the job feeling wholly unprepared for what was ahead, but he reported, "The one consolation was that the 600 OMB career staff were dedicated antibureaucrats. They weren't in the business of giving things away. They were in the business of interposing themselves between the federal Santa Claus and the kids and saying, 'Whoa'. . . " (Stockman 1986, 101).

This antibureaucratic reputation has important consequences for OMB-agency relations, for information-sharing between OMB and agencies, and potentially for budgetary outcomes. Furthermore, the institutional history and culture together illustrate OMB's bent on being a watchdog over more parochial forces that vie for public resources; on neutrality or merit-based decision making; and on efficiency, both in terms of process and in terms of government operation. In examining the budget formulation process and the role OMB plays in that process vis-à-vis the departments and agencies, these themes are repeated. Perhaps nowhere do we see the counterbalancing force that OMB exerts on the American system of government more than in its relationship with other agencies during the budget process. In that process

OMB engages in its most deliberate effort to tame the potential excesses and mitigate the potential unintended consequences of democratic processes and institutions.

The Federal Budget Process—How Democratic?

The federal budget is first and foremost a political document. The president's budget proposal represents the blueprint for implementing the agenda the president sets forth during the campaign. Like any political endeavor, the budget process is replete with pressures from various constituencies trying to garner support for their pet programs. The result of the year-and-a-half-long budget process is a policy statement about national priorities for spending the more than $2 trillion that make up the federal budget. There are very few forces in the process that work to limit such spending. OMB is one such force.

The annual budget cycle, which begins with the agency formulation process and ends with annual appropriations by Congress, is dominated by OMB during its middle phase. OMB begins to review agency budget requests in the September or October during the fiscal year preceding appropriations. Before agencies submit their budget requests, OMB typically transmits budget guidance, which conveys the expected parameters of the agency's request (i.e., spending targets) as well as the priorities on which the president will focus in his submission. OMB guidance is analogous to the budget resolution that the congressional budget committees typically pass during the following summer—it outlines broad targets and goals for spending and priorities.

Once agencies submit their requests, the OMB review process begins. The review involves career staff, top political appointees (PADs), the OMB director, and ultimately the president. In September and October OMB holds hearings with the agencies. These hearings are different from most congressional hearings in that they are not open to the public, no witnesses are called, and no formal

report of the proceedings is published. The hearings are designed to get clarifying information about the agency's submission and to understand the agency's main priorities for the coming year. They also provide the opportunity for OMB staff to reiterate the president's position on various relevant policies and programs. The overall intent is to understand the details of the numbers that make up the agency's request.

OMB examiners do not tend to rely on "outside" influences such as interest groups or political organizations in the course of their analysis (although they may consider what political influences are at play and inform their higher-level bosses about such factors). In this sense, one could argue that the OMB budget process is quite undemocratic. No constituencies are given a direct voice during the development of spending targets and priorities. Furthermore, the public is not privy to the questions or answers exchanged during the OMB hearing period, and no OMB decision sees the light of day before it is published in the president's budget. In fact, even after Congress passes the final budget, all details about the agency's budget request, OMB's recommendation, and the dialogue that took place between OMB and the agencies is embargoed. That is, all of the information that was considered in the derivation of the published president's budget is considered "predecisional" and is not released for public consumption. On the other hand, the president's general budget priorities undoubtedly are derived in consideration of political factors; indirectly, agency budgets also are derived with their politically active constituencies in mind.

After the OMB hearing process, examiners make funding recommendations to their bosses (first branch chiefs, then division directors, then PADs). At each step in the organizational chain, funding recommendations can change. Usually in late October and early and mid-November the director holds a review. This process typically involves examiners presenting funding recommendations to the director and other top OMB policy officials who have not previously been involved in the details. Traditionally, examiners have been expected to include some commentary on how the agency, Congress, and interest groups might react to the various funding recommendations (Tomkin 1998, 123). Although the inclusion of this commentary implies that politics enter into examiners' recommendations, there is a sense that staff members pay closest attention to more neutral information, with a strong concern that all assertions made in the issue papers are backed by facts. OMB's training manual advises examiners, "You look objectively at the program. The fact that it 'serves' a 'needy' population is immaterial to you if the service is not effective, is not adequately or efficiently provided, or is not worth the investment. Think about the program in this way. You will be surprised how few people do" (Tomkin 1998, 124).

Tomkin's extensive examination in the 1970s found that the OMB career level emphasized four main factors in providing budget recommendations to policy officials and the president: first, the guidance that was received by the policy level at OMB or the White House; second, budget constraints or the need to protect the taxpayer's dollar; third, the examiner's personal evaluation of the value of the program; and fourth, the information provided by the agency in its budget submission and during the fall process (Tomkin 1998, 124). Thus, although political priorities appear to hold the most sway in staff assessments of agency programs, Tomkin argues, "objective, substantive program analysis was uppermost in the staffers' minds"; this analysis was coupled with a strong "measure of political sensitivity and realism" (Tomkin 1998, 124–25). As we shall see, my examination of career staff role perceptions found similar evidence of a conscious balancing of this kind of neutral advice-giving with political awareness.

In sum, although the part of the budget process that is dominated by OMB's career staff is hidden from public view and devoid of the kind of inclusive discourse usually associated with democratic decision making,

there appears to be cognizance of and an accounting for the political realities that drive budget formulation—both in the sense that agency submissions are likely to be influenced by their clientele groups and by virtue of the fact that OMB staff members are expected to understand and report on political realities. The process mainly promotes two kinds of efficiency, however: micro- and macro-efficiency. Specifically, nondeliberative processes tend to move decisions along quickly, allowing OMB to meet appropriations-cycle deadlines, and closed processes facilitate hard decision making about budget cuts that enable the government to hit the bottom line. These efficiency goals serve the interests of the common good and provide a counterbalance to the other, more political, parts of the budget formulation process.

OMB Political Staff, the White House, and the Federal Budget Process— How Democratic?

Although political influence is felt in the budget process prior to the director's review in terms of the priorities and parameters set for OMB career staff and agency officials, the director's review marks the point at which political officials weigh in on the programmatic particulars. Not every issue or program is presented during the director's review. Traditionally, less politically visible programs or highly complex or technical questions may be decided at the branch or division level, with the PAD providing tacit approval. Thus, there are still opportunities for examiners to play a central role in decisions that may affect an agency's budgets in significant ways.

During the director's review, examiners often are expected to make an oral presentation about the programs, issues, and funding recommendations on which they expect the director to decide. Branch chiefs and division directors (deputy associate directors) also may present information, depending on the political salience of the issue and the branch chief's and division director's personal styles. During this process the director and the director's top lieutenants usually ask the examiners detailed questions about their programs and their funding recommendations.

Once the director makes funding and policy decisions, he or she may take certain issues to the White House for presidential review before making them final and communicating them to the agencies. Presidents differ substantially in their involvement in this part of the process: Some get very involved in these issues and spend significant amounts of time on them; others delegate decision making to key lieutenants (Tomkin 1998, 131). After the director's decisions are sanctioned by the White House, OMB provides a "passback" to the agencies. The passback can take several forms, depending on the administration and the historical precedent that has been set between the particular agency and OMB staff. It can be as formal as a written letter from the director to a department secretary detailing account-by-account funding levels and specific policy instructions; it can be a phone call (usually from a policy official) providing an overall funding level for the entire agency (a "top-line"); or it can be almost anything in between.

Agencies with less political clout usually are less likely to appeal OMB passback than agencies with considerable political backing, either in Congress or by powerful interests. Once appeals are filed and reviewed, final decisions usually are made within two or three weeks. Depending on the administration, the White House review process can involve the OMB director making presentations before the president and the president's top aides (Bill Clinton ran the process this way); it can be a "board" of decision makers (George W. Bush has a committee of three top economic advisors and the vice president review budget decisions and appeals); or it can be almost anything else. The presidential appeals process is not prescribed in law. Like the organization of the White House, the chief executive has considerable discretion in determining the process through which the major agencies of government will be funded—at least before the numbers are transmitted to Congress.

The budget decision process usually concludes around the middle of December, and production of the actual publication—the aggregate accounting and narrative descriptions that make up the president's budget—usually consumes the month of January. The president's final budget request to Congress is submitted on the first Monday in February, as prescribed by law, usually shortly after the president has delivered the State of the Union address.

There are several noteworthy patterns in this process. First, even though the political actors change from administration to administration, the career staff, which holds longer relative tenure, has exercised a considerable amount of influence over the policy and budgetary outcomes—even during the relatively politicized periods in OMB's history. Some of the decisions made by the unelected cadre have a significant impact on the amounts agencies bring forward and request from Congress.

Although career-level decisions have political sanction, civil servants' influence may be a cause of some concern to those who support democratic principles of representation. Specifically, a premium is placed on examining federal programs with an eye toward making them more efficient. Furthermore, the process itself focuses not on weighing the multitude of viewpoints about governmental priorities but on hitting fiscal targets (albeit targets often prescribed in law). Thus, the process favors macroefficiency more than satisfying representational interests. On the other hand, the political level of OMB tends to involve itself most closely and personally in the issues that are the most politically salient and most important to the president—and, initially have a perceived electoral mandate. This political involvement provides a check on OMB's power, just as OMB provides a check on a political system that has the potential to reward special pleaders rather than serve the broader public interest.

OMB's Balancing Act—Regulators, Agency Budget Maximizers, and Neutral Competence

OMB is situated at the top of the federal pyramid organizationally as well as in terms of the executive budget process. This position affords it a less parochial view of federal spending than the departments and agencies have. One of the original intents of having a central budget office was to offer a cohesive and controlled federal spending plan. OMB still plays that role, although, as a "regulator," it must rely heavily on the entities it is charged with overseeing for the information it uses to make budgetary decisions. To fully understand the nature of OMB's role in budget making, it is important to grasp the relationship OMB has with executive agencies, the agencies' incentives during the budget process, and OMB's understanding of its responsibility to the president. These roles and relationships provide insight into the balance OMB strikes internally, as well as the counterbalance it offers in terms of the tensions inherent in a democratic system.

Regulating the Regulators

In general, regulators must strike a balance between cooperating with the regulated entity to get required information and providing unbiased oversight in support of good government. There is an inherent danger for the regulator in being cooperative in this relationship because it increases the possibility of being coopted by the entity over which it has supervision (agency "capture"). Marver Bernstein's seminal book, *Regulating Business by Independent Commission,* concludes that regulating agencies—specifically, the commissioners of those agencies—tend to be ineffectual in providing real oversight for regulated entities. Bernstein (1955) argues that the generally mediocre appointees who are charged with carrying out the public interest are so focused on and influenced by the regulated industry they are supposed to be overseeing that impartial, honest policy judgment often is impossible.

Bernstein attributes commissioners' oversight failure most specifically to the relationships the parties create. He says that "close contacts between a commission and regulated groups dull the perspective of the [regulating] agency" (Bernstein 1955, 157). Bernstein further argues that the commissioners' myopic views prevent them from serving the broader public interest because regulatory decisions tend to be made in the context of special knowledge and special interest in the regulated industry. In fact, many of the commissioners are appointed because they have special ties to (and therefore special knowledge of) the industry they are charged with regulating.

More generally, Bernstein argues that we cannot take the politics out of democracy, which is what the independent commission movement tried to do. Although independence "insures judge-like wisdom, balance, and insight," the commissions he examined were not successful in providing this kind of service because they were not focused on the broader social, political, and economic context in which they were regulating. Bernstein acknowledges that there must be bias in regulatory arrangements, but he argues that the regulatory agency's bias must be in accepting the statutory goal so that it is responsive to its purposes. He concludes that regulators' ability to remain free from the influences of regulated parties depends largely on the "prestige and competence of the regulatory officials" (Bernstein 1955, 265). Bernstein goes on to argue that the support the regulator has from the president and Congress, support for the regulation among the public at-large, and the potency of the regulated groups are critical in the regulator's ability to oversee and sanction effectively.

OMB appears to fit well with Bernstein's notion of effective "regulator" even though he and others examine independent commissions regulating various private industries. Specifically, OMB is "exercising governmental control" (Bernstein 1955, 3) over federal agencies when it reviews their budgets because it makes determinations about whether funds are being spent effectively and whether funding requests meet federal fiscal targets. Moreover, although Bernstein's work focuses on examples of commissions that fail to regulate effectively, the reasons he gives for such failures—inept commissioners who are in bed with the regulated agencies and tend to have parochial views—do not seem to apply to OMB.

First, OMB staff tend to be highly educated; about 60 percent have master's degrees, and more than 10 percent have doctorates.[8] Although educational attainment is not always the best measure of quality, Tomkin says that most reports indicate that OMB is able to attract top talent from top graduate schools, and these staff members are almost universally regarded as the best and brightest in government (Tomkin 1998, 24).

Second, in terms of being coopted by the agencies, the historical evidence as well as more recent information suggests that OMB may suffer from being too adversarial rather than being in bed with the agencies it "regulates." Even during periods when OMB was accused of being more political, as opposed to focusing on its "economy and efficiency" mantra, it seemed to maintain its bad-guy image. It has carried its "naysayer" image through eight decades; indeed, agencies still seem to regard OMB more as an agency that denies than as one that facilitates. For example, when I asked one agency official what biases he thought OMB had, he said, "OMB is focused on reducing budget requests." He also felt that although the situation had improved in recent years, OMB was bad about "giving [his agency] discretion in distributing overall funding increases [provided during passback]." OMB staff members also agreed that the relationship with agency counterparts is not particularly affable. One examiner remarked, "[The relationship between OMB and the agencies] is generally adversarial. Unless an agency is among the chosen few that are the president's highest priorities, it never gets all it wants. Most count on the Congress to

make them whole. That makes control of information of primary importance."

There also appears to be a keen sense among the examiners and managers I interviewed that OMB must keep a larger mission in mind as it works with agencies in the formulation of the president's budget. This mission typically is regarded as being the purveyor of fiscal responsibility. One examiner said, "In the fall [when the budget is formulated], more than any other time of the year, there is a pronounced emphasis on thriftiness, making the analyst something akin to a guardian of the nation's purse strings." Similarly, OMB's strategic plan says that it "has the lead role within the Executive Branch for maintaining Federal fiscal discipline . . . and promoting program efficiency and effectiveness" (OMB 2000, 2).

Most of the OMB interviewees agreed that it was critical to protect sensitive budget information, and little in their comments pointed to a fear of being unduly influenced by agencies. Despite the basic distrust that exists in the OMB-agency relationship, no one I interviewed at OMB worried that they would be "captured" by the agency, and none saw examples of this in the institution at large. Even a manager who argued that one could not stay at arm's length from the agency and still be effective called for viewing agency information with healthy skepticism.

In addition, there is evidence of a keen focus on broader economic goals and administration policy. Each of the OMB employees I interviewed mentioned the overall fiscal targets and the government-wide priorities and tradeoffs that must be considered during formulation. Although there undoubtedly are parochial interests within OMB, the evidence of a broader view seems especially consistent with Bernstein's conception of good regulation. Arguably, meeting fiscal targets and achieving positive economic outcomes are the "public interest" OMB is attempting to serve. In this sense, OMB adopts a presidential perspective, assuming a budget that spends wisely is in the president's interest.

In the end, however, OMB is between a rock and a hard place in terms of getting the information it needs to provide the responsible spending proposals to which it seems so dedicated. Bernstein and others of his ilk would probably approve of OMB's *modus operandi*, but the jury probably is still out on whether this style leads to the most effective budget outcomes. Furthermore, in emphasizing fiscal responsibility over open, transparent processes, OMB sacrifices some democratic values in the name of economic efficiency—which it believes is in the public interest.

Information Asymmetry and Budget Maximization

The adversarial role OMB plays with executive branch agencies comports with a particular view of the incentive structure during budget formulation. William Niskanen (1971) argues that budgets will naturally grow because bureaucrats are driven by self-interest. Such a paradigm leads to budget maximization because senior bureaucrats' utility functions—power, money, income, security, perquisites of office, patronage, and the easy life—are fed by large and rapidly growing budgets.

In terms of communication during the bargaining process, Niskanen argues that bureaucrats give bad information (e.g., poor analysis, self-serving reports) to sponsors when the bureau is in a "demand-constrained" environment. Such misinformation helps agencies justify "bad" spending to the sponsor. In a budget-constrained environment, however, bureaucrats have incentive to find efficiencies, and they provide sponsors with information that favorably portrays improvements. Niskanen argues that the effect of such efficiencies is an increase in output and an increase in budgets. In these cases, bureaucrats prefer that accurate information be disseminated to sponsors and to the public.

Niskanen's notions of budget maximization and information asymmetry also appear to fit with OMB's view of the agencies, although with some important qualifications.

Parkinson, Niskanen, and others argue that budgets will necessarily grow because agencies have that incentive, and they also have the advantage over sponsors in terms of information about their budgets. OMB, at least, seems to regard agencies as budget maximizers, which tends to drive the moderate distrust it feels toward them during budget formulation. One OMB manager said, "All too many times, the department ignores [OMB] guidance and sends to OMB a budget that does not include a good scrubbing, nor a sense of prioritization. Consequently, OMB literally [has to] build the budgets. . . ." Another manager labeled agency budget requests "self-serving." Indeed, agencies themselves admit to this goal—at least marginally. When asked about his agency's main goal during budget formulation, one agency official said, "To provide a basis to defend a budget request that maximizes resources and meets the needs of our constituents." At the same time, many agency officials admitted that OMB is not the only party that focuses on fiscal responsibility: Agency budget offices share a degree of this responsibility.

In terms of gathering information about budgets, there is a sense that some of the information required to develop analytical spending plans simply does not exist, and information that might be damaging to the agency's case for more funding is not provided. One examiner said, "Overall, I'd say that departments typically do a poor job of providing information, which simply reflects that department requests are based less on analysis than on wish lists." Another emphasized the incentives that agencies have to withhold important information: "There is political incentive for the agency to not be completely forthcoming about past spending, program performance, and the basis for budget requests. Some important information is usually provided, but full information is not unless the agency believes providing it will lead to its getting the budget request."

Another disadvantage OMB has in gathering information from the agency is the time pressures under which it operates. Logically, the short time frames cause OMB to focus on its adversarial role because that is more expedient than developing longer-term and friendlier relationships with the agencies. It is interesting that the longest-tenured OMB official whom I interviewed argued for more informal and closer relationships with the agencies than did others with shorter tenures. Similarly, examiners with longer tenures were more comfortable gathering information from "less official sources" within the agency than was the examiner with only two years of experience. In short, it appears to take time to get comfortable with the complicated relationship OMB has with the agencies (not to mention the generally accepted "steep learning curve" examiners face), but it also appears that a longer-term perspective yields an information-gathering style that may be more efficient over the long haul. One oldtimer told me that his cohort of examiners (in the 1970s) typically stayed at OMB for about ten years. During this time they got to know their programs very intimately, and the agency rarely could "pull the wool over their eyes." Furthermore, examiners had cumulative knowledge that they drew upon, which meant that as time went on they were able to ask more sophisticated questions and explore information sources that supplemented what they already had learned. Logically, once an examiner had a base of information on which to build, learning about the increment for that budget year was relatively quick and easy.

Today most examiners leave after three years. Those who remain see high turnover as an institutional threat. In a recent survey, 72 percent of OMB analysts said that the high turnover rate was a barrier to OMB's success.[9] Thus, OMB's short-term focus also may be a function of the short tenure of many of its examiners, which appears to affect both its style and its effectiveness in gathering information from the agencies and ultimately may detract from its ability to serve presidents and the presidency. Short tenures portend limited expertise on programmatic issues, as well as limited politi-cal sophistication. Ultimately, such personnel trends also may undermine the institutional traits that help OMB provide a counterbalance to parochial thinking, budget maximization, and information asymmetry.

Neutral Competence versus Political Responsiveness

Another important element of OMB's role centers on its unique position as the "institutional presidency." As such, it has had to balance neutral, merit-based analysis with the political agenda of the president. Different scholars call for different degrees of tipping on the neutrality-political responsiveness scale. Terry Moe (1985, 239), for example, says that presidents seek "responsive competence" (an executive system that is responsive to the president's political needs), not "neutral competence." Moe argues that from its creation, BOB was an embodiment of the politics-administration dichotomy, "neutral competence," and their conceptual relatives; it was designed to ferret out efficiency and economy in the federal system. Because modern presidents really needed responsiveness more than neutral analysis, however, the institutional arrangement was incongruous with serving administrations that aimed to expand government and implement other activist policy goals (e.g., the presidency of Franklin Roosevelt). As a result, presidents tended to look for support in places other than BOB, such as White House staff. Thus, although Moe does not explicitly call for greater politicization of OMB, he believes that politicization is a rational response to the environment in which it operates. He calls for a "presidential version of neutral competence" (Moe 1985, 266), which he argues would examine political problems and offer nonpolitical solutions to them, making executive agencies more responsively competent.

Other scholars are more cautious about mixing politics into OMB's operation.[10] Some argue, for example, that neutral competence provides the institutional staying power of the executive branch and should not be forfeited in the name of political expediency (see especially Heclo 1975 and Seidman 1998). Others argue that the goals of presidents are not well served by increasing the numbers and power of political officials; neutrally competent advisors (such as those at BOB/OMB) provide better service to the president and the presidency (see especially Campbell 1986 and Light 1995). Colin Campbell, in particular, argues that the debate between trading off neutrality and responsiveness is misguided. Campbell advocates that presidents adopt a combination of the two, which he says will lead to "policy competence." Still others argue that OMB's neutral competence actually has improved its ability to be responsive to certain presidents, refuting the claims Moe made in 1985. Patrick Wolf (1999, 163) concludes that neutral competence survived as a "core" value at OMB even during its most politicized periods. Like Campbell, Wolf does not believe in trading the two concepts off. He calls a choice between neutral competence and responsiveness a false one and argues that a balance between them can be struck: "[OMB] preserved its dedication to professionalism and objectivity even while regularly responding to presidential needs and directives."

Does OMB believe that oversight is necessary so that the budgetary "facts" are presented in an unbiased way, or does OMB aim to serve the political agendas of presidents by providing budgetary options that are consistent with those agendas? My examination found evidence that OMB does both. Its mission statement provides some support for this claim: "The Office of Management and Budget serves the *President* by preparing the annual United States Budget and carrying out other statutory requirements, developing integrated fiscal, budget, program and management policies, leading government-wide coordination in policymaking, and ensuring, through management oversight, government-wide effectiveness and consistency in policy implementation in accordance with Presidential priorities" (OMB 2000, 1; emphasis added).

This statement makes clear that the OMB's focus is on the administration it serves. It is important to note that the president is identified as the key customer—not the presidency. This emphasis implies some measure of political responsiveness and a focus on democratic values embodied in the elected representative of the people. At the same time, embedded in the statement are the phrases "coordination in policy making," "management oversight," and "ensuring . . . government-wide effectiveness." Thus, in describing itself OMB strikes a balance between its role as an agency in the service of particular presidents and an institutional coordinator and overseer of government operations. This notion of balance also came through in the interviews I conducted. Specifically, although the examiners described their efforts to "scrub" the agency's budget request to determine where it was not reasonable, they also emphasized the importance of the prioritization of budget expenditures consistent with the president's program. In many ways the responsiveness-neutrality debate is more on the minds of scholars than on the minds of practitioners. OMB staff members do not perceive much of a contradiction between serving the political agenda of a president and providing solid and defensible program analysis.

Thus, Wolf is right to assert that choosing between neutrality and responsiveness is a false choice. The former supports the latter. Perhaps the best way to understand this dynamic is by concluding that OMB emphasizes its analytical capacity because it serves the president. The neutral analysis of agency budgets lends credibility to the president's budget, and OMB's funding recommendations aim for consistency with the president's priorities. Thus, OMB endeavors to serve the president by critically evaluating agency proposals for consistency with the political agenda and more generally for "good government" practices. To the extent that the president's agenda is consistent with the will of the people, OMB serves a democratic purpose. If the majority does not favor the agenda, the next presidential election will provide the mechanism for change. More broadly, however, OMB provides the mechanism for evaluating the ongoing operations of government as well as new proposals with an eye toward efficiency and effectiveness. This kind of evaluation, if effective, serves the long-term health of the system and meets the demands of the public at large.

What Does the Public Say?

Although Americans rarely if ever are asked about their views of the executive budget process or the effectiveness of OMB, we do know that the public tends to value fiscal responsibility. In 1996, when Americans were asked by the Pew Center for the People and the Press how important it was to them to balance the federal budget, 88 percent said it was very important (62 percent) or somewhat important (26 percent).[11] Interestingly, more than half of those respondents thought that balancing the budget would hurt (20 percent) or not have much of an effect (35 percent) on them personally.[12] These results point to a broader concern on the part of the public—beyond personal finances, that of fiscal discipline for the country. More recently, when reports of the eroding budget surplus were made public, an overwhelming majority of Americans (73 percent) said they thought it was a very or somewhat serious problem.[13] In a 2002 Brookings Institution survey, 56 percent of Americans believed that inefficient government programs were a bigger problem than misplaced government priorities (28 percent).[14]

At the same time, Americans don't tend to feel that government programs should be cut back greatly when given the choice between cutting back to reduce the federal government's power and maintaining government programs to deal with important problems. Twice as many said that programs should be maintained as those who said they should be cut back greatly, and on average respondents placed themselves closer to maintaining federal programs than to cutting them.[15]

In terms of Americans' perceptions about how democratic the federal government is, a 1999 Council for Excellence in Government poll found that Americans do not generally feel connected to government, and fully two-thirds say that the government pursues its own agenda rather than the people's agenda.[16] Americans also tend to blame special interest groups, the media, and politicians for government's problems. Sixty-three percent said the government serves special interests; only 25 percent said government serves the public interest.[17] In terms of trust and confidence in government, only 29 percent of those surveyed said that they could trust government in Washington to do what's right just about always or most of the time, and only 21 percent said they had a great deal or quite a lot of confidence in the federal government (34 percent said they had very little confidence).[18]

Interestingly, the public does not tend to perceive federal employees as a significant part of the government's problem. In the Council's 1999 poll, only 6 percent of the respondents said that federal employees are responsible for what's wrong with government—compared to 38 percent who said it was special interest groups, 29 percent who said it was the media, 24 percent who said it was elected officials, 24 percent who said it was political parties, and 14 percent who said the public itself was responsible for what's wrong with government.[19] Furthermore, data from a May 2002 Brookings Institution survey showed that Americans had a more favorable general opinion of federal government workers than they had of elected officials. Sixty-nine percent had a very favorable or somewhat favorable attitude toward government workers, whereas 62 percent had a positive view of elected federal officials such as members of Congress.[20] Although these results are not conclusive, they do provide some evidence that the public values fiscal responsibility and efficiency; thinks government priorities are often misplaced but views effective program operations as a more critical problem; has limited trust and confidence

Conclusion

In terms of OMB's perspective, the evidence presented above confirms its focus on being the president's watchdog over executive agencies. First, there is a strong sense that OMB is aware of its role as protector of the public's resources. Thus, although it does not seem to be preoccupied with "agency capture," OMB does seem dedicated to a broader goal of reining in the agencies. Because OMB tends to think agencies are not focused on federal fiscal outcomes (with the potential exception of the agency budget offices), it assumes a skeptical and even adversarial posture toward them. The 1921 law that created this presidential budget institution implies that there is a natural incentive for agencies to think parochially, serve client groups, and attempt to extract more dollars from the federal coffers. OMB was created and designed to protect the executive branch from itself (or, at least, to protect the president from his underlings). OMB also gave Congress some cover. Since 1921 Congress has not had to face each agency pleading its own special case for more money. Thus, OMB's organic statute, its history, the culture that grew out of that history, and its current role perception give it a focus on the long-term success of the government's programs more than any particular president's personal success—although efficient and effective government operations reflect on individual presidents as well.

Agencies believe that OMB's main goal is to cut their budgets and exercise other unwanted controls. This belief tends to engender distrust. Distrust seems to beget less-than-optimal information sharing, secrecy, and undemocratic processes. Furthermore, OMB starts at a disadvantage because agencies, almost by definition, know more about "where the bodies are buried" in their bud-

gets (information asymmetry). OMB also is at a disadvantage because of its short-term focus, owing to increased turnover and demands. Thus, OMB has to make tradeoffs between cozying up to agencies to get information and remaining at arm's length to avoid becoming (or even appearing to become) biased. By avoiding agency capture, OMB is better situated to view the broader economic implications of federal programs and to ensure that the public at large is served efficiently and effectively by those programs. The distance between agencies and OMB, the "us-and-them" mentality, and the secrecy of the process provide a check on government programs that might not exist if OMB did not play the role it does. While agencies focus on their particular constituencies, OMB focuses on the broader constituency—the American taxpayer.

OMB also is caught between the poles of neutral competence and political responsiveness. It tends to regard itself as the president's watchdog over budget-maximizing agencies while it is watchdog over the president's budgetary and policy priorities. In this regard, OMB provides the president with an institutional barrier to parochial thinking on budgetary matters, and it provides the venue through which a democratically elected president can implement an agenda knowing that policies and programs have been analyzed and evaluated on their technical merits. This aspect of OMB's role may be the best example of the balance that exists in our system between merit and pure politics. OMB's perception seems to be that one can serve the other. When political decisions are made with the benefit of good, solid analysis, they can serve the public interest more effectively than they would in the absence of such analysis. Furthermore, politics is part of the analysis because OMB must serve the current president, who is democratically elected by the people. In this sense, OMB's balancing act between merit and politics seems not only reasonable but quite democratic. Politicians make better decisions, in theory, when they have the benefit of technical advice and an unbiased review of the potential effects of political decisions.

Thus, OMB brings us face to face with many of the tensions that are natural in a democracy: tensions between special interests and the "common good," tensions between open and deliberative processes and efficient processes aiming for effective outcomes, tensions between innovative policymaking and routine program implementation, and tensions between politics and merit. OMB through its unique history and culture, its part in the budget process, and its relationship with federal departments and agencies provides a counterbalance to the more democratic elements of the system, but its overall effect is democratic nonetheless. In particular, there is evidence that the public values fiscal responsibility and effective federal programs. There also is evidence that the public has reservations about special interests controlling government decision making. Furthermore, the federal budget process in its entirety provides democratic checks on OMB. In particular, if the parameters are drawn more broadly, the budget process includes both the agencies' formulation process and the congressional budget and appropriations processes. Arguably these processes are more open and participatory than OMB's. Federal agencies deal more directly with public constituencies because their policies and priorities are more transparent. Congress must answer directly to voters, which gives it greater political incentive to publicize its decisions, especially when they are popular decisions. Conversely, OMB's hidden processes afford it the luxury of making more unpopular decisions (e.g., cutting programs) without the threat of electoral backlash. If the opinion data are to be believed, these "unpopular" decisions may be just what the public wants. Ironically, OMB's insulation from democratic processes may allow it to generate outcomes that represent the people's collective interests quite well.

Finally, and perhaps most important, OMB serves the longer-term health of the government because its focus is on economic responsibility, efficient government programs, effective public management, and merit-based analysis. Although its success in fulfilling this responsibility is beyond the scope of this study, an organization such as OMB provides an important counterbalance in any democratic system. In a pluralistic system marked by malleable opinions and ambitious politicians, the longer-term focus and stability OMB provides maintains the kind of equilibrium that our democracy needs to endure.

Notes

I would like to express my deep appreciation to staff members at OMB and the agencies who agreed to talk to me about the work they do. I also would like to thank Stephen J. Wayne for another round of guidance and patience. Finally, thanks to Sam Yarnell, who makes the work worthwhile, and Sue Ann Ross, who provides perennial support.

1. I interviewed three OMB examiners (line staff responsible for recommending funding levels on all budgetary accounts): one from the national defense area, one with experience working on two different domestic discretionary budgets, and one who works on construction appropriations and entitlements. Two of the three examiners have had relatively long tenures at OMB (six and eight years, respectively); one is relatively new to examining (two years). I also interviewed two OMB management officials—one branch chief (the first level of management at OMB, which usually is considered to be "in the trenches") and one deputy associate director (second-level management in charge of multiple branches, and top-level career staff at OMB). Finally, I interviewed two agency staff members who have had significant dealings with OMB during budget formulation. One has more than fifteen years of experience in this role, the other approximately seven. The questions were open ended and specifically focused on role perception and executive branch relationships. Although this methodology does not afford the advantage of generalizing to the entire federal government (or even the OMB population), it does offer richness and texture to the analysis. Thus, although I do not claim that the very few interviews I conducted are a representative sample, they do provide an "insider's perspective" on the budget process and the role OMB plays in it.

2. All historical information is taken from the OMB Examiner's Handbook for 1999, particularly a section titled "The Evolution of Budgeting in the United States," dated September 7, 1994.

3. The Circular referred to here is A-10. David Stockman strengthened this circular in 1982 and included it in Circular A-11 (Budget Formulation).

4. Tomkin (1998, 35) cites Fredrick Mosher and Larry Berman as attributing this culture to Harold Smith.

5. From the diary of Harold Smith, May 25, 1940, Franklin Delano Roosevelt Library, as cited in Berman (1975, 20).

6. This figure comes from discussions with OMB employees; these data are not published.

7. Taken from "Toward a More Perfect OMB: The Branch Chiefs' Perspective," 1997, p. 6, (internal OMB document in which OMB branch chiefs forwarded solutions to organizational problems).

8. Demographic information from OMB Internal Climate Survey (unpublished), 1996, p. 1.

9. OMB Internal Climate Survey, 1996, results of questions 23 through 32.

10. See especially Heclo (1975), Berman (1975), Campbell (1986), Light (1995) and Seidman (1998). There is a vast public administration literature on "neutral competence" and the politics-administration dichotomy. The scope of this chapter prohibits a full discussion of that literature.

11. Pew Center for the People and the Press, January 11–14, 1996. Question: "How important is it to you that Congress balance the federal budget . . . is it very important to you, somewhat important, not too important, or not important at all?" See Pew Center for the People and the Press (1998).

12. Pew Center for the People and the Press, January 11–14, 1996. Question: "What's your opinion . . . if the federal budget is balanced in seven years do you think this will help you and your family financially, hurt you and your family financially, or not affect you and your family too much?" See Pew Center for the People and the Press (1998).

13. CNN/USA Today/Gallup poll, August 24–26, 2001. Question: "Do you think the decrease in the budget surplus is a very serious problem, somewhat serious, not very serious, or not a serious problem at all?"

14. Brookings Institution, Center for Public Service, May 30, 2002. Question: "What do you personally feel is the bigger problem with government? Government has the wrong priorities, OR government has the right priorities

but runs the programs inefficiently?" See Mackenzie and Labiner (2002).

15. Brookings Institution, Center for Public Service, May 30, 2002. Question: "If 1 represents someone who generally believes that, on the whole, federal government programs should be cut back greatly to reduce the power of government, and 6 represents someone who feels that federal government programs should be maintained to deal with important problems, where on the scale of 1 to 6 would you place yourself?" See Mackenzie and Labiner (2002).

16. Council for Excellence in Government, May 1999. Agreement with the statements "Government generally pursues the people's agenda"; "Government generally pursues its own agenda."

17. Council for Excellence in Government, May 1999. Agreement with the statements "Government serves the special interests"; "government serves the public interest."

18. Council for Excellence in Government, May 1999. Questions (in sentence order): "How much of the time do you think you can trust the government in Washington to do what is right—just about always, most of the time, only some of the time, or never?" and "I am going to read a list of institutions in American society, and I'd like you to tell me how much confidence you have in each one—a great deal, quite a lot, some, or very little."

19. Council for Excellence in Government, May 1999. Question: "Among the following, which one or two would you say are most responsible for what is wrong with government today—special interest groups, the media, elected officials, political parties, the public, government employees?"

20. Brookings Institution, Center for Public Service, May 30, 2002. Question: "Generally speaking, what is your opinion of (Insert a—elected federal officials such as members of Congress; Insert c—federal government workers)? Is it very favorable, somewhat favorable, somewhat unfavorable, or very unfavorable?" See Mackenzie and Labiner (2002).

References

Berman, Larry. 1975. *The Office of Management and Budget and the Presidency*. Princeton, N.J.: Princeton University Press.

Bernstein, Marver. 1955. *Regulating Business by Independent Commission*. Westport, Conn.: Greenwood Press.

Campbell, Colin. 1986. *Managing the Presidency*. Pittsburgh: University of Pittsburgh Press.

CNN/*USA Today*/Gallup. Nationwide poll, August 24–26, 2001. Available at www.gallup.com/poll/releases/pr030423.asp (accessed July 2, 2002).

Council for Excellence in Government. 1999. "America Unplugged: Citizens and Their Government." [Poll.] May. Available at www.excelgov.org/publication/poll1999/1.html (accessed July 2, 2002).

Heclo, Hugh. 1975. "OMB and the Presidency—The Problem of "Neutral Competence." *Public Interest* 38: 80–98.

Light, Paul. 1995. *Thickening Government*. Washington, D.C.: Brookings Institution Press.

Mackenzie, G. Calvin, and Judith Labiner. 2002. "Opportunity Lost: The Decline of Trust and Confidence in Government after September 11." In Brookings Institution Center for Public Service reports [online]. Washington, D.C.: Brookings Institution, May 30. Available at www.brook.edu/gs/cps/opportunityfinal.pdf (accessed July 2, 2002).

Moe, Terry. 1985. "The Politicized Presidency." In *The New Direction in American Politics*, ed. J. E. Chubb and P. E. Peterson. Washington, D.C.: Brookings Institution Press.

Niskanen, William A., Jr. 1971. *Bureaucracy and Representative Government*. Chicago: Aldine Press.

Office of Management and Budget (OMB). 2000. "Strategic Plan." October 2. Available at www.omb.gov (accessed June 30, 2002).

Pew Center for the People and the Press. 1998. "How Americans View Government: Deconstructing Distrust." March 10. Available at http://people-press.org/reports.

Seidman, Harold. 1998. *Politics, Position, and Power*, 5th ed. New York: Oxford University Press.

Stockman, David. 1986. *The Triumph of Politics*. New York: Harper & Row.

Tomkin, Shelley L. 1998. *Inside OMB: Politics and Process in the President's Budget Office*. New York: M. E. Sharpe.

Wildavsky, Aaron. 1964. *The Politics of the Budgetary Process*. Boston: Little, Brown.

Wolf, Patrick J. 1999. "Neutral and Responsive Competence: The Bureau of the Budget 1939–1948, Revisited." *Administration and Society* 31: 142–67.

Part IV

A DEMOCRATIC JUDICIARY?

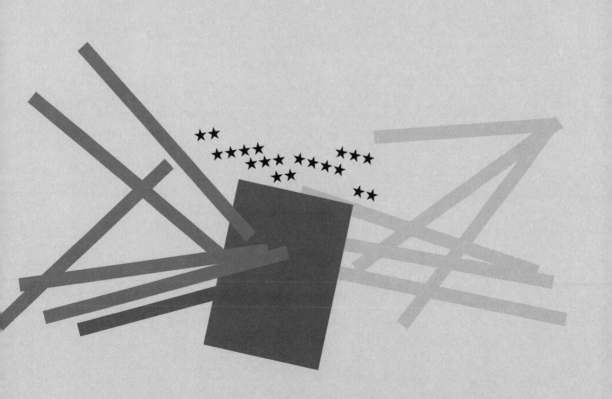

Chapter 10

Does a Real Democracy Need Judicial Review? The Supreme Court as an Antidemocratic Institution

Emily H. Hoechst

Whoever attentively considers the different departments of power must perceive, that, in a government in which they are separated from each other, the judiciary . . . will always be the least dangerous to the political rights of the Constitution....

Alexander Hamilton,
Federalist 78

There is hardly a political question in the United States which does not sooner or later turn into a judicial one.

Alexis de Tocqueville,
Democracy in America

Constitutional scholarship on the issue of judicial review frequently seems to be a Dickensian exercise—the kind we might recognize as a Tale of Two Courts. Judicial review is the best of practices, it is the worst of practices; it is an exercise in wisdom, it is an exercise in foolishness; it is the zenith of freedom, it is the nadir of servitude. Only superlative degrees of comparison seem to suffice. On one point, however, all commentators seem to agree: Judicial review is an extraordinary institution within a liberal democracy—one that seems *prima facie* to be at odds with the principle of rule by the people. As Alexander Bickel pointed out several decades ago, "When the Supreme Court declares unconstitutional a legislative act or the action of an elected executive, it thwarts the will of representatives of the actual people of the here and now; it exercises control, not in behalf of the prevailing majority, but against it. That, without mystic overtones, is what actually happens" (Bickel 1962, 16–17).

The practice of judicial review has long been defended on the grounds that it is necessary to protect against a potentially serious malfunction in the democratic process. A democracy depends for its legitimacy on the consent of the governed, which is secured under conditions in which all citizens have an equal opportunity to participate. Equal opportunity is always threatened, however, by the possibility that an overreaching majority (or a powerful minority, for that matter) may ignore or injure the rights of citizens who cannot politically protect themselves. The framers of the Constitution recognized this possibility and enacted several safeguards— among them the separation of executive, legislative, and judicial powers—to prevent majoritarian abuses. Therefore it is plausible, even necessary, that the Supreme Court should use judicial review to protect minority rights in the service of the Constitution. "Rights-based constraints on the political process are necessary for a well-functioning democracy; they are not antithetical to it. Unchecked majoritarianism should not be identified with a democracy. A system in which majorities are allowed to repress the views of those who disagree could hardly be described as democratic" (Sunstein 1993a, 142).

How can we describe as democratic, however, a system in which nine (or fewer) unelected and politically unaccountable judges can override majority will? Rights-based constraints on the majority may be necessary, but it is not at all certain that Supreme Court justices—unelected, politically insulated, and tenured for life—should formulate and apply these constraints. When the Supreme Court strikes down legislation as unconstitutional, it perpetuates a paradox within our democratic system. As John Hart Ely points out, "It will not do to say the majority rules but the majority does not rule" (Ely 1980, 8).

So how do we reconcile judicial review with democratic principles? One way is to grant that judicial review is undemocratic but to claim that it is justifiably so given the conflicting demands of democratic politics. The concept of democratic government, after all, includes diverse elements that often are in tension with one another. As Stephen Wayne points out in chapter 1 of this book, democratic principles attempt to preserve, among other things, both individual liberty and the collective good. These aims frequently conflict, and where a conflict involves a constitutional issue, perhaps it is permissible for the judiciary to settle the matter decisively. Such an admittedly undemocratic practice is at least arguably reconcilable with a democratic government.

This line of argument claims that although judicial review may be *undemocratic*, it is not *antidemocratic*. The semantic distinction bears great significance. What scholars such as Bickel and Ely claim is that as long as judicial review does not weaken democracy, it is permissible even though its methods are undemocratic. Thus, judicial review supports certain democratic principles—such as individual liberty, equality, or the common good—when they may be unpopular or difficult to enforce. In this context, the argument goes, judicial review does not undermine the larger democratic framework of which it is a part, despite the fact that decisions rendered by the Supreme Court are neither representative nor repealable.

My aim in this chapter is to caution us against becoming too comfortable with this justification. I raise the possibility that judicial review is indeed antidemocratic. In this chapter I argue that judicial review undermines the bases of democratic practice in ways that make our democracy weaker, while it aims to protect and preserve democratic principles. In its most simplified form, my argument is that aggressive judicial review robs citizens and legislators of the opportunity to practice self-government by removing from the realm of the political certain important constitutional issues. I have in mind here not only the phenomenon Mark Tushnet identifies as "judicial overhang," wherein the Supreme Court acts as a safety net for legislators who choose not to be bothered with the constitutionality of the laws (Tushnet 1999, 55–67). I have in mind also the negative effects judicial review may have on our belief that we are *capable* of self-government, including resolution of knotty constitutional issues, without assistance from the Supreme Court. Our sense of political efficacy, I propose, is what is most threatened by an exclusive judicial review of constitutional questions.

Central to this argument is an understanding of the importance of *deliberation*—the process through which citizens, legislators, and judges discuss, debate, and decide important political issues. Deliberation, as we will see, was essential to the framers' understanding of democracy and was intended to be a political skill that all three branches of government, as well as citizens, would undertake. Today that process, within the legislative branch at least, has been all but stifled by the enormous practical demands of our modern democracy. The judiciary, however, still retains the indicia of deliberation, largely because of its insulation from political pressure and its institutional proclivity for cautious and incremental decision making. In effect, the judiciary appears to have assumed the responsibility of political deliberation in the face of legislative abdication (Sunstein 1993a; Tushnet 1999).

Such an assumption of deliberative practice, I argue, weakens our democracy regardless of the ideological bent of any given decision, whether liberal or conservative. The mechanism of judicial review removes the resolution of a political problem from the democratic arena. In exercising exclusive control over difficult political and constitutional issues, the Supreme Court removes from American citizens and legislators the opportunity to figure out for themselves, by themselves, where they stand on matters of constitutional import. Judicial review therefore corners the market on constitutionality, with the undesirable effect of rendering citizens' and representatives' political skills increasingly passive.

In this chapter I examine the antidemocratic nature of judicial review in three sections. In the first section I argue that the process of deliberation has been vital to democratic practice but that current theoretical and empirical descriptions of legislative politics show that we have fallen short of the founders' vision of a deliberative democracy. In the second section I argue that although it is understandable that the Supreme Court has taken upon itself the role of constitutional deliberator, such a practice may have the unwelcome effect of reinforcing the reluctance of legislators and citizens to deliberate themselves. I examine two common justifications for judicial review and demonstrate how each relies on and reinforces legislative abdication of political deliberation. In the last section, drawing on arguments made by Alexis de Tocqueville and the work of Mark Tushnet and Cass Sunstein, I begin to illustrate how democratic self-government suffers under an aggressive practice of judicial review, and I outline the ways in which the Supreme Court might begin to return some political power to the legislatures without completely abandoning its role as guardian of constitutional rights.

Deliberative Democracy

One of the strongest arguments in support of judicial review in recent years has been that the judiciary in general, and the Supreme Court in particular, are more well-suited to deliberate about knotty constitutional issues than are federal or state legislatures. In our understanding of the separation of powers, we apparently have come to accept that the judiciary and the legislature must have very different goals and do very different things. To put it crudely, legislatures do what people want, but the Supreme Court does what is right. As Alexander Bickel writes,

> Courts have certain capacities for dealing with matters of principle that legislatures and executives do not possess. Judges have, or should have, the leisure, the training, and the insulation to follow the ways of the scholar in pursuing the ends of government. This is crucial in sorting out the enduring values of a society, and it is not something that institutions can do well occasionally, while operating for the most part with a different set of gears. It calls for a habit of mind, and for undeviating institutional customs (Bickel 1962, 25–26).

It seems odd for scholars to imply that legislatures should defer to the judiciary in "sorting out the enduring values of society." After all, we entrust our elected officials with the power to legislate to secure those very values. Justifications for judicial review, however, rely on a specific vision of legislative politics that assumes that our legislatures are beholden to the desires of the people, unhampered by considerations of constitutionality. Thus, legislative politics is a politics of preference. As one prominent commentator puts it, "Legislatures are of an entirely different order. They are not ideologically committed or institutionally suited to search for the meaning of constitutional values, but instead see their primary function in terms of registering the actual, occurrent preferences of the people—what they want and what they believe should be done" (Fiss 1979, 10). In contrast to merely satisfying constituent preferences, the judiciary operates at a higher level, above the political fray, as it were. "The task of the judge is to give meaning to constitutional values, and he does that by working with the constitutional text, history, and social ideals. He searches for what is true, right, or just. He does not become a participant in interest group politics" (Fiss 1979, 9).

Of course, it has long been a staple of academic commentary to pit "a principled, deliberative judiciary" against "a reflexive, interest-ridden political process" (Sunstein 1993a, 146). Indeed, there seem to be good reasons to insist that the legislature take its cue from the wishes expressed by the people. A representative government, as we understand it, is supposed to take citizens' desires as they are and is not to attempt to evaluate or change them. We expect our legislatures to be "impartial" or "neutral" among our competing interests, and we are justifiably skeptical of any democratic theory that does not respect the existing preferences of the electorate. Representatives are not supposed to substitute their judgment for our own or to impose their view of what is good on us. We call such actions paternalistic and regard them as an abridgment of our freedom.

The difficulty with the foregoing picture is that it accepts wholesale the view of politics as a process devoid of deliberation. Under this view, legislatures operate as clearinghouses for voter preferences rather than as deliberative bodies themselves. This image, however, is not the way the framers of the Constitution envisioned our democracy at work. Deliberation is supposed to be a widely shared political skill, not restricted to the judiciary. In support of this idea of a deliberative democracy, we can turn briefly to the constitutional debates between the Federalists and the Anti-Federalists. Despite their divergent views on the appropriate form of government, both sides emphasized the need for a deliberative politics within the legislature.

Under neither view was representation supposed to be an unconsidered reflection of constituent preferences and demands.

Initially, of course, the Anti-Federalists were not in favor of a national legislature at all. They devoted their efforts to opposing a strong, distant, centralized government on the grounds that such a government would be too far removed from the daily life of its citizens and therefore potentially abusive. For the Anti-Federalists, civic virtue was an animating principle; they argued for a decentralized government because they believed that true civic responsibility and participation were possible only in small communities. Political participation was important for the Anti-Federalists because it educated people in seeking a common good rather than simply pursuing private self-interest. If citizens were deprived of the opportunity for direct participation, they argued, the principle of civic virtue would be seriously undermined.[1] Eventually, some Anti-Federalists came to accept the practical necessity for representation; nevertheless, they thought that it should be representation of a particularly reflective type:

> When we speak of representatives
> . . . they should be a true picture of
> the people; possess the knowledge
> of their circumstances and their
> wants; sympathize in all their distresses, and be disposed to seek their
> true interests. The knowledge necessary for the representatives of a
> free people, not only comprehends
> extensive political and commercial
> information . . . [i]t calls for a knowledge of the circumstances and ability of the people in general, a discernment how the burdens imposed
> will bear upon the different classes
> (Smith 1985, 340).

The Federalists rejected the Anti-Federalist argument that civic virtue in a people and its representatives would adequately control corruption and rule by faction. For the Federalists, the natural inclination toward self-interest would always arise, even (or maybe especially) in a democracy. In a small republic, a self-interested group could too easily gain power and oppress others by using the political system solely for its own gain. Thus, the Federalists argued, a large republic with many and diverse interests would be better protection against oppression and factional tyranny (Madison 1990, 43–48). More important, however, Madison argued that representation itself might eliminate the threat of a tyrannical faction because it would allow a body of legislators to engage in a form of collective reasoning about the common good. The delegation of power to representatives would allow them to "refine and enlarge the public views, by passing them through the medium of a chosen body of citizens, whose wisdom may best discern the true interest of their country, and whose patriotism and love of justice, will be least likely to sacrifice it to temporary or partial considerations" (Madison 1990, 47).

Both the Federalists and the Anti-Federalists anticipated that the national legislature would be a deliberative body—that it would be able to operate somewhat above the fray of constituent pressures and deliberate on matters of public importance and the common good. This Madisonian ideal, however, stands in sharp contrast to the operations of the national legislature today. The shift away from a deliberative legislature seems to invite aggressive judicial review. Sunstein argues persuasively that the failure of the legislature to deliberate collectively about the laws it enacts necessarily triggers intervention by the courts.

> The original constitutional framework was based on an understanding that national representatives should be largely insulated from constituent pressures. Such insulation, it was thought, would facilitate the performance of the deliberative functions of government. That system of insulation has broken down with the decline of the electoral college, direct election of senators, and,

most important, developments in technology, travel, and communications that have enabled private groups to exert continuing influence over representatives. In these circumstances, it is neither surprising nor entirely inappropriate that the judicial role has expanded and that at least a few of the deliberative tasks no longer performed by national representatives have been transferred to the courts (Sunstein 1993b, 198).

Some empirical research draws an even starker picture. Not only does there appear to be no time or inclination for extended ruminations and deliberations about legislation, there appears to be an increasing amount of pressure against such deliberation. Roger Davidson, a specialist in government and public policy, describes the situation as follows:

> It is well to recall the leading characteristics of lawmaking in today's Congress. First, lawmakers are torn, as always, between the conflicting demands of Capitol Hill and their home constituencies. Second, rising demands upon their time make it virtually impossible for members to devote sustained attention to legislative problems. Third, senators and representatives have responded to burgeoning work loads by delegating the mechanics of lawmaking to staff aides. Fourth, while committees are the main processors of legislation, they are more likely these days to combine their efforts to produce legislative packages or omnibus bills. Finally, ideological conflict . . . produces legislation that is full of compromises and ambiguities (Davidson 1988, 115).

If this description is at all accurate, we are very far indeed from the deliberative representation envisioned by the Federalists and the Anti-Federalists alike. What we have instead is an open marketplace of competing interests, complete with all the freedom and all the structural inequalities of the economic marketplace. As Sunstein is careful to note, however,

> There is a crucial difference between the economic principle of "consumer sovereignty"—by which consumers, in markets, decide on the allocation of goods and services through registering their "preferences"—and the Madisonian principle that vests ultimate sovereignty in the people. On the Madisonian principle, citizens and representatives are supposed not to seek and pay for "what they want," but to deliberate about social outcomes. They are required to offer reasons on behalf of one view rather than another. They are required to listen and talk to one another. The goal, in Madison's own words, is a system of "discussion" in which "minds [are] changing," in which "much [is] gained by a yielding and accommodating spirit" and in which no man is "obliged to retain his opinions any longer than he [is] satisfied of their propriety and truth, and . . . open to the force of argument" (Sunstein 1993a, 164).

If legislative politics operates on the model of the free market, focusing on constituent satisfaction, it would seem to be a positive development that the judiciary assumes more of the deliberative function regarding constitutional issues. Such an assumption may have the unfortunate effect, however, of reinforcing legislative abdication and weakening this aspect of democracy over time. Indeed, when we examine the most prominent arguments offered in support of judicial review, we find that they operate on the assumption that the legislature is not capable of resolving the hardest constitutional issues. Such an assumption is extremely detrimental to representative democracy.

Judicial Review and Political Practice

When we look at the strongest arguments in favor of judicial review, we find embedded within them the belief that legislators and citizens are unfit to divine the constitutional "truth." Such arguments fall roughly into two categories, which I call retrospective and prospective justifications. Beneath both justifications lies the unquestioned assumption that legislatures do not subject their constituent or interest group preferences to constitutional scrutiny or review and that they do not deliberate about a broader common good. As a result, both the retrospective and the prospective arguments in favor of judicial review tend to reinforce significant abdication of deliberation by the legislature.

A retrospective justification recalls the democratic roots of the Constitution and claims to adhere to its original framework in evaluating current legislation. Retrospective justifications for judicial review argue that the Supreme Court intervenes against the political majority only when that majority threatens to subvert the constitutional intent of the framers. Judicial review, in this line of argument, is not an unjustified grasp for power. It is the enforcement of historically enacted restraints on political power—a balancing of rights in the face of potentially abusive democratic processes. "Of course side constraints on majority rule are necessary, but as the framers wisely decided, it is saner and safer to set them down in advance of particular controversies than to develop them as we go along. . . . It is also . . . more democratic, since the side constraints . . . have been imposed by the people themselves" (Ely 1980, 8).

Retrospective justifications come in a variety of types, variously labeled originalism, formalism, and (less helpfully) judicial conservatism. Sometimes historical conservatives raise retrospective justifications in an attempt to criticize modernity out of nostalgia for an older, allegedly more virtuous time.[2] Retrospective justifications claim legitimacy on the basis of an almost totemic adherence to some "factual" basis, such as the text of the Constitution or the historical record of the framers' intentions. Retrospective justifications therefore can provide a modicum of security in the flux of politics.

Of course, retrospective justifications have their problems. To begin with, we know that the adoption of the Constitution was not as democratic as we would have liked because votes for its ratification excluded slaves and women. We also know that judicial review was not an explicit part of the Constitution; it was cleverly fashioned by Chief Justice John Marshall in *Marbury v. Madison*. The point is not to critique retrospective justifications. It is that by rejecting current political decisions in favor of past interpretations, retrospective justifications imply that the Supreme Court alone is capable of pronouncing constitutionality. The Court must be the one to interpret the Constitution because only it recognizes that the framers' (considered, deliberative) solutions are superior to our own (hasty, ill-considered) preferences.

Prospective arguments in favor of judicial review spring from the democratic commitment to enduring values such as liberty and equality. Prospective justifications argue that judicial review supplies a much-needed corrective to the inevitable myopia of democratic politics. Under these kinds of arguments, the Supreme Court exercises its power to support and nurture the long-range view of democratic aspirations, which legislatures by their nature cannot indulge. Prospective justifications remind us that a democratic government seeks both short-term solutions and deeper, more stable values, which will help to buffer society from the freely changing whims of the majority.

In addition, the prospective justification keeps alive the thought that our democracy exists not only for ourselves but also for our posterity. "The heart of the democratic faith is government by the consent of the governed. The further premise is not incompatible that the good society not only will want to satisfy the immediate needs of the greatest number but also will strive to support and maintain enduring general values" (Bickel 1962, 27).

Yet prospective justifications of judicial review implicitly claim that the future good of our government is more secure in the Supreme Court's hands than in our own. From this standpoint, our public values are too important to languish in the legislative arena. The Court must step in where Congress fears to tread.

Both the retrospective and the prospective defenses of judicial review take as their starting point the inadequacy of the legislature and the public to the task of principled deliberation about constitutional values. Judicial review is defended either as an artifact of a more intelligent and reasonable time or as the only way to ensure that we do not gamble away our children's political inheritance. As we will see in the final section, however, relegating constitutional deliberation to the Supreme Court has enormous consequences for the practice of self-government.

The Antidemocratic Tendencies of Judicial Review

Judicial review has always had its critics, who argue that the Supreme Court should take a limited role in constitutional interpretation. Gerald Rosenberg's research leads him to conclude that "court decisions are neither necessary nor sufficient for producing significant social reform" (Rosenberg 1991, 35). Donald Horowitz reaches much the same conclusion, based on his understanding of the unique features of adjudication that make it particularly ill-suited to solving broad social issues (Horowitz 1977). Rosenberg and Horowitz focus on the institutional inefficiencies of judicial review; their arguments take for granted the desirability of social change, but they criticize the Supreme Court as a vehicle for such change. My argument is complementary but slightly different.

The argument that judicial review actually harms democratic practice—that it is antidemocratic—applies whether we consider the Supreme Court effective or ineffective with regard to social change. It applies whether we think the Court is right or wrong, capable or incapable, too liberal or too conservative. This argument claims that even if the Supreme Court is extremely skillful at resolving constitutional issues (and, of course, especially if it is not), judicial review is not good for democratic government because it removes the decision and the responsibility for its outcomes from the people and their representatives.

James Thayer perhaps most forcefully captures the antidemocratic nature of judicial review in his book on John Marshall:

> It should be remembered that the exercise of [judicial review], . . . even when unavoidable, is always attended with a serious evil, namely, that the correction of legislative mistakes comes from the outside, and the people thus lose the political experience, and the moral education and stimulus that comes from fighting the question out in the ordinary way, and correcting their own errors. The tendency of a common and easy resort to this great function . . . is to dwarf the political capacity of the people, and to deaden its sense of moral responsibility. It is no light thing to do that" (Thayer 1901, 22).

The political experience and education of which Thayer writes is intimately connected to the practice of deliberation that both the Federalists and the Anti-Federalists agreed was necessary. The Federalists and Thayer inhabited a very different world, however, from the one in which we find ourselves today. The biggest challenge to democratic deliberation comes not from theoretical but from practical concerns: How can a nation of this size and scope possibly be governed by an antiquated system of representation and an idealized notion of deliberation on the common good? The breadth of issues that the Supreme Court decides may seem overwhelming—First Amendment issues of freedom of speech and religion, the constitutionality of election reform and campaign finance laws, the legal status of the right to abortion, a myriad of privacy issues concerning the family and homosexuality, questions of criminal procedure under the Fourth Amendment, regulation of interstate commerce, the equal protection clause, states' rights concerns, duties and liabilities of federal agencies, and the legitimacy of election outcomes, to name a few. Perhaps our choice (if indeed it is a choice) to delegate resolution of constitutional issues to the judiciary is wise, given that we the electorate, and our representatives, have neither the time nor the inclination to engage all of these issues.

By delegating the deliberative function to the judiciary, we relieve ourselves of a great many pressing concerns and free ourselves for more enjoyable pursuits. Moreover, whether we agree or disagree with the outcome, there is a welcome measure of security in a Supreme Court decision. The Court gives us one answer per issue, and the answer has the force of law. Political solutions are rarely so clear and so certain; they often contain compromises and ambiguities. The Supreme Court, however, enjoys a kind of superior position; like an institutional father figure, the Court weighs the issues and then informs us of its decision. We political children are expected to abide by the rules.

As I hope I have made clear, allowing the judiciary to assume the deliberative role carries particular political and psychological costs. Politically, we place ourselves at a distance from the issues at stake; we lose touch with the particular manifestations of constitutional questions. Constitutional law becomes something that happens "out there," in the specialized arena of the courts, rather than in our midst and within our communities. Not only do we lose a measure of control over the outcome, we also lose the experience of confronting an issue by confronting one another, exchanging views and assessing evidence, making judgments and voicing arguments. We divest ourselves of political responsibility because the issues are too complicated, too important, or both.

Tocqueville expressed precisely this concern when he wrote of the kinds of despotism democratic nations have to fear. It is not the violent tyranny of ages past that threatens democracy but the subtle and persistent paternalism of a government that Tocqueville describes as "an immense protective power" that guards the people and "is alone responsible for securing their enjoyment and watching over their fate. That power is absolute, thoughtful of detail, orderly, provident, and gentle. . . . It provides for their security, foresees and supplies their necessities, facilitates their pleasures, manages their principal concerns, directs their industry, makes rules for their testaments, and divides their inheritances. Why should it not entirely relieve them of all the trouble of thinking and all the cares of living?" (Tocqueville 1969, 692).

The lure of security is powerful, particularly in the global climate of fear we experience today. Limiting uncertainty seems worth the tradeoff in intangible democratic benefits. Again, however, such a delegation has psychological costs that seem innocuous but are in fact disastrous for democratic practice. "Thus [the government] daily makes the exercise of free choice less useful and rarer, restricts the activity of free will within a narrower compass, and little by little robs each citizen of the proper use of his own faculties" (Tocqueville 1969, 692).

Within current constitutional scholarship there are two proposals for ameliorating the deleterious effects of judicial review. The more radical proposal, offered by Mark Tushnet, advocates "ending the experiment" of judicial review over the next five years or so (Tushnet 1999, 154*ff.*). To his credit, Tushnet is honest about the uncertainty inherent in his proposal. "What would a world without judicial review look like? It might look like Stalinist Russia. Or it might look like Great Britain, which does not have a written constitution, or the Netherlands, which has a written constitution that the courts do not enforce" (Tushnet 1999, 163). Tushnet argues that constitutional law does not disappear without judicial review but that it becomes a *populist* constitutional law, the practice of which he asserts already occurs in many

places outside of the judiciary. Ending judicial review, Tushnet argues, would have "one clear effect: It would return all constitutional decision-making to the people acting politically. It would make populist constitutional law the only constitutional law there is" (Tushnet 1999, 154).

Here, however, our need for certainty and security may become acute. Although judicial review might usurp our opportunities for deliberation, a populist constitutional law throws our most important rights and securities up for political contestation. Leaving issues such as equal opportunity or abortion to the political process and the voting public may cause even a staunch populist to think twice. Tushnet has no guarantee against the possibility of political error, though he does offer some reassurance. "Populist constitutional law returns constitutional law to the people, acting through politics. Just as judges can, the people can give wrong answers to important questions. Populist constitutional law offers no guarantees that we will end up with progressive political results. But, of course, neither does elitist constitutional law" (Tushnet 1999, 186).

A less radical solution, proposed by Cass Sunstein, is that the Supreme Court voluntarily restrict the practice of judicial review to cases that concern an abridgment of the right to equal political participation. This approach, Sunstein claims, would leave the Court with more than enough to do, and it would ensure that the political process operates reasonably fairly in deciding the "substantive" issues (Sunstein, 1993a). Nonetheless, there is a difficulty with regard to line-drawing: Sunstein is in favor of a broad conception of "political" rights. Securing equal political participation, in his view, means providing redistributive economic assistance, guaranteeing certain educational opportunities, and preventing wealthy corporations from monopolizing political speech under the protection of the First Amendment (Sunstein 1993a, 197–231). One wonders whether this list really restricts judicial review at all because a great many rights could arguably be linked to political participation. This observation seems to be Tushnet's objection to this approach, and it is why he supports a more radical break with the practice of judicial review. Sunstein's conceptual point, however, supports the argument here: It is better for our democracy to leave certain constitutional decisions to the political process, with the proviso that the Supreme Court must do everything it can to protect the political process itself.

Conclusion

Under either proposal, it is difficult to put aside the anxiety that we will undoubtedly feel upon staying the hand of the Supreme Court to try our own at politics. Sunstein and Tushnet ask us to trust our legislatures before those legislatures have proven themselves trustworthy. They ask us to risk our rights, our views, and our ways of life in the open forums of public deliberation. They ask us to admit the possibility of errors and accept responsibility for correcting them. They ask us to trade a comfortable judicial certainty for the arduous and insecure political unknown.

In this regard, our longing for security should not induce us to shirk our democratic responsibilities, lest we find ourselves incapable of self-government at all. Both Tushnet's radical proposal and Sunstein's more gradual curtailment of judicial review make progress in the direction of reclaiming our democratic practices. Neither theorist claims that the reclamation will be easy or even successful. They know, as did Tocqueville, that "nothing is harder than freedom's apprenticeship. The same is not true of despotism. Despotism often presents itself as the repairer of all the ills suffered, the supporter of just rights, defender of the oppressed, and founder of order. . . . But liberty is generally born in stormy weather, growing with difficulty amid civil discords, and only when it is already old does one see the blessings it has brought" (Tocqueville 1969, 240).

Notes

1. For this overview of the Anti-Federalist position I am indebted to Sunstein (1993b), 174–81.
2. Justice Hugo Black and, more recently, Robert Bork have both favored retrospective justifications in this sense.

References

Bickel, Alexander. 1962. *The Least Dangerous Branch: The Supreme Court at the Bar of Politics.* New Haven, Conn.: Yale University Press.

Davidson, Roger H. 1988. "What Judges Ought to Know about Lawmaking in Congress." In *Judges and Legislators,* ed. Robert A.. Katzmann. Washington, D.C.: Brookings Institution.

Ely, John Hart. 1980. *Democracy and Distrust.* Cambridge, Mass.: Harvard University Press.

Fiss, Owen. 1979. "Foreword: The Forms of Justice." *Harvard Law Review* 93: 1.

Horowitz, Donald. 1977. *The Courts and Social Policy.* Washington, D.C.: Brookings Institution.

Madison, James. 1990. *The Federalist* No. 10. Edited by George Carey and James McClellan. Dubuque, Iowa: Kendall-Hunt Publishing.

Moore, Wayne D. 1996. *Constitutional Rights and Powers of the People.* Princeton, N.J.: Princeton University Press.

Rosenberg, Gerald. 1991. *The Hollow Hope: Can Courts Bring About Social Change?* Chicago: University of Chicago Press.

Smith, Melancton. 1985. *The Anti-Federalist.* Edited by Herbert J. Storing. Chicago: University of Chicago Press.

Sunstein, Cass. 1993a. *The Partial Constitution.* Cambridge, Mass.: Harvard University Press.

———. 1993b. "The Enduring Legacy of Republicanism." In *A New Constitutionalism: Designing Political Institutions for a Good Society,* ed. Stephen Elkin and Karol Soltan. University of Chicago Press.

Thayer, J. B. 1901. *John Marshall*. Boston: Houghton Mifflin.

de Tocqueville, Alexis. 1969. *Democracy in America*. Translated by George Lawrence, edited by J. P. Mayer. New York: Harper & Row.

Tushnet, Mark. 1999. *Taking the Constitution Away from the Courts*. Princeton, N.J.: Princeton University Press.

★★★

Chapter 11

Entering the "Political Thicket": The Unintended Consequences of the Supreme Court's Reapportionment Decisions

Steve Glickman

All, too, will bear to mind this sacred principle, that though the will of the majority is in all cases to prevail, that will to be rightful must be reasonable; that the minority possess their equal rights which equal law must protect, and to violate would be oppression.

—Henry S. Commager, *Majority Rule and Minority Rights*

As Thomas Jefferson articulated in his first Inaugural Address, the American political system encapsulates the inherent tension between two fundamental principles: majority rule, under which people can make government conform to their will, and individual rights, which places certain limits on the authority of such a government (Commager 1943, 4–8). Although majority rule often has been cited as the central tenet of democracy, arguably the preservation of individual rights has historically been regarded as foremost to *American* democracy. Only through protection of these rights can our government achieve legitimacy in the eyes of people of all races and classes—a sentiment embodied by the Equal Protection Clause of the Fourteenth Amendment to the Constitution. On the heels of the Civil War, Congress expressly included a guarantee through the Fourteenth Amendment that "No State shall make or enforce any law which shall abridge the privileges or immunities of citizens of the United

States . . . nor deny to any person within its jurisdiction the equal protection of the laws."

Nonetheless, federal and state legislatures occasionally have created policy that has fallen short of this constitutional mandate, forcing the judiciary to inherit the often precarious and difficult responsibility of safeguarding the delicate balance between majority rule and minority rights. Some of the most controversial recent Supreme Court decisions have been cases dealing with voting rights issues, particularly in response to discriminatory methodologies that many Southern state legislatures utilized in apportioning their legislative seats. Through a broad examination of the Supreme Court's regulation of legislative apportionment, I explore in this chapter the inherent problems the Court faces in exerting its institutional power of judicial review within the fundamentally political sphere of the electoral process.

Although many eminent scholars have applauded the Supreme Court's reapportionment decisions as necessary interventions within the traditional legislative sphere of redistricting (and with the understanding that it may be unfair to criticize the Court's involvement in retrospect through counterfactual arguments), in this chapter I argue that the courts lack the tools or foresight effectively to adjudicate what are essentially legislative issues. Despite the Supreme Court's initial efforts to chisel out a system that would guarantee equal access to the political process, the Court has only superficially improved minority "descriptive" representation, at the expense of the far more crucial objective: minority "substantive" representation. The racial gerrymandering that has resulted from these "reapportionment cases" has served as a temporary band-aid, but it also unintentionally has provided a formula for the suppression of African American voters in the South and a subsequent reduction of representatives sympathetic to their political concerns.

Debating the Judiciary's Role in Protecting Minority Rights

Racial discrimination has been deeply embedded within the constitutional framework from its inception, and both the document itself and those empowered to interpret and enforce its provisions have been extraordinarily resistant to formal change.[1] In fact, the framers had very specific reasons for ensuring that the American political structure would maintain its status quo. For example, *Federalist 10* warns against the dangers of majority tyranny and suggests ways to design institutions to prevent the abuse of minority rights by the majority in power. Although the *Federalist Papers* do not explicitly provide a role for the courts as watchdogs, *Federalist 78* does allude to the responsibility the judiciary has for enforcing the Constitution's underlying principles, and some courts have interpreted this duty as a demand for active judicial oversight (Winter 1979, 33).

Many scholars have criticized such oversight, known as "judicial activism," on the grounds that it usurps the legislature's role to respond to the majority's wishes. In a landmark work, *The Least Dangerous Branch*, Alexander Bickel (1962) argues that "judicial review is a deviant institution in the American democracy" because its existence prevents a representative majority from having the power to reverse a Supreme Court decision (made by unelected justices) (Bickel 1962, 18). For Bickel, the central characteristic of American democracy was popular representation through elections, and judicial review clearly runs counter to this charac-

teristic. Although Bickel certainly was aware that American government was built on a system of checks and balances and that judicial review can be understood as an additional check against the elected branches, Bickel believed that judicial review was unique because of its finality (Bickel 1962, 19–23).

On the flip side of this debate is the school of thought that argues that the United States is a constitutional democracy and that the Constitution specifies or places limits on majority rule and the normal operation of electoral democracy—limits that are widely accepted by the American people. When judicial review is used to enforce these limits, it simply functions as a further check on majority will. Usually the limits that the Supreme Court enforces are those having to do with individual liberties—rights considered to be especially vulnerable to majoritarian violations. Thus, judicial review differs only in degree, and not kind, from other countermajoritarian restraints built into the American political system, such as legislative bicameralism, the Electoral College, and the presidential veto.

The Court Begins to Carve Itself a New Role: *Carolene Products* and Its Critics

The modern debate about judicial review was spurred in the 1930s, when the Supreme Court began to take upon itself the responsibility of defending individual rights—particularly rights related to the political process. When the power of judicial review has been used to protect individual rights, it has been justified on the grounds that the exercise of such rights by minorities is least likely to be protected by the democratic process. If majorities have an incentive to deprive their opponents of their political rights—because doing so helps the majority retain and exercise power—the Court can play a legitimate role in defending against majoritarian incursions, or so the argument goes.

This reasoning emerged clearly in the famous footnote 4 of the Supreme Court's *United States v. Carolene Products Company*

(1938) decision.[2] In this footnote, Justice Harlan Fiske Stone contended that the Court should strictly enforce the Constitution when the legislation in question clearly infringes a specific right identified in the text of the Constitution, excludes citizens from the political process, or results from prejudice against "discrete and insular minorities." The latter two criteria suggest that there is a special need for the Supreme Court to intervene when minority rights are being violated, even when no specific provisions of the Constitution are contravened (Griffin 1996, 105).

In "The Origins of Judicial Activism in the Protection of Minorities," Robert Cover notes that Stone's decision extends the scope of judicial review "not in terms of the special value of certain rights, but in terms of their vulnerability to perversions by the majoritarian process" (Cover 1982, 1291). In defense of the *Carolene Products* decision, Cover emphasizes that because of the discreteness and insularity of certain minorities, such as African Americans, we cannot trust "the operation of those political processes ordinarily to be relied upon to protect minorities" (Cover 1982, 1296).

Martin Shapiro (1964) takes this line of argument further in *Law and Politics in the Supreme Court: New Approaches in Political Jurisprudence*. Shapiro contends that when the other two branches will not act—for whatever reason—to remedy racial discrimination, the Supreme Court *must* step in and take action, particularly in cases involving discrimination against racial minorities. According to Shapiro, providing equal opportunity through protection of minority rights does not deviate from democracy because majority rule serves only as the means by which political equality can be achieved.[3] Shapiro's arguments certainly are attractive on their face; in retrospect, however, they fail to recognize fully the potential political repercussions of such Supreme Court attempts to regulate the political process.

The 1960s "Reapportionment Revolution"

In the 1960s the Supreme Court engaged in its most systematic exploration of the meaning of political equality. Beginning with its decision in *Baker v. Carr* (1962), the Court took on some of the issues that are central to American democratic theory. *Baker* originated with a lawsuit against the state of Tennessee, which had not reapportioned its legislative districts in sixty years—even though its state constitution and a 1901 act of its legislature called for reapportionment every ten years. The Supreme Court declared in *Baker* that the issue of legislative districting was "justiciable" under the Fourteenth Amendment—meaning that the Court had the authority to assess the fairness of the electoral schemes undergirding representation in state legislatures. In a famous dissenting opinion, Justice Felix Frankfurter criticized the majority for leading the Court into a "political thicket" that could ensnarl it in partisan political conflicts and thereby rob it of its legitimacy:

> The notion that representation proportioned to the geographic spread of population is so universally accepted as a necessary element of equality between man and man that it must be taken to be the standard of a political equality preserved by the Fourteenth Amendment . . . is, to put it bluntly, not true . . . every strand of this complicated, intricate web of values meets the contending forces of partisan politics. The practical significance of apportionment is that the next election results may differ because of it. Apportionment battles are overwhelmingly party or intra-party contests.[4]

Although Frankfurter overstates his case to a certain extent—because the Supreme Court probably does have a certain role in ensuring equal voting opportunities for all citizens—his warning has proven to be remarkably prophetic. As reapportionment and redistricting more commonly became judicial matters, the Court literally has invited legal challenges to apportionment schemes in nearly every state. Within twenty months of the *Baker* decision, thirty-nine states faced lawsuits challenging prevailing districting arrangements, thereby providing the groundwork for the second major reapportionment case: *Reynolds v. Sims* (1964) (Hacker 1964, 37).

The background for the *Reynolds* case was similar to that in *Baker.* Voting districts in Alabama had not been redrawn for fifty years. During that time frame, Alabama's population had shifted from farming communities to cities and suburbs, but the rural counties (comprising just one-quarter of the population) remained in control of both houses of the state legislature. Several Birmingham residents went to court, charging that their votes had only one-sixteenth the weight of rural voters. In its decision, the Supreme Court struck down all state legislative systems in which apportionment was based on geography rather than population. The opinion enunciated three principles concerning the "right" to vote and voter equality that have set the standard for all subsequent court cases: Voting is a fundamental right because it preserves all rights; equal representation means that one person's vote is worth as much as another's, and the constitutional standard therefore is "one person, one vote"; and the individual, rather than the group, is the fundamental political unit of representative government.

Most notably, by creating a "one person, one vote" standard that superseded districting along geographic lines, the Supreme Court unintentionally created a formula for gerrymandering.[5] Ironically, this formula made group politics even more prevalent—in direct violation of the third *Reynolds* principle. As a result of the *Reynolds* decision, legislative districting became a permanent part of the Court's docket. As Frankfurter had envisaged, these reapportionment cases plunged the Supreme Court into a political thicket from which it would not be able to extract itself.

The Voting Rights Act of 1965 and the Shifting Legal Sands

The *Baker* and *Reynolds* decisions did not alter the political atmosphere singlehandedly. Just one year after *Reynolds* was decided, Congress passed the Voting Rights Act (VRA) of 1965 with the ostensible goal of increasing opportunities for African Americans to select adequate political representation to Congress. Originally this legislation was proposed to enforce the Fifteenth Amendment in states that excluded African Americans from the ballot. At the time, the percentage of voting-age African Americans registered in the South was only 35.5 percent, compared with 73.4 percent of voting-age whites (Grofman, Handley, and Niemi 1992, 21). The most powerful provision of the VRA was Section Five, which mandated that the U.S. Attorney General had to "preclear" all redistricting plans in certain states to ensure that the changes did not perpetuate voting discrimination. (Essentially, if a plan decreased the ability of minority voters to elect minority candidates, it discriminated). Thus, the VRA gave the Justice Department distinct but overlapping responsibilities: to exercise preclearance powers *and* to urge its own interpretation on the courts through litigation (Cunningham 2001, 67).

Several Supreme Court decisions have relied on Section Five to strike down attempts by white majorities to diminish African American political success or to maintain their own political success founded on racially discriminatory practices.[6] The central issue— the right to participate fairly in an electoral contest with the prospect of being able to elect the candidate of one's choice—was framed in terms of minority and majority group interests (Burke 1999, 64–70). In its decisions, the Court indicated that a lack of equal access to the political process was necessary to establish a constitutional violation; in addition, for the first time it established relatively formal guidelines for the evaluation of equal opportunity (Grofman, Handley, and Niemi 1992, 33). For example, in *Allen v.*

State Board of Elections (1969), the Court determined:

> The right to vote can be affected by a dilution of voting power as well as by an absolute prohibition on casting a ballot. . . . Voters who are members of a racial minority might well be in the majority in one district, but a decided minority in the county as a whole. This type of change could therefore nullify their ability to elect the candidate of their choice just as would prohibiting some of them from voting.[7]

Particularly important was the fact that *Allen* reemphasized "vote dilution"—an issue that Chief Justice Earl Warren had indicated in *Reynolds* should be dealt with as an actionable wrong under the Constitution. In Warren's words, "Diluting the weight of votes because of place of residence impairs basic constitutional rights under the Fourteenth Amendment just as much as invidious discriminations based upon factors such as race."[8]

The VRA and these Supreme Court decisions pressured state attorneys general to remedy the effects of vote dilution by requiring the maximum number of safe minority districts. Packing minority voters into single-member districts was thought to be the most effective way of assuring minority electoral success. By the mid-1970s, state governments were *de facto* required to gerrymander their districts along these racial lines, thereby creating the so-called majority-minority districts (Burke 1999, 71). The underlying premise was that minority candidates more effectively and legitimately represented members of racial minority groups—a claim that has recently been subject to extensive debate.

Voting Rights in the 1980s: Institutional Juggling of the VRA

The case of *City of Mobile v. Bolden* (1980) forced both Congress and the Supreme Court to reexamine the implications and effects of

the VRA. In *Bolden*, the African American plaintiffs argued that the at-large procedure of electing city commissioners diluted their votes because a majority of 50 percent plus one vote could win 100 percent of the seats. Although African Americans constituted 40 percent of the population in Mobile, no African American had been elected to public office in seventy years. In a plurality opinion written by Justice Potter Stewart, the Court required plaintiffs challenging dilutive electoral practices to demonstrate a racially discriminatory *purpose*. Although Stewart emphasized that the Equal Protection Clause did not require proportional representation of minority groups, the Court still focused its analysis on group electoral identity (Burke 1999, 74–75):

> The mere fact that a number of citizens share a common ethnic, racial or religious background does not create the need for protection against gerrymandering. It is only when their common interests are strong enough to be manifested in political action that the need arises. For the political strength of a group is not a function of this ethnic, racial or religious composition; rather it is a function of numbers—specifically the number of persons who will vote in the same way.[9]

Because it is difficult to predict how people will vote—despite the fact that a group of people may share the same ethnic, racial, or religious ties—critics of the *Bolden* decision contended that it established an exceedingly burdensome and irrelevant evidentiary standard that would make it nearly impossible to win lawsuits against racially discriminatory electoral systems. These criticisms led Congress to resolve the dispute over the evidentiary standard needed to establish vote dilution claims under the VRA by amending Section Two in 1982. The amendments eliminated the obligations of minority plaintiffs to prove discriminatory intent and instead required that plaintiffs demonstrate lack of electoral success in electing a representative of their choice. This action, however, begged the question: What constitutes a legitimate group for the purpose of such choice?

The Supreme Court attempted to answer this question in *Thornburg v. Gingles* (1986). Because minority communities were presumed to be politically homogeneous and thought to be better represented by candidates of their own racial makeup, fair representation was defined to mean proportional group representation, despite the Court's attempt to counter this notion in *Allen* (Burke 1999, 86). In its decision in *Gingles*, the Court established a three-pronged test for analyzing vote dilution claims involving multimember districts:

> These circumstances are necessary preconditions for [a violation]. . . . First, the minority group must be . . . sufficiently large and geographically compact to constitute a majority of a single-member district. . . . Second, the minority group must be . . . politically cohesive. . . . Third . . . the white majority votes sufficiently as a bloc to enable it . . . usually to defeat the minority's preferred candidate.[10]

Following the *Gingles* case, there was strong agreement within state legislatures that the law, as interpreted by the Supreme Court, continued to require the creation of majority-minority districts whenever possible. In other words, failure to establish majority-minority districts in situations where the three *Gingles* prongs were present could result in vote dilution lawsuits.

The partisan divisions resulting from this legal environment became significantly clearer as the 1990 redistricting began. On one hand, Democrats needed both to create new majority-minority districts and to protect white Democratic incumbents. To do so, Democratic-controlled state legislatures used very creative cartography. On the other hand, although Republicans regarded racial redistricting as an opportunity to increase the GOP's partisan representation, the party did not control the redistricting process in any of the states where majority-minority districts were to be added (Canon 1999, 73–75, 78). Therefore, the Justice Departments under Republican presidents Ronald Reagan and George H. W. Bush were all too eager to help this apportionment process along. The Republicans had the best of both worlds: the ability to take credit for increasing minority representation while packing minorities into a few districts to "bleach" the other districts within a state—to their party's political advantage.

Shaw v. Reno and New Definitions of Fair Representation in the 1990s

The redistricting after the 1990 census resulted in the election of an increased number of African Americans to Congress, so racial gerrymandering seemed to be effective on its face. The 1992 elections raised African American representation in the House from twenty-five members to thirty-eight members (Jacobson 2001, 10). On the other side of the coin, in the few years between the Supreme Court's 1986 *Gingles* decision and its early 1990s decisions, the Court's membership experienced an ideological shift to the right. Three conservative iconoclasts—Antonin Scalia (1986), Anthony Kennedy (1988), and Clarence Thomas (1991)—joined the Court, and this changing of the guard ensured that the legal framework for redistricting would undergo a serious transformation.[11]

Three decisions in the mid-1990s underscored both the Supreme Court's new agenda and the type of partisan quandary foreshadowed by Frankfurter in his *Baker* dissent. First, *Shaw v. Reno* (1993) opened the door to challenges of majority-minority districts under the Equal Protection Clause. Then, in *Miller v. Johnson* (1995) and *Bush v. Vera* (1996), the Supreme Court struck down redistricting plans that created black-majority districts even though they had been drawn in compliance with Justice Department interpretations of the VRA. In doing so, the Court questioned the constitutionality of ever using race to determine district lines (Rush 1998, 7).

The debates in *Shaw, Miller,* and *Vera* about whether the Justice Department could require states to take extraordinary measures to "increase" minority representation (at least superficially) had less to do with the bizarre shape of the districts or the dilution of minority or majority votes than with the principles under which the districts were drawn. Insofar as the Justice Department had consciously sought to condition redistricting to favor specific groups—minority or otherwise—the Rehnquist Court perceived such action to violate basic precepts of fairness (Rush 1998, 12).

In *Shaw v. Reno*, a group of white voters in North Carolina sued the U.S. Attorney General, following a preclearance approval under Section Five of the VRA of two majority-minority congressional districts in the state. One of the districts cut diagonally across the state, following Interstate 85, and in some areas was no wider than one or two highway lanes. (*Shaw* became infamous as the "I-85" case.) The plaintiffs argued that the district constituted a racial gerrymander and therefore violated the rights of the racial majority under the Fourteenth Amendment. The Supreme Court agreed with the plaintiffs, arguing that the bizarre shape of the district seemed to have no other rational basis than linking individuals solely by race (Scher, Mills, and Hotaling 1997, 93). Justice Sandra Day O'Connor wrote in her majority opinion:

> A reapportionment plan that includes in one district individuals who belong to the same race, but who are otherwise widely separated by geographical and political boundaries, and who may have little in common with one another but the color of their skin, bears an uncomfortable resemblance to political apartheid. It reinforces the perception that members of the same racial group—regardless of their age, education, economic status, or the community in which they live—think alike, share

the same political interests, and will prefer the same candidates at the polls. We have rejected such perceptions elsewhere as impermissible racial stereotypes.[12]

Yet hadn't the Supreme Court previously suggested in its interpretation of the VRA that an effective means of enhancing minority representation, particularly in the South, was the creation of majority-minority districts? Had the Court not also required plaintiffs to show that they were injured by both a discriminatory purpose and a discriminatory effect? It does not seem plausible to contend in the I-85 case that North Carolina intended to discriminate against the racial majority or that they were underrepresented as a result of congressional districting.[13] Yet O'Connor's decision required only the demonstration that a racial classification existed; no discriminatory intent or discriminatory effect was necessary.

A year later, in *Johnson v. De Grandy* (1994), Justice David Souter, writing for the majority, argued that maximizing the number of majority-minority districts might, in fact, do a disservice to minority voters. In reality, there may not be a single voice of the minority community but a multiplicity of voices. Maximizing majority-minority districts reaches one measure of minority political potential (descriptive representation), but it gives minorities few incentives or opportunities to form coalitions with other voters in their districts; nor do majority voters outside majority-minority districts have an impetus to seek the support of minority voters within those districts (substantive representation) (Burke 1999, 109). Moreover, incumbents in such districts have less incentive to promote the interests of their districts when their seats are guaranteed through a racial supermajority.[14] Souter wrote:

> [T]here are communities in which minority citizens are able to form coalitions with voters from other racial and ethnic groups, having no need to be a majority within a single district in order to elect candidates

of their choice. Those candidates may not represent perfection to every minority voter, but minority voters are not immune from the obligation to pull, haul, and trade to find common political ground, the virtue of which is not to be slighted in applying a statute meant to hasten the waning of racism in American politics.[15]

In the next major apportionment case to reach the Supreme Court, *Miller v. Johnson* (1995), the Court continued to redefine apportionment by arguing that although race can be used as a criterion for redrawing legislative districts, it cannot be the "overriding, predominant factor" or force in making decisions about districts. Instead, race must be subordinate to "race-neutral considerations," such as "compactness, contiguity, respect for political subdivisions or communities defined by actual shared interests," among others.

Because *Shaw* broached the possibility that "bizarre" districts may be evidence of a racial gerrymander, an inquiry into possible equal protection violations against majority voters might have meant an examination of the actual shape of legislative districts (Burke 1999, 103–4). Justice Kennedy sought to clarify this possibility in *Miller* when he wrote, "Our observation in *Shaw* of the consequences of racial stereotyping was not meant to suggest that a district must be bizarre on its face before there is a constitutional violation."[16] Nor is it necessary that plaintiffs demonstrate a "threshold" of "bizarreness" before they can allege an equal protection violation. Shape is relevant only because it might be suggestive of something deeper—namely, that a district was designed with race as the "overriding and predominant factor," above and beyond all other districting principles (Canon 1999, 104). Thus, *Miller* is best read as a compromise decision between ideologies in the Supreme Court, with the right wing wishing to move toward a color-blind interpretation of the Constitution and the left wanting to maintain the *Gingles* approach. In

Miller the Court asserted that it wished to downplay race on the American political and legal agenda but probably not eliminate it altogether (Scher, Mills, and Hotaling 1997, 105–6).

Finally, in *Bush v. Vera* (1996), Justice O'Connor attempted to provide a coherent summary of the Supreme Court's rules for assessing the fairness of state redistricting plans. O'Connor identified four major principles that the courts would have to follow in making determinations about fair reapportionment schemes:

- Majority-minority districts will survive judicial scrutiny as long as they don't subordinate "traditional districting principles" to the use of race "for its own sake."

- Section Two of the VRA essentially compels creation of majority-minority districts where the three *Gingles* factors are present.

- States have a compelling interest in drawing majority-minority districts to avoid Section Two liability, but this compelling interest does not justify deviating from traditional districting principles.

- Bizarre, noncompact districts drawn for racial reasons are unconstitutional (Rush and Engstrom 2001, 118).

The reapportionment decisions of the 1990s were driven by philosophical differences within the newly conservative Supreme Court regarding the Constitution and representative democracy. Largely for this reason, the Court could not consistently settle the question of the constitutionality of many majority-minority districts, even as it took initiative away from federal and state actors in the executive and legislative branches that were trying to hammer out the difficulties of race politics. It had become clear that the Supreme Court had entered into an area—reapportionment—where manageable judicial standards remained inevitably elusive and partisanship continued to reign supreme (Burke 1999, 117–22).

Conclusion: (Un)intended Consequences and *Georgia v. Ashcroft*

When the Supreme Court chooses to take on reapportionment disputes, it inevitably will find its legal principles in conflict with political considerations. Even the political parties have found themselves in quandaries of their own. Democrats learned that pursuing the principle of enhanced minority representation, though achievable, has resulted in a loss of Democratic seats. Republicans, though opposed to the principle of "leveling the playing field" artificially to restore social inequities, have benefited from the application of that principle in practice.

Baker and *Reynolds* asked the Supreme Court to consider the constitutionality of state apportionment schemes, and the Court initially entered the realm of political representation with trepidation. The passage of the Voting Rights Act proved to be a turning point for redistricting litigation, and new statutory causes of action proved easier and more effective than constitutional claims. In particular, Section Two of the VRA dispensed with the necessity of proving purposeful discrimination for a vote dilution claim. A plaintiff merely had to demonstrate that the results of the electoral process did not produce as many minority representatives as would be indicated by their percentage in the population. This new "discriminatory effect" approach in the VRA promoted the creation of majority-minority districts in vote dilution cases, which were reviewed under the *Gingles* "totality of the circumstances" analysis.

As a result of this legal atmosphere, African American leaders, voting rights activists, and the Department of Justice (unlikely partners at the time to be sure) pursued a policy of maximizing the number of majority-minority districts, with proportional congressional representation of African Americans as the unwritten goal (Burke 1999, 2–8).

This increase in "descriptive representation" consequentially increased the number of Republican officeholders as the remaining majority districts lost minority (and largely Democratic) voters; thus, this strategy sacrificed a certain level of African American "substantive representation."[17] Moreover, these newly elected Republican members of Congress had few minority voters remaining in their districts, which created a far more conservative Republican majority in the House, particularly among the representatives in the South.

Racial redistricting also reduced the number of white moderate Democrats serving in the House. States that failed to enact Democratic gerrymanders designed to protect majority incumbents saw a particularly sharp decline in the percentage of moderate Democratic representatives: The percentage of Democratic representatives in these states fell from 46 percent in 1990 to 15 percent in 1994. Moderates lost ground even in states with Democratic gerrymanders; the proportion of moderates in these states shrank from 52 percent in 1990 to 32 percent in 1994. Unfortunately for African American substantive representation, liberal gains failed to account for the decline of the white moderates. Republicans gained nine additional seats in 1992 in states with new African American districts. Thus, racial redistricting has greatly altered the makeup of Congress and has resulted in the election of a Congress that is less likely to enact more liberal measures favored by the African American community (Burke 1999, 110–14).

Seemingly in recognition of this representation dilemma, in June 2003 the Supreme Court announced a decision that extensively analyzed the merits of substantive versus descriptive representation: *Georgia v. Ashcroft*. The central part of the Court's determination—whether legislative redistricting plans in Georgia resulted in racial retrogression, in violation of the VRA—identified three major factors in assessing a minority group's opportunity to participate in the political process: whether the plan adds or subtracts "influence" and/or coalitional districts; the comparative positions of legislative leadership, influence, and power of representatives of majority-minority districts; and (unimportantly) whether the representatives elected from the districts created and protected by the VRA support the plan. Citing *Gingles*, Justice O'Connor's majority opinion laid out the fundamental dilemma of the VRA:

> In order to maximize the electoral success of a minority group, a State may choose to create a certain number of "safe" districts, in which it is highly likely that minority voters will be able to elect the candidate of their choice. Alternatively, a state may choose to create a greater number of districts in which it is likely—although perhaps not quite as likely . . . that minority voters will be able to elect candidates of their choice.[18]

On one hand, the creation of majority-minority districts "risks isolating minority voters from the rest of the state" and "narrowing political influence to only a fraction of political districts." The Court recognized that the increase in descriptive representation comes at the cost of limiting representation to fewer areas. On the other hand, "spreading out minority voters over a greater number of districts creates more districts in which minority voters may have the opportunity to elect a candidate of their choice," which increases substantive representation "by creating coalitions of voters who together will help to achieve the electoral aspirations of the minority group."[19]

Yet just when there is some hope that the Supreme Court had finally come to maximize minority representation and facilitate voting coalitions, O'Connor introduces two suspect concepts: "influence districts" and "comparative positions of legislative leadership." "Influence districts" are created when "minority voters may not be able to elect a candidate of choice but can play a substantial, if not decisive, role in the electoral process." How would a court determine if this were the case? O'Connor asserts that it is important to consider "the likelihood that candidates elected without decisive minority support would be willing to take the minority's interests into account."[20] Furthermore, if a state's redistricting plan has failed to create minority-friendly coalition or influence districts, the state can prove that its reapportionment scheme is not retrogressive by demonstrating that the existing representatives of majority-minority districts have extensive legislative influence. O'Connor writes, "A lawmaker with more legislative influence has more potential to set the agenda, to participate in closed-door meetings, to negotiate from a stronger position, and to shake hands on a deal. Maintaining or increasing legislative positions of power for minority voters' representatives of choice, while not dispositive by itself, can show the lack of retrogressive effect under § 5."[21]

Justice Souter's dissent provides a powerful case for placing the burden to prove increased minority voter influence squarely in the laps of the states. Largely relying on *Johnson*, he writes:

> Before a State shifts from majority-minority to coalition districts, however, the State bears the burden of proving that nonminority voters will reliably vote along with the minority. It must show not merely that minority voters in new districts may have some influence, but that minority voters will have effective influence translatable into probable election results comparable to what they enjoyed under the existing district scheme. And to demonstrate this, a State must do more than produce reports of minority voting age percentages; it must show that the probable voting behavior of nonminority voters will make coalitions with minorities a real prospect. If the State's evidence fails to convince a factfinder that high racial polarization in voting is unlikely, or that high white crossover voting is likely, or that other political and demographic

facts point to probable minority effectiveness, a reduction in super-majority districts must be treated as potentially and fatally retrogressive, the burden of persuasion always being on the State.[22]

As Souter's dissent further elaborates, in presenting states with a choice between tangible majority-minority districts and several other intangible, abstract options without the benefit of formal guidelines, the Supreme Court has again created an environment that is easily subject to exploitation. Although the Court had the right idea in placing stronger emphasis on the need to evaluate substantive representation, its means to do so has largely diluted the Justice Department's ability to regulate the apportionment process under the VRA. Rather than placing more tools in the hand of the Attorney General to prevent retrogression, the Court has created a set of opaque principles that not only guarantee additional supervision by the Court but essentially place minority interests back at square one. Although the Court in *Georgia* identified many of the important modern voting rights conflicts, it failed to create a truly workable solution. At the same time, the Court predictably divided along partisan/ideological lines, demonstrating again the conflict between its legal and political principles.

Although the Supreme Court has had much to say in voting rights cases, the major philosophical questions invoking the relations between minority and majority voting rights are unlikely to be resolved with finality any time soon. Indeed, it might be a feature of our democratic legal and political systems that few fundamental questions are ever resolved once and for all; they continue to be the focus of public debate and political controversy. In the 1960s, perhaps, the Court could not have feasibly remained on the sidelines in cases dealing with redistricting disputes that

clearly were examples of unbridled racial discrimination, where no legislative relief was forthcoming. Yet the Court predictably found itself unable to escape or prevent the intense political forces surrounding these critical electoral issues.

The Supreme Court's continued efforts to create some sort of lasting doctrine to govern reapportionment prevent it from remaining above the political fray. Arguably, the Court's involvement in this arena has severely tarnished its reputation as the nonpartisan branch of government (particularly following its controversial *Bush v. Gore* decision). Ultimately, the major unintended consequences of the Court's decisions from *Baker* to *Bush* are not their substantive repercussions (at least until *Georgia v. Ashcroft*) but the discrediting of the Court as the last remaining nonpartisan haven for legal-political relief. Although this conclusion may be presenting an unfair paradox, in some sense, the Court should have chosen its involvement much more judiciously, leaving politics where it belongs: to the legislatures.

At the end of O'Connor's *Georgia* opinion, she writes:

> While courts and the Department of Justice should be vigilant in ensuring that States neither reduce the effective exercise of the electoral franchise nor discriminate against minority voters, the Voting Rights Act, as properly interpreted, should encourage the transition to a society where race no longer matters: a society where integration and color-blindness are not just qualities to be proud of, but are simple facts of life.[23]

The term "color-blindness" itself is mere politically correct jargon to mask the Supreme Court's recent efforts to strip the VRA of its authority and significance. Rather than serving as the protector of "discrete and insular minorities," as it had during the Warren era, the Court—through its own changing politics—has drastically affected the politics of the nation. In the end, the Supreme Court's new conservatism has proven unable or unwilling to protect that which is most fundamental to American democracy—proof that the Court is less an apolitical haven for legal relief and more a third *political* branch of government.

Cases Cited

Allen v. State Board of Elections, 393 U.S. 544 (1969)

Baker v. Carr, 369 U.S. 186 (1962)

Beer v. United States, 425 U.S. 130 (1976)

Bush v. Vera, 517 U.S. 952 (1996)

City of Mobile v. Bolden, 446 U.S. 55 (1980)

City of Richmond v. United States, 422 U.S. 358 (1975)

Georgia v. Ashcroft, 123 S.Ct. 2498 (2003)

Johnson v. De Grandy, 513 U.S. 804 (1994)

Miller v. Johnson, 515 U.S. 900 (1995)

Reynolds v. Sims, 377 U.S. 533 (1964)

Shaw v. Reno, 509 U.S. 630 (1993)

Thornburg v. Gingles, 478 U.S. 30 (1986)

United States v. Carolene Products Company, 304 U.S. 144 (1938)

Whitcomb v. Chavis, 403 U.S. 124 (1971)

White v. Regester, 412 U.S. 755 (1973)

Notes

1. Amendments to the Constitution require a two-thirds vote of both the House of Representatives and the Senate and then ratification by three-quarters of the state legislatures.
2. For complete case citations, see "Cases Cited."
3. Martin Shapiro (1964, 220) writes, "Majority-rule elections are not democratic goals or even essential elements *per se* of democracy. They are simply expediential and rather rough means of achieving the real goals of democracy: government by the people and political equality among the individuals composing the people."
4. *Baker*, 369 U.S. at 301–24.
5. The term "gerrymander" originates from a controversy over the drafting of a Massachusetts legislative district in 1882, in which the governor of Massachusetts, Elbridge Gerry,

created a district that looked so odd it sparked a journalist to comment that its shape resembled a salamander (Rush 1998, 9). Rush and Engstrom (2001, 4) have defined gerrymandering as "discriminatory districting which operates unfairly to inflate the political strength of one group and deflate that of another."

6. See *Allen v. State Board of* Elections, 393 U.S. 544 (1969); *Whitcomb v. Chavis*, 403 U.S. 124 (1971); *White v. Regester*, 412 U.S. 755 (1973); *City of Richmond v. United States*, 422 U.S. 358 (1975); *Beer v. United States*, 425 U.S. 130 (1976).
7. *Allen*, 393 U.S. at 569.
8. *Reynolds*, 377 U.S. at 566.
9. *Mobile*, 446 U.S. at 88.
10. *Gingles*, 478 U.S. at 31.
11. The term "iconoclast" is probably an overstatement in relation to Justice Kennedy, who has settled into the middle (though strongly leaning right) of the Supreme Court's current ideological spectrum.
12. *Shaw*, 509 U.S. at 647.
13. According to Lowenstein (1998, 67), whites constituted 78 percent of North Carolina's population, but they were the majority in 83 percent of the congressional districts.
14. David Lublin (1997), in his analysis of racial redistricting, provided some empirical research in response to Justice Souter's proposition. First, Lublin claims that racial redistricting in the South has made the House less likely to adopt legislation favored by African Americans, whereas racial redistricting in the North generally does not have the same effect. This observation would help to explain why there was such a large number of Supreme Court cases from southern states. In addition, Lublin noticed that racial redistricting results in the election of more Republicans unless mapmakers purposely adopt Democratic gerrymanders with bizarre district lines to avoid this outcome, so the creation of new majority-minority districts assured the Republicans solid control of the House in 1994.

    Lublin goes on to argue for modified gerrymandering that would allow African Americans to achieve substantive representation without having to pack districts with a supermajority of black voters, but he also argues that the election of more than token numbers of African American representatives requires majority-minority districts. On one hand, election of minorities to Congress legitimizes the political process for members of these previously powerless and excluded groups: Electing some group members to positions of authority empowers members of any group because the very existence of minority representatives provides direct evidence that members of such groups can influence the choice of elected officials and participate actively in the political arena. Although black majority districts assure the election of African American representatives, they also impede efforts to maximize African American substantive representation. Using the same African American population base to create a new Democratic district or a second 40 percent black district results in greater gains in substantive representation (members of Congress sympathetic to black interests). On the other hand, concentrating African American voters in black majority districts actually undermines African American substantive representation if it prevents redistricters from placing African American voters in districts where they can help elect an additional Democrat or raise the African American share of the population above 40 percent.

15. *Johnson*, 512 U.S. at 1020.
16. *Miller*, 515 U.S. at 912.
17. Hannah Fenichel Pitkin is widely recognized as the foremost modern scholar dealing with these categories of representation, and it is largely in her book *The Concept of Representation* (Pitkin 1967) that this representative dichotomy originated.
18. *Georgia*, 123 S.Ct. at 2511.
19. Ibid. at 2512.
20. Ibid.
21. Ibid. at 2513.
22. Ibid. at 2518.
23. Ibid. at 2517.

References

Abraham, Henry J. 1986. "Contemporary Judicial Processes and a Democratic Society." *Political Science Quarterly* 101, no. 2: 277–88.

Bickel, Alexander M. 1962. *The Least Dangerous Branch: The Supreme Court at the Bar of Politics*. New Haven, Conn.: Yale University Press.

Burke, Christopher M. 1999. *The Appearance of Equality: Racial Gerrymandering, Redistricting, and the Supreme Court*. Westport, Conn.: Greenwood Press.

Canon, David T. 1999. *Race, Redistricting, and Representation: The Unintended Consequences of Black Majority Districts*. Chicago: University of Chicago Press.

Commager, Henry S. 1943. *Majority Rule and Minority Rights*. London: Oxford University Press.

Cover, Robert M. 1982. "The Origins of Judicial Activism in the Protection of Minorities." *Yale Law Journal* 91, no. 7 (June): 1287–1316.

Cunningham, Maurice T. 2001. *Maximization, Whatever the Cost: Race, Redistricting, and the Department of Justice*. Westport, Conn.: Praeger Publishers.

Griffin, Stephen. 1996. *American Constitutionalism: From Theory to Politics*. Princeton, N.J.: Princeton University Press.

Grofman, Bernard, Lisa Handley, and Richard G. Niemi. 1992. *Minority Representation and the Quest for Voting Equality*. Cambridge, U.K.: Cambridge University Press.

Hacker, Andrew. 1964. *Congressional Districting: The Issue of Equal Representation*. Washington, D.C.: Brookings Institution Press.

Jacobson, Gary C. 2001. *The Politics of Congressional Elections*. New York: Addison-Wesley.

Lowenstein, Daniel H. 1998. "Race and Representation in the Supreme Court." In *Voting Rights and Redistricting in the United States*, ed. Mark E. Rush. Westport, Conn.: Greenwood Press.

Lublin, David. 1997. *The Paradox of Representation: Racial Gerrymandering and Minority Issues in Congress*. Princeton, N.J.: Princeton University Press.

Pitkin, Hannah F. 1967. *The Concept of Representation*, Berkeley: University of California Press.

Rush, Mark E. 1998. "Representation in Theory and Practice." In *Voting Rights and Redistricting in the United States*, ed. Mark E. Rush, Westport, Conn.: Greenwood Press.

Rush, Mark E., and Richard L. Engstrom. 2001. *Fair and Effective Representation?: Debating Electoral Reform and Minority Rights*. Lanham, Md.: Rowman & Littlefield.

Scher, Richard K., Jon L. Mills, and John J. Hotaling. 1997. *Voting Rights and Democracy: The Law and Politics of*

Districting. Chicago: Nelson-Hall Publishers.

Shapiro, Martin. 1964. *Law and Politics in the Supreme Court: New Approaches to Political Jurisprudence*. London: The Free Press of Glencoe.

Winter, Ralph K., Jr. 1979. "The Growth of Judicial Power." In *The Judiciary in a Democratic Society*, ed. Leonard J. Theberge. Lexington, Mass.: Lexington Books.

Further Reading

Baker, Gordon E. 1966. *The Reapportionment Revolution: Representation, Political Power, and the Supreme Court*. New York: Random House.

Ball, Howard. 1971. *The Warren Court's Conceptions of Democracy: An Evaluation of the Supreme Court's Apportionment Decisions*. Rutherford, Pa.: Fairleigh Dickinson University Press.

Butler, David, and Bruce Cain. 1992. *Congressional Redistricting: Comparative and Theoretical Perspectives*. New York: Macmillan.

Cameron, Charles, David Epstein, and Sharyn O'Halloran. 1996. "Do Majority-Minority Districts Maximize Substantive Black Representation in Congress?" *American Political Science Review* 90, no. 4 (December): 794–812.

Cortner, Richard C. 1970. *The Apportionment Cases*. Knoxville: University of Tennessee Press.

Dahl, Robert. 1957. "Decisionmaking in a Democracy: The Supreme Court as a National Policymaker." *Journal of Public Law* 6: 279–95.

Dixon, Robert G. 1968. *Democratic Representation: Reapportionment in Law and Politics*. New York: Oxford University Press.

Ely, John Hart. 1980. *Democracy and Distrust: A Theory of Judicial Review*. Cambridge, Mass.: Harvard University Press.

Engstrom, Richard L. 1980. "Racial Discrimination in the Electoral Process: The Voting Rights Act and the Vote Dilution Issue." In *Party Politics in the South*, ed.

Robert Steed, Laurence Moreland, and Ted Baker. New York: Praeger.

Glazer, Nathan. 1975. "Towards an Imperial Judiciary?" *The Public Interest* 41 (fall): 104–23.

Lloyd, Randall D. 1995. "Separating Partisanship from Party in Judicial Research: Reapportionment in the U.S. District Courts." *American Political Science Review* 89, no. 2 (January): 413–20.

Lublin, David, and D. Stephen Voss. 2000. "Racial Redistricting and Realignment in Southern State Legislatures." *American Journal of Political Science* 44, no. 4 (October): 792–810.

Mason, Alpheus Thomas. 1966. "Understanding the Warren Court: Judicial Self-Restraint and Judicial Duty." *Political Science Quarterly* 81, no. 4 (December): 523–63.

McCloskey, Robert G. 1960. *The American Supreme Court*. Chicago: University of Chicago Press.

McCubbins, Mathew D., and Thomas Schwartz. 1998. "Congress, the Courts, and Public Policy: Consequences of the One Man, One Vote Rule." *American Journal of Political Science* 32, no. 2 (May): 388–415.

McKay, Robert B. 1965. *Reapportionment: The Law and Politics of Equal Representation*. New York: Twentieth Century Fund.

Mishler, William, and Reginald S. Sheehan. 1993. "The Supreme Court as a Countermajoritarian Institution? The Impact of Public Opinion on Supreme Court Decisions." *American Political Science Review* 87, no. 1 (March): 87–101.

O'Rourke, Timothy G. 1980. *The Impact of Reapportionment*. New Brunswick, N.J.: Transaction Books.

Pritchett, C. Herman. 1964. "Equal Protection and the Urban Majority." *American Political Science Review* 58, no. 4 (December): 869–75.

Rush, Mark E. 1993. *Does Redistricting Make a Difference?: Partisan Representation and Electoral Behavior*. Baltimore: Johns Hopkins University Press.

Schubert, Glendon. 1965. *Reapportionment*. New York: Charles Scribner's Sons.

Schwab, Larry M. 1988. *The Impact of Congressional Reapportionment and Redistricting*. Lanham, Md.: University Press of America.

Swain, Carol M. 1993. *Black Faces, Black Interests: The Representation of African Americans in Congress*. Cambridge, Mass.: Harvard University Press.

Uhlmann, Michael M. 1979. "The Supreme Court and Political Representation." In *The Judiciary in a Democratic Society*, ed. Leonard J. Theberge. Lexington, Mass.: Lexington Books.

CONCLUSION

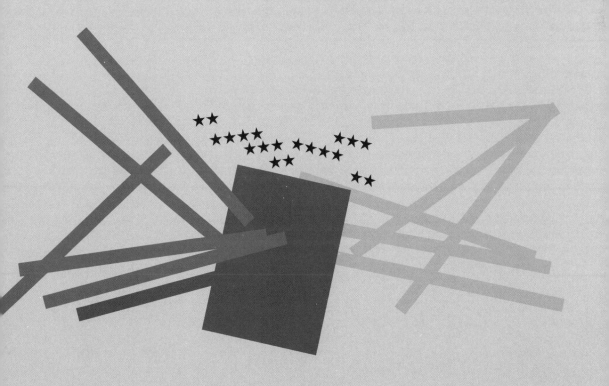

Chapter 12

Is This Any Way to Run a Democratic Government?

Stephen J. Wayne

We began our study by asking two basic questions: How democratic is the government of the United States? Does its democratic character generally promote good government? We now turn to the answers the contributors to this book have provided.

Although the American system of government was not designed to be a representative democracy, it was intended to be broadly reflective of the public's interests. Its goals—"to form a more perfect Union, establish Justice, insure domestic Tranquility, provide for the common defence, promote the general Welfare, and secure the Blessings of Liberty" (Preamble, U.S. Constitution)—were national in scope. To achieve them, a central authority was necessary. Fearful of distant government with concentrated power, the framers settled on a framework that separated institutions and their powers, internally checked and balanced those powers, and imposed a federal structure in which the authority for governing was both shared and divided.

The good news is that the constitutional design is alive and well and has worked to deter any one person or group from dominating the government for extended periods of time. The bad news is that this same design has impeded governing, making it difficult to meet the increasing demand for government services efficiently, effectively, and equitably.

Democratic pressures for government to be more inclusive in its composition, more responsive to diverse economic and social interests, and more even-handed in its distribution of the country's resources have created tensions to which the institutions of that government have tried to respond. The contributors to this book have provided an evaluation of that response.

Representation, Responsiveness, and Issues of Good Government

Representation in government, responsiveness of government, and the equity of public policy decisions have become issues in and of themselves, as well as criteria by which we can evaluate the democratic character of the system of governing.

Representation is a function of Congress as a body and its members individually in the performance of their roles. How equitable is that representation? The perceived link between special interests and the special benefits they provide members of Congress, particularly with regard to reelection, has contributed to the conventional wisdom that America's government is of, by, and for the wealthy and powerful—that those with the greatest resources exercise the most influence. Although chapters 4 and 5, on the subject of money and Congress, do not refute this allegation, they raise questions about its accuracy and applicability across the board. Campaign contributors are not a microcosm of society or the electorate. They are a group of people distinguished by their interest in politics, their activity within the electoral and governing arenas, and their willingness to spend their own money in support of their political beliefs and interests.

There is a relationship between giving money to members of Congress and personally contacting them. Donors do so with greater frequency than do nondonors. The relationship between campaign contributions, influence peddling, and public policy outputs is very complex, however, and is not easily demonstrated in a systematic way, even though anecdotes about the "buying" of Congress persist. Although the jury is still out on the tie between campaign contributions and political contacts and favorable public policy decisions, most scholars agree that the more the electorate resembles the population, the more contributors resemble the electorate, the more those who contact members of Congress reflect broad-based societal views, the more likely it is that legislative outcomes will meet society's needs as a whole—and do so equitably.

Much the same theoretical argument underlies chapter 5, on the relationship between demographic and substantive representation. A legislature that does not reflect the composition of the population is less likely to respond adequately to the issues, needs, and interests of citizens who are not fairly represented. The reason is straightforward: Malrepresentation limits decision makers' perceptions, experiences, and emotional and intellectual understanding, thereby skewing public policy outcomes in the direction of those who are in positions of power.

Although the public perceives Congress as more prone to special interest and male-dominated politics than the other institutions of the national government, this perception may not be entirely accurate. The executive branch also is very sensitive to pressures from individuals and groups outside the government. As in Congress, the exercise of these pressures can obscure or warp the national interest in favor of special interests. Within the executive branch, such pressures produce tensions between the president, who has a national constituency and must pursue national

priorities, and the departments and agencies that provide a functional service to an issue-based clientele.

Although the executive branch does not mirror America in composition or attitude, it may suffer less from representational distortion than Congress—not because it is a more representative body but because civil servants and, to a lesser extent, political appointees have professional credentials that are considered appropriate criteria for serving their representational roles. They operate according to standard operating procedures that limit personal discretion. Moreover, they are judged more by their professional competency than by their political pedigree. In addition, the appointive and merit-based hiring and promotional processes in recent years have been increasingly geared toward achieving a more equitable demographic composition for the executive.

Because the bureaucracy looks and thinks more like America than it did in the past, the public might be expected to express more confidence in its decisions and greater approval of its performance. Yet the record here is mixed. Survey data do indicate that the public regards most civil servants and, to a lesser extent, political appointees more favorably and as less self-interested than they perceive elected officials (Pew Research Center for the People and the Press 1998). Nonetheless, this perception has not replaced the overall judgment that the federal government remains too large, too inefficient, and too removed from the public's general needs and concerns (Pew Research Center for the People and the Press 1999).

To impose a unified perspective over the executive branch, presidents have depended on their surrogates in the Executive Office—particularly the Office of Management and Budget—to coordinate and, if need be, police the departments and agencies in their legislative, budgetary, and regulatory activities. Whereas presidents and their surrogates usually can force outcomes that coincide with their political objectives, congressional leaders have more difficulty doing so unless they have the support of a cohesive partisan majority. The hierarchy of the executive branch gives the president institutional advantages that congressional leaders lack because of the legislature's horizontal organization and decentralized power bases.

The Supreme Court was not intended to be a representative body; nonetheless, its representative character has been called into question when its decisions in major cases appear to be out of sync with predominant views for an extended period of time. The Supreme Court's interpretation of the Constitution occasionally constrains the other branches of government; a persistent pattern of judgments, however, that reverse laws enacted by the people's elected representatives jeopardizes the Court's reputation as an impartial judicial body and undercuts public support for its decisions.

This review has not specifically discussed how groups use the judicial process to further their own interests. They do so by initiating test cases, filing friend of the court briefs, waging public campaigns to affect the confirmation of federal judges, and generating a debate over legal issues that they hope will have an effect on the judiciary's judgment. Here too, groups with the resources to affect these judgments are advantaged.

Accessibility of Public Officials

Responsiveness is a corollary of representation. A government that mirrors society in its composition but impedes accessibility in practice does not meet the criteria for an operational democracy. To achieve responsiveness, government officials must be accessible to citizens who wish to express their views on the issues of the day, as well as knowledgeable about the opinions of citizens who do not go out of their way to express them. Moreover, decision-making processes must be visible, and decision makers must be held accountable for their actions. How well does the American national government meet these criteria? And how do these criteria affect issues of good governance?

In Congress the constituency influence is strongest, fueled by the reelection incentive of members of the legislature. When that incentive becomes dominant, it functions as a prism through which public policy is perceived, positions are taken, and votes cast. Representatives, who use such a prism to make their policy judgments, act more like delegates than trustees. As such, they need to be accessible. Those who can demonstrate the most constituency-based clout exercise the most influence, which is why interest groups seeking to affect legislative policy judgments do so in a constituency-relevant way.

The special interest connection in the executive branch is similar except that the connection is with functional departments and agencies, not geographic electoral constituencies. The electoral impact outside groups can wield is clearly noted, however, by presidents and their political aides—a reason for as well as a consequence of their turning regularly to public opinion pollsters as advisors. Although national surveys do not dictate policy decisions, they do provide information that often sets the parameters for these decisions and frames the language that will be used to explain them to the public.

The Supreme Court makes no pretense of being open and accessible. There are a limited number of public seats in its chamber, live coverage by the electronic media is not permitted,[1] opinions are announced without advanced warning, and the Court's decision-making process is shrouded in secrecy. Following the presentation of oral arguments, the Court closes itself off to all but the justices and their clerks. The public has access to oral arguments, *amicus curiae* briefs, and Court decisions, but often after the fact.[2] Despite the closed nature of judicial decision making, the Supreme Court's traditional disinclination to reach out to make constitutional determinations, and its reluctance—until recently—to get involved in political questions, its judgments have been affected by political and social reality and by the external pressures exerted on the Court through appropriate legal channels.

CONCLUSION

A Democratic Paradox

The constitutional framework protects individual liberties and civil rights by requiring institutional interaction and by placing specific prohibitions on the government. That interaction and those prohibitions constrain democratic decision making. They place the burden on those who wish to formulate new policy, not those who wish to maintain existing policy. That burden requires them to build and sustain a consensus that crosses the institutional divide. Moreover, the Constitution places some policy decisions out of reach of that consensus entirely.

Despite these impediments and prohibitions, the people's legislative representatives and their elected executive officials are still oriented to respond to public demands and satisfy group interests in their formulation and administration of public policy. Sometimes, in doing so, the rules the Constitution establishes to protect everyone, including and especially a minority, may run counter to policies that are enacted or promulgated. Where such laws or executive actions are challenged, the federal judiciary must decide the matter. In doing so, the courts periodically confront a major democratic paradox: how to ensure the rights of all without undermining the very principle on which political equity rests—that all individuals be able to exercise equal influence on public policy decisions.

Addressing this paradox, the authors of chapters 10 and 11 on the judiciary are critical of the Supreme Court's efforts to right "legislative wrongs." Should political activity or judicial interpretation be the decisive force to resolve social issues? Is the Supreme Court in the best position to discern the most desirable outcome, let alone to achieve it? The current quandary over legislative redistricting is an example of a political thicket into which the Court has entered and from which it has been unable to extricate itself.

Summary: Two Basic Questions Revisited

How Democratic Is the Governmental System Today?

Descriptive representation has improved, although not to the point that the government mirrors society. According to democratic theory, the improvement in descriptive representation should have resulted in better substantive representation. It may have, although clearly not in every case.

Government has become more open to public view most of the time, and public officials are more responsive to a growing number of organized interests. There are more voices that find expression and more interests that are represented. These developments have enhanced the democratic character of the system.

How Democratic Should the U.S. Government Become?

The greater the representation of social groups, the more interests that must be addressed, the more information about the public and its desires that must be considered, and the more public scrutiny that must be given to decision making. The increasing orientation of policymakers and administrators to their electoral and functional clientele and the special organized interests that represent them also has produced more public posturing by elected officials and their staffs, constant campaigning by those in power, and an increase in the stridency of political rhetoric—none of which facilitates compromise, builds consensus, or makes it easier to discern a national interest.

The more interest groups, the greater the political pressures that tie benefits elected officials desire to their behavior in office. The unequal distribution of resources that some of these groups possess and use has created a damaging perception of government of, by, and for the special interests—a perception that has contributed to public cynicism and distrust of American government.

The more open the government, the more difficult it is to achieve efficiency, decisiveness, and expert-driven decision making, or even the making of unpopular decisions themselves. These decisional difficulties have generated inventive legislative solutions, such as laws that trigger a specific response if Congress does *not* act (e.g., the War Powers Resolution of 1973) or permit only up-or-down voting (e.g., fast-track authority and military base closings).

The increasingly difficult burdens placed on the presidency to influence Congress in its lawmaking capacity also have created greater incentives for presidents to use the unilateral powers at their disposal to circumvent Congress. They also have encouraged presidents to adopt a crisis mentality as a vehicle for enhancing their power, such as wars on poverty, energy, and, more recently, terrorism. Although democracies can withstand an expanded executive in times of crisis, they can do so only if the crisis is authentic and the expansion of executive power temporary.

Notes

1. The Supreme Court did make available the oral arguments that were presented in *Bush v. Gore,* 531 U.S. 98 (2000), as well as the justices' interchange with the attorneys, but it did so after—not during—the session.
2. Much of this information is now available now on various law-related websites.

References

Pew Research Center for the People and the Press, 1998. "Deconstructing Distrust: How Americans View Government." March. Available at http://people-press.org.

———. 1999. "Retropolitics." November. Available at http://people-press.org.

Contributors

Michael A. Bailey (Ph.D., Stanford University) is an associate professor in the Department of Government at Georgetown University. An expert on Congress, political economy, and political science methodology, he has published articles on congressional elections, trade policy, and interstate policy competition.

Courtenay W. Daum is a Ph.D. candidate in government at Georgetown University. She received her M.A. from the University of Delaware. Her primary fields of research and teaching include women and politics, judicial politics, and constitutional law.

Joseph A. Ferrara (Ph.D., Georgetown University) is an independent political consultant. From 1982 to 2000 he served in the federal government in staff and management positions in the House of Representatives, the Office of Management and Budget, and the Department of Defense. He has published articles on public management and public opinion in a variety of scholarly journals. He also is an adjunct professor at Georgetown University.

Peter L. Francia (Ph.D., University of Maryland) is a research fellow and program coordinator at the Center for American Politics and Citizenship at the University of Maryland.

Steven G. Glickman is a law student at Columbia University. He received his M.A. from Georgetown University.

John C. Green (Ph.D., Ohio State University) is professor of political science and director of the Ray C. Bliss Institute of Applied Politics at the University of Akron. An expert in religion and politics, he has written numerous books and articles.

Paul S. Herrnson (Ph.D., University of Wisconsin) is director of the Center for American Politics and Citizenship and professor of government and politics at the University of Maryland. An expert on American politics, he has written and edited numerous books on elections, interest groups, and politics in the United States.

Emily H. Hoechst is a Ph.D. candidate in political theory in the Department of Government at Georgetown University. She received her J.D. from Georgetown University and practiced law for four years before returning to academia.

Lynn Kirby (Ph.D., Georgetown University) is a visiting assistant professor at Towson University. Her research interests include public opinion, the presidency, and democratic theory.

Wesley Joe is a Ph.D. candidate at Georgetown University. His areas of interest include American politics and economic policy.

Jeremy D. Mayer (Ph.D., Georgetown University) is an assistant professor in the School of Public Policy at George Mason

University. He is the author of *Running on Race: Politics in Presidential Campaigns* and *The Giant Awakes*.

Lynda W. Powell (Ph.D., University of Rochester) is a professor of political science at the University of Rochester. Her publications include *Term Limits in the State Legislatures* (with John Carey and Richard G. Niemi) and *Serious Money: Fundraising and Contributing in Presidential Nominating Campaigns* (with Clifford W. Brown, Jr., and Clyde Wilcox).

Lynn Ross is a Ph.D. candidate at Georgetown University. She received her M.P.A. from Syracuse University. She worked as a program examiner in the Office of Management and Budget for seven years. Her areas of interest are bureaucratic politics and the presidency.

Beth Stark is a Ph.D. candidate in the Department of Government at Georgetown University. Her current areas of research include civil society and women's political participation.

Margaret Tseng (Ph.D., Georgetown University), is a visiting assistant professor at the University of Delaware. Her research interests include presidential politics and minority politics.

Stephen J. Wayne (Ph.D., Columbia University) is a professor of government at Georgetown University. He specializes in the American presidency and electoral politics. His books include *The Road to the White House*, *Presidential Leadership* (with George C. Edwards III), and *Is This Any Way to Run a Democratic Election?*

Ben Webster is a Ph.D. candidate in the Department of Government at Georgetown University. He received his M.S. from Georgetown. His areas of interest include environmental politics and public policy.

Clyde Wilcox (Ph.D., Ohio State University) is a professor of government at Georgetown University. He is the author or editor of a variety of book and articles on campaign finance, religion and politics, and gender politics. Prior to coming to Georgetown, he worked at the Federal Elections Commission as an analyst.

Index

Index

Dahl, Robert, 19n1
Daniels, Mitch, 127
Daum, Courtenay, ix. *See also* women in Congress
Davidson, Roger, 149
Declaration of Independence, 4
Dekker, Paul, 22, 25
deliberative democracy, 146–50. *See also* judicial
    review
Democracy and Association (Warren), 29
Democracy in America (Tocqueville), 22
Democracy in Capitalist Times (Dryzek), 72–73
democratic governance, 3–20, 175–79
    and citizen indifference/inattention, 6
    and the collective good, 4–5
    and constitutionalism, 10
    crises and suspensions of civil liberties, 13–14
    and decisional rules, 10–11
    and descriptive versus substantive representa-
        tion, 8–9, 178
    and executive branch decision making, openness
        of, 14–15, 176, 177
    and executive power, 12–13
    foundations of, 3–6
    and individual liberty, 4
    and judicial review, 15–16, 178
    and the judiciary as an antimajoritarian
        institution, 15
    and legislative processes, 11–12, 178
    and political equality, 4, 19n1, 71–72
    the presidency and public opinion, 13
    and public accessibility, 5–6, 177
    and public policy, 16–18, 60–63, 178
    representation and constituencies, 7–8
    representation and responsiveness, 6–10, 175–77
    representatives and delegate versus trusteeship
        roles, 9–10, 69–70
    the rule of law, 5
    and rules for decision making, 10–16
    See also civic foundations of American democracy
Democratic National Committee, 109, 111
Democrats
    and congressional donors, 42–44, 43t, 44t,
        53–54, 60, 63
    congressional fundraising events, 36
    Democratic presidents and executive orders, 120
    and the Patients' Bill of Rights, 60–63
    and reapportionment decisions, 9, 162, 165,
        168n14
    self-funding candidates and race outcomes, 55t,
        56–57, 57t
    and soft money, 53–54, 63
descriptive representation, 8–9, 70, 165–66, 178
    and "doubling up," 76–78, 79n8
    and multimember districts, 72, 76–78
    and reapportionment decisions, 9, 165–66
    and single-member districts, 72, 75–78,
        79nn5, 7
    and substantive representation, 8–9, 70, 72,
        165–66, 178

    and women in Congress, 70–72, 73, 74, 75–78,
        79nn5, 6, 7
    See also women in Congress
direct democracy, 6, 73
Dodson, Debra, 78n3
Dolan, Kathleen, 79n6
Dole, Robert, 109
donors, campaign. *See* campaign contributions
"doubling up" and proportional descriptive represen-
    tation, 76–78, 79n8
Dryzek, John, 72–73

Eisenhower, Dwight D.
    and presidential polling, 104
    proclamations by, 118
    and unilateral presidential powers, 118
Electoral College, 7
electoral constituencies, 7–8. *See also* reapportion-
    ment decisions and the Supreme Court
electoral system. *See* women in Congress
Ely, John Hart, 146
Engendering Democracy (Phillips), 71–72, 78n2
Environmental Protection Agency (EPA), 93, 94t, 95t
Equal Protection Clause, Fourteenth Amendment,
    157, 159, 161, 162, 163
Erikson, Robert, 57
executive branch
    decision making and openness of, 14–15, 176, 177
    executive power and democracy, 12–13
    responsiveness and accessibility of, 177
    See also federal budget process and the Office
        of Management and Budget; federal bureau-
        cracy and the reflection of America; polling,
        presidential; presidency and issues of demo-
        cratic governance; presidential powers,
        unilateral
executive orders, 119–20, 120f, 123n1, 127

FamiliesUSA, 62
Federal Aviation Administration (FAA), 93, 94t, 95t
federal budget process and the Office of Management
    and Budget, 125–42, 176–77
    and Bureau of the Budget, 127, 136
    and Congress, 127–28, 132, 139
    and crisis management environment, 129
    and culture of OMB, 128–30, 134, 139
    democracy and the review process, 131, 140
    and the director's review, 131–32
    funding process and staff roles, 131, 132
    funding recommendations by OMB, 130–31
    information asymmetry and budget maximiza-
        tion, 135–36, 139
    and "naysayer" image of OMB, 129, 134, 139
    neutral competence versus political responsive-
        ness, 136–38, 139
    and OMB–agency relations, 127, 129–30, 133
        36, 139
    and OMB–president relations, 136–38, 139
    and OMB's balancing act, 133–38, 139

Index

Index

INDEX

Index